Haunted Wisconsin

Terrace Books, a trade imprint of the University of Wisconsin Press, takes its name from the Memorial Union Terrace, located at the University of Wisconsin–Madison. Since its inception in 1907, the Wisconsin Union has provided a venue for students, faculty, staff, and alumni to debate art, music, politics, and the issues of the day. It is a place where theater, music, drama, literature, dance, outdoor activities, and major speakers are made available to the campus and the community. To learn more about the Union, visit www.union.wisc.edu.

Haunted Wisconsin

Michael Norman

Terrace Books

A trade imprint of the University of Wisconsin Press

Terrace Books
A trade imprint of the University of Wisconsin Press
1930 Monroe Street, 3rd Floor
Madison, Wisconsin 53711-2059
uwpress.wisc.edu

3 Henrietta Street
London WCE 8LU, England
eurospanbookstore.com

Library of Congress Cataloging-in-Publication Data
Norman, Michael, 1947 June 29–
Haunted Wisconsin / Michael Norman.—3rd ed.
          p.   cm.
First ed.: Sauk City, Wis.: Stanton & Lee, c1980.
Includes bibliographical references and index.
ISBN 978-0-299-28594-4 (pbk.: alk. paper)
ISBN 978-0-299-28593-7 (e-book)
1. Ghosts—Wisconsin.   2. Legends—Wisconsin.   I. Title.
BF1472.U6S37   2011
133.109775 — dc22
2011015991

Earlier versions of "Summerwind" and "The Phantom Congregation" appeared in *Haunted Heartland*,
published by Stanton & Lee, copyright © 1985 by Beth Scott and Michael Norman. An earlier account
of the Davis Theatre ghost in the chapter "No Exit" appeared in *Haunted Homeland*, published by
Forge Books, copyright © 2006 by Michael Norman. A story about the Walker House, Mineral
Point, in the chapter "Someone to Watch over Me," appeared in *Haunted Heartland*, published by
Stanton & Lee, copyright © 1985 by Beth Scott and Michael Norman.

A name marked with an asterisk (*) indicates the use of a pseudonym.

This book is dedicated to my mother,

Elizabeth Jean "Bette" Norman

Contents

Part II: Southern Frights

Preface

Come over here, sit by me. I'll tell you a ghost story.

Those words, or some variation of them, have been spoken over the millennia and within every society of the inhabited world. Whether young or old, rich or poor, famous or obscure, many of us find extraordinarily compelling those tales of a hidden world coexisting with our own, one that on occasion allows us a glimpse of its denizens—in the form of ghosts or apparitions or spirits or poltergeists or whatever you want to call them. I am amazed at that. When Beth Scott and I set out in 1977 to collect Wisconsin ghost stories, our biggest concern was that, for any contemporary "true" stories, people might be reluctant to share their experiences. Could we even find enough material to fill our pages? That is certainly not the case in 2011. The supernatural has gone mainstream. From cable channels endlessly programmed with all manner of "ghost hunter" series to bookstore shelves groaning (*hideously?*) under stacks of books devoted to haunted places and "true" ghost encounters and on to Halloween tours of haunted hot spots in hundreds of communities around the nation, we seem to be awash in stories about apparitions of the dead and (not quite) gone. Has there been a noteworthy surge of interest in "things that go bump in the night"? I'll leave the heavy analysis to others, but it seems to me there has been, and there may be a few reasons for interest in the supernatural to have moved closer to center stage.

First, and contrary to some popular opinion, we have become more tolerant of, or at least we're more used to, diverse beliefs and ideas even if some of them, such as alleged encounters with the supernatural, are contrary to the laws of physics as we know them. We see and hear some rather amazing things on the unfiltered Internet or via one of the hundreds of available cable or satellite channels. It seems everyone has an opinion or belief about *something,* and it all comes at us in tsunami waves of information. It seems too that more of us are willing to share our own personal experiences—however trivial—with the wider world, or some small portion of it. This would undoubtedly apply to relating an encounter with dear, departed Aunt Edna when she comes visiting. Again. Also, the very definition of *privacy* is changing so that a greater percentage of the general public seems to be more comfortable spilling once closely guarded secrets.

Second, although there have been no known scientific "breakthroughs" by way of confirming the existence of the paranormal, there continues to be enough anecdotal "evidence" to feed the audience for such material. Thirty years ago, when the first edition of *Haunted Wisconsin* was published, we were amazed to find so many *common* people describing very *uncommon* experiences with what they took to be the supernatural. Today, they seem to be every-where. I don't know if that's progress or not. Perhaps there always were far more individuals who brushed up against the "unknown" than we realized, but back then social norms, personal uncertainty about what actually took place, or pressure from family or friends might have kept them quiet. Many people told us we were the first outside their immediate circle of friends or family who heard their story. Then, too, there were far fewer platforms available from which they could talk about their extraordinary encounters if they so desired.

Third, we never fully leave behind us our childhood fear of the dark, of the unknown, of the *unseen*. Nor can we understand with absolute certainty—and I know this differs from the spiritual beliefs of some—what happens to us *after death*. So just as we did and do squirm at the notion of walking into a deserted cemetery on a moonless night or blanch at the thought of our name whispered hoarsely from somewhere behind us in an otherwise empty room, so also do we search for answers to that deepest and darkest fear of all—that when we die, it is unequivocally, undeniably *finis*. That there is no spiritual *Great Beyond . . .* beyond the immediate physical universe we inhabit. That we won't be returning in any manner, shape, or form. Ashes to ashes. Dust to dust.

And yet there are those occasional intimations of immortality that this may *not* be the case. That we are a long, long way from understanding the universe and its infinite possibilities. That's where those ghost stories that do not spring from a novelist's fertile imagination come into play. Those are the stories derived from the experiences of those individuals to whom something extraordinary has happened, something they believe may be of supernatural origin, or at least they are open to the idea. Scoff if you will, but there are legions of us out there.

Us? Yes, that legion now includes this author among its number. I won't say that what happened to me was of "supernatural" origin—it was a brief, single incident so I'm not ready to climb up on that rock quite yet. What transpired took place not long ago, after years of interviewing scores of other people about their own ghost stories, of visiting countless allegedly haunted places, and all the while, unfortunately, never seeing, hearing, or feeling anything even remotely supernatural. I've been an open-minded skeptic on the subject. So with that in mind let me tell you what happened to me.

I was performing in a summer stock production of *Love Letters* by A. R. Gurney in a theater on a college campus. There is at least one substantiated story that the ghost of a former faculty member who designed the theater complex nearly forty years earlier haunts the place. He seems benevolent enough, even protective of the space he planned but didn't live long enough to work in.

So on that particular June evening a few years ago, I found myself in the Gurney play, which is a touching piece, relatively easy to rehearse and perform as it doesn't require script memorization. Two actors, a man and a woman, sit at a table on stage reading the correspondence they've written to each other over a lifetime. It's not a technically challenging show. A few light cues and that's about it. For that reason the stage manager was positioned up in the light booth at the rear of the theater and not backstage. In fact there was no one backstage, which I wasn't entirely happy about. It's always good to have a crewmember back there during a performance in case someone wanders in or, God forbid, a fire breaks out. I voiced my concerns, but no one was available. The stage manager locked the doors to the backstage area before the perform-ances, and we thought all would be well. The show must go on.

We were in the second night of a three-performance run. The first act went well; the audience laughed at the right moments and we got some nice applause. As I recall, we—Sandee, my fellow actor, and I—sat backstage during the intermission and quietly visited. Around us were the set pieces being used during rehearsals for the next production that summer, the musical *Forever Plaid*. I noticed that offstage to the left were a couple of tables full of the quirky props used in that popular show—a sombrero, castanets, a ukulele, a cardigan sweater, scarves . . . you get the idea. We saw no one else during that ten-minute break.

We took our places for act 2. Lights up, and we began. A few minutes into the act, I came to the end of a short piece of dialogue. Then, as Sandee began her lines, from backstage to my left came the clear, distinct resonance of someone running a finger over the strings of that ukulele I'd seen on the prop table. A single, distinct riff.

I tried to remain focused on the show and said my next line. Yet I was thinking someone was backstage goofing around. After all, a ukulele doesn't play by itself! What's next, a drunk staggering out to disrupt the performance?

Well, what happened next was . . . *nothing*.

No one walked out on stage. No one followed up with a quick ukulele solo. I didn't break character and yet I wondered what the heck was going on. More than anything, I wanted to get up, go backstage, and solve this peculiar mystery. But of course I didn't.

I also wondered whether I might be hearing things, perhaps having an auditory hallucination. It's been known to happen.

The play ended, we took our bows, and we left the stage. Once we got backstage, the first words out of my mouth were: "Sandee, did you hear that?!" I described the ukulele strum and when I'd heard it, and she allowed that she had been aware of "something" offstage at that point in the second act but she had been preoccupied with her line reading.

Was I certain of what had happened? Absolutely. I might have become less confident but for what happened a few minutes later, when we went out into the lobby: the house manager, who had been standing at the back of the theater during the performance, and the stage manager up in the light booth, listening to us on headphones via a microphone backstage, told me they heard the same thing I did—the single strum of a ukulele that seemed to come from backstage. Both were as puzzled as I was.

There was, as far as I could determine, no easy access to backstage during the performance—the stage manager had locked the stage door. A heavy set of metal "barn doors" leading to the scene shop were closed (and anyway rattle when they're slid open), and a narrow, poorly lighted spiral staircase in a backstage corner that leads to storage space under the stage was not in use for the show.

There it is. Not a roaring, disembodied apparition. Not a levitating table. Not even errant footfalls in the night. A small event, some might say. Yes, it was. Except it's a riddle I've not been able to solve. Is it possible *someone* got backstage, walked over to the prop table, and then, for some unexplainable reason, ran his (or her) finger across the ukulele strings before making a hasty exit? Yes. Is it probable? No.

What I offered by way of explanation, and only half in jest, was this: the ghost in that theater—his name is Sanford Syse—assumed the role of backstage crew that night (and perhaps on other nights as well), and this was his rather astonishing way of letting us know that he was on the job making certain that nothing unexpected transpired backstage. Far-fetched? Perhaps. But I have trouble coming up with any other explanation.

You can read more about the ghost at this theater in the chapter "No Exit."

This third edition of *Haunted Wisconsin* includes most of the stories from the two earlier volumes. I've added a few new stories and updated others where I've become aware of additional incidents. As in the earlier editions of this book, some sources asked that their real names not be included. In those instances where a pseudonym is used, you'll find it marked with an asterisk (*).

The origins of *Haunted Wisconsin* over thirty years ago are relatively straightforward. Writer Beth Scott and I decided to write a book. Period. Looking back, it seems such a simple decision, undoubtedly one that is made daily by scores of authors. Little did I think that three-plus decades later I'd be compiling a new edition of the book.

We didn't even have a subject, though we had narrowed it down to the vague notion that it would be nonfiction and about Wisconsin. In time, I discovered a passage in the book *Wisconsin Lore*, by Robert Gard and L. G. Sorden, that claimed the state "contains, if the yarns are an indication, more ghosts per square mile than any state in the nation." While I realized it simply may have been an extravagant, unsupportable claim by these two authors (after all, who counted?), I pointed out the passage to Beth and suggested that maybe here was our subject—a book of some choice Wisconsin ghost stories that could be added to the state mix of brats, beer, and cheese. Though Gard and Sorden included a short chapter of primarily historical ghost tales, there was no book on the subject. Indeed, there were only a handful of regional ghost story collections, and most of those focused on the American South or the New England states, as might be expected.

Early on, we made the decision that we would strive for an impartial, open-minded point of view in our stories. Both of us were journalists by inclination and training and wanted the facts to carry the story; in that way we thought readers might draw their own conclusions. In a very few cases, we did try to explain what might have happened or solve the "mystery," as with the relatively famous Paulding Light. If the haunting took place some years before—perhaps as long as a century removed from the present—it was simply not feasible, so we relied heavily on what witnesses and participants at the time had to say about the events. For contemporary accounts for which we were able to interview witnesses, we believed—and I continue to think—that they were honest and sincere in relating their experiences. And, of course, a few years ago I had my own slight experience, which I related earlier. That certainly helped me understand how anomalous events such as these can be unnerving, possibly even leading to a revision of one's outlook on events termed "supernatural."

Any book is the result of numerous contributions, either in the writing process or as it wends it way through a publisher's prudent hands. The author(s) have received assistance from many individuals for each edition of *Haunted Wisconsin*, especially the following: Dennis Boyer, Dodgeville; Beverley Christ, Ripon; Krista Clumpner, Houghton, Michigan; Marjorie Davies, Wisconsin Dells; Al Denninger, Rhinelander; John Dettloff, Couderay; Betsy Doehlert, Madison; Tim Ericson, River Falls; Deb Fenske and Steve Fenske, Waupaca; Charles "Chuck" Golden, River Falls; Richard Heiden, Milwaukee; Tom Heinen, Milwaukee; Ervin Kontowicz, Milwaukee; Stacy Kopchinski, Rochester; Elizabeth Lefebvre, Madison; Jeanie Lewis, Ridgeway; Carol Matara, River Falls; Barb McMahon, Hayward; the late Willis Miller, Hudson; Jerry Minnich, Madison; Mary Beth Mueller, Milwaukee; LaDonna Nieland, Waupaca; Steve Nieland, Waupaca; Kathy Olson, Stone Lake; the late C. W. Orton, Ridgeway; the late Dick Owens, Renton, Washington; Don Petzold, River Falls; Phil Pfuehler, River Falls; Will Pooley, Eau Claire; Gerald Schneider, Milwaukee; Debbie Schuerman, Rochester; Mara Westerhouse, Waupaca; Paul Woehrmann, Milwaukee; Mrs. Verne Worthing, Evansville; Ezra Zeitler and Micah Zeitler. For this third edition, thanks to the wonderful staff at the University of Wisconsin Press, including Raphael Kadushin, Sheila Leary, and former sales manager Fred Lauing for their generous support and encouragement; and to my editor, Sheila McMahon, who was incredibly patient and thorough throughout the editing process. Finally, thanks to my treasured friend, literary colleague, and the man who first steered *Haunted Wisconsin* to publication thirty years ago, Mark E. Lefebvre, Madison, without whom this book would not have been possible; and to the memory of Beth Scott, my friend and coauthor on the first edition of this book.

June 2011

Part I
The Haunted North

The Gmeiner Enigma

Henry DeLong does not like anyone closing the guest bedroom door in his home. In fact he is so insistent that he's been known to slam it open if he finds it shut. There would be nothing wrong with this except that Henry is a ghost and the family that lives in his former home got mighty perturbed with his behavior.

It took Deb Fenske—who lives there with her husband, Steve—some time to figure out what was going on in her house.

"I thought maybe it was because the door wasn't closing properly, so I'd close it and push on it to make sure it was shut tight. Again a few minutes later it would be open."

Then came the day when she "got the message," as she put it.

She had returned home for lunch one winter day and found that bedroom door standing wide open. She wanted to keep it closed for very practical reasons—it's a rambling, century-old, two-and-a-half-story brick house that's expensive to heat in the cold months, and closing off some rooms made good sense. That upstairs guest room was one of them.

Once again Fenske shut the door tight, then went up to the top floor for a few minutes. *Thud!!* She thought it sounded like a door somewhere below her crashing open and hitting a wall. Fenske found the guest room door wide open once more.

"I got the message," she said, smiling with resignation. "I stood on the landing facing the guest room and made a deal with Henry. I told him we would keep the door open, but that when we have guests who stay in that room, that he not open the door if they had closed it."

So far, Henry has kept his promise. The Fenskes haven't had another problem with that particular door.

Sometimes it's not easy living in an older home under the best of circumstances, but even more so if the many oddities that unfold within its walls hint that a previous owner has not altogether vacated the property. Deb and Steve Fenske had heard something of those stories that went along with the historic Henry and Elizabeth DeLong House, on West Fulton Street in Waupaca, when they bought the place in July of 2000. On one occasion, a young woman who had previously lived there told Deb Fenske, apprehensively, that she had wanted to speak with her about the house for quite some time. When Fenske said she wasn't sure what the woman was talking about, the latter blurted out, "Your house is haunted!" Fenske smiled back and assured her she didn't see it as a problem. She preferred to use the word "spirit" rather than "haunted." The DeLong House is a classic boxy, American foursquare, turn-of-the-twentieth-century home of brick and concrete construction. The broad front steps, guarded by two small stone lions, lead to a wide, enclosed front porch. Above, a dormer protrudes from the steeply pitched roof. The low, ornamental banister stretching around the porch roofline and framed windows with interesting, decorative woodwork add pleasing touches to the post-Victorian "prairie box" building style. The uniqueness of the house as early twentieth-century domestic architecture and the loving care with which it has been treated over the last century has earned it a place on the local, state, and national registers of historic places.

Conrad Gmeiner built the house in 1903 as a gift for his wife's parents, Henry and Elizabeth DeLong. Gmeiner, who owned the Waupaca Brick Yard from 1903 to 1944, also put up three other houses adjacent to the DeLongs', all of them made of brick from the Waupaca brick kilns.

Henry DeLong was a commercial potato farmer who sold his produce as far away as Madison, Milwaukee, and Chicago. The Fenskes found the remains of what they believe was the potato-weighing station near the driveway. At the turn of the last century, even though the area surrounding the homes remained farmland, new housing was drawing residents away from central Waupaca. Trolley cars rattling down Fulton Street made their way to and from the Wisconsin Veteran's Home in the nearby town of King, and in the summer they carried tourists from the train station to popular resorts along the scenic Chain O'Lakes area southwest of the city.

The DeLongs loved the house, according to Deb Fenske. Henry and Elizabeth's great-granddaughter told her that a spirit in the house was more than likely that of "Grandpa Henry."

Both Fenskes soon discovered that even though Henry DeLong "agreed" to keep the guest room door closed when someone visited, that didn't mean he had vacated the room, let alone his old house. For instance, there was the time Deb went in to tidy up the guest room. She found an indentation on the bed, and a pillow sham was turned vertically when it had been horizontal. The pillow showed an indentation, as if someone had been sleeping on it.

She asked her husband whether he had been in there. He was puzzled, because he hadn't for some time.

"Well, somebody has!" she said pointedly.

Henry as the culprit made sense to her. They had figured out it had been *his* old bedroom after all, and he may even have died in it. Deb said Henry's spirit was happy in there; she was even resigned to the occasional, odd ways in which the departed owner decided to say hello.

The Fenskes no longer expect their resident spirit to wander only the upstairs bedrooms. Deb fell asleep one evening on the living room couch and awoke to find a man—she was quite certain it must have been Henry—standing next to her. He was older, wearing baggy, bib overalls, a denim jacket, and a broad-rimmed straw hat. He stared at her for a few seconds before vanishing. "He loved this house so much. If that's who [the ghost] is, he's never done anything bad to us."

Although the family assumes the ghost they live with is Henry DeLong, they can't be entirely certain. Oddly, Henry DeLong must have been camera shy, because they haven't been able to locate a single photograph of him. Deb, for one, would like to know if the fleeting figure she saw was indeed DeLong.

The couple remain unsure because they've discovered at least one other male ghost in the house. As Deb woke up one morning, she saw him standing by their bedroom window, staring in the couple's direction. He didn't seem to be focused on them, however. This was a bigger man than the earlier ghost she'd seen. He was dressed all in white and had dark hair.

There is some evidence that Elizabeth DeLong could not care for her husband adequately as he became elderly, and they hired someone to help with his medical needs. The Fenskes think the person Deb saw might have been someone like a hospital orderly working for the DeLongs. This person's old bedroom might have been Deb and Steve's bedroom. Deb has also seen him a few times hanging about the hallway outside their bathroom.

Both Steve and Deb Fenske readily admit that their stories about living in a haunted house sound "weird" and "bizarre" to strangers, but both are very comfortable sharing their extraordinary experiences. Deb Fenske is the product and marketing manager for a Waupaca corporation, while Steve is the hazardous material training coordinator for Wisconsin's Emergency Management Department.

Neither of them has been harmed nor exceptionally frightened. Events are usually more "startling" than frightening. For example, there was the time she saw the man in white looking down at her in bed. She tried to awaken Steve, but by the time he sat up the image had vanished. It's also just plain discomfiting to have a ghost popping up in one's bedroom. "I'd just as soon they stayed out of there," she said firmly.

Yet it was an incident in the couple's bedroom that gave Deb the notion that someone or *something* else shared their home. Shortly after they moved in, she placed three small, carved statues on the bedroom dresser. Before long she noticed that one statue in particular, a delicate carving of a woman, was in a different position. She pointed it out to Steve and they decided to "test" whether it might have been caused by vibrations, perhaps from opening dresser drawers. They pulled the drawers out and although the statues moved slightly, none of them turned. One night the couple made sure the female statue was facing out, toward their bed. In the morning, it had turned one hundred eighty degrees, so that it was looking away from them. They didn't turn it back around, but when they got home from work, the statue was facing outward again. No one had been in the house since the couple left in the morning.

Perhaps it's coincidence, but the statue is thought to represent a goddess of fertility. The Fenskes have no children.

The couple has decorated their home to match its historical, turn-of-the-century charm. Throughout the ground floor, gleaming bird's-eye maple floorboards complement the original dark oak woodwork. A parlor just inside the front door features a full-width, built-in cloister bench that opens to reveal a storage compartment. For Halloween trick-or-treaters, Deb puts a "body" inside with its arm dangling out. In one corner of the small room is a spinning wheel handmade by Deb's father-in-law.

A formal dining room contains several shelves and tables with the Fenskes' collection of Christmas antiques, including several dozen folk art Santa Claus figures, which they display year-round. Early American prints decorate most of the walls.

But it's in the living room—in a corner that has a formal Abraham Lincoln portrait looking out into the room—where the Fenskes have found there is an especially significant amount of ghostly "activity." In that corner, a brightly patterned, two-piece sectional forms an "L." Deb described it as a "portal . . . like there is something right in that area."

"I've been on that couch wide awake watching television and had a blanket pulled right off my legs. I saw it in midair. Then I touched the spot on my leg where the blanket was, and it was like somebody had put dry ice on it."

Once it was as if someone they couldn't see had been sitting there and then rose to take a stroll. Again, the television was on, the couple sitting at opposite ends of the long sectional, when Deb dozed off. Their Dalmatian dog was under his own blanket on the couch between them.

"I heard someone and thought Steve had gotten up to go to bed. I thought . . . it was strange he didn't wake me up."

As she snuggled under a blanket, Deb heard him go up the stairs and stop on the landing. Out of the corners of her eyes, she saw him there turning to look at her before continuing on up. She heard him walk around a bit more upstairs.

She was still wondering why her husband hadn't told her he was going to bed when she decided to turn off the television and go upstairs herself, but first she wanted to throw a blanket that had fallen to the floor over their "very spoiled" Dalmatian. She leaned over to pick it up, and that's when she realized Steve hadn't gone upstairs. He was asleep, curled up at the far end of the sofa.

Yet someone *had* gone up that staircase, someone she thought had been Steve, someone who started out at least in the vicinity of the sofa.

They have now heard those same sorts of footfalls so often over the years that they've lost track of all the occasions. Sometimes Deb will insist that her husband look around the house because it seems as if someone is there, but they've yet to discover a prowler. They laugh now because Steve says he does it more to "humor" his wife than out of any belief that he'll find an intruder.

In fact it took some time for Steve to fully appreciate the impact of what his wife was telling him. They had both seen the small statue change positions, but other than that Steve hadn't witnessed anything out of the ordinary. He had no reason to doubt his wife's stories about the two men she'd seen on separate occasions, or the night someone definitely not Steve walked upstairs, but yet remained unconvinced. For a time.

One night as Steve was going upstairs, he stopped on the landing midway up. Directly in front of him someone else was moving up the next flight of steps to the upstairs hallway. The figure—really nothing more than a separate, distinct shadow—stopped for a few seconds before moving off down the hallway. Both Steve and Deb have taken to calling these apparitions "shadow people."

"I didn't really believe all these things for the longest time, until I saw that shadow. I wanted to, but it was always her that saw figures," Steve recalled.

More recently, an extraordinary episode with a folding chair in their dining room caught Steve and a friend off-guard. Deb found some satisfaction in knowing her husband was now fully in the "haunted loop."

The Fenskes were hosting a birthday party for the daughter of some friends. They had temporarily leaned several wooden folding chairs against a wall in the dining room. Steve and the girl's father were in the front living room chatting when Deb came out of the kitchen carrying a couple of beers for the men. As she passed the folding chairs, there was a sharp *SLAP!* She looked down to see that a seat on one of the folding chairs had snapped open. She glanced over toward Steve and their friend. Their mouths fell open.

"Steve was practically hyperventilating," she remembered. "His eyes were bugging out."

Both men were pointing to the chair. It had not only fallen open, but also then *turned* nearly ninety degrees, as if inviting someone to sit down. Deb had only seen it slide away from the wall and open.

"I will never forget the looks on their faces," she remarked with a laugh. "I didn't think Steve's eyes could get any bigger, and I've never seen [our friend] speechless. He's going *ah-ah-ah-ah-ah*. A chair falling down from against a wall is one thing, but falling down and turning is something else."

The Fenskes' matching Dalmatians—Lexi and Luther—also seemed sensitive to a presence in the house. Both dogs have since died . . . but may now be presences themselves.

Before the couple moved in, they brought the dogs to the house to get used to their new surroundings. Lexi in particular would run up to the finished, walk-up attic and stare at the ceiling. She would run in circles, yipping and looking as if trying to keep something in sight.

Later, if the dogs were sitting with Deb and Steve in the living room, the dogs frequently looked up at the stairs and seemed to follow something passing through the living room and on into the dining room. "Their heads were in perfect synchronization," she said. Neither Deb nor Steve saw or felt anything.

Lexi died unexpectedly a few years after they moved in. The couple was devastated by her loss, especially because Luther had health problems of his own, including becoming blind and diabetic after eating some herbicide. Deb and Steve were able to keep him alive through medication for three years. The Dalmatians always seemed perfectly in sync in life, so perhaps it shouldn't be surprising that the departed Lexi paid an unexpected visit one day.

Steve was in the living room when the aged Luther jumped up on the sofa next to him. A few minutes later Deb came out of the kitchen.

"Oh my god!" she cried. At that moment, Luther's head—right down to a Dalmatian's distinctive black spots—had changed to become Lexi's. His head changed, his face changed. But then he shook himself and returned to his normal self.

Lexi had always begged for back rubs. She would back up into Deb's lap hoping for a good massage. If Deb complied, the dog moaned in delight. Luther, on the other hand, wanted nothing to do with someone touching his back. Right after Luther's head seemed to morph into Lexi's, he jumped off the sofa and went over to Deb and nuzzled her, something that he rarely did. She petted him carefully. He turned around and backed into her as if he now wanted a back rub. He even plopped his rear end onto her lap. As Deb rubbed his back—for the first time—he whimpered with pleasure, just as his pal Lexi used to do.

Since the dogs' deaths, Deb in particular still hears their toenails clicking across the hardwood floors, especially in the winter when the house is more tightly shuttered.

At times she's been sitting on the couch when she's felt one of the dogs leap up and sit on her legs. "I'm thinking I've got a ninety-pound ghost dog on me," she says. "I could feel her weight, I mean she was on me!"

But as with the two human ghosts in their house, Deb and Steve Fenske are perfectly comfortable with these friendly, although unseen, canine companions.

The Henry DeLong House is one of a cluster of four brick homes Conrad Gmeiner put up a century ago, but the only one with the notable designation as an official historic site. Next door to the Fenskes is the original Gmeiner home, a late "Victorian transition" house with a wide, open front porch. Mara Westerhouse and Danny Tamburrino bought it in late 2009. Remarkably, that house along with the Fenskes' and another home across the street might be the center of a "haunted historic district" in that part of Waupaca.

The Gmeiner house has had sweeping changes made to it over the years, but not enough to prevent the appearance of revenants from the past.

Mara and Danny's baby girl—named Bella after her grandmother—was born in the February after they moved into the house. Late one night Mara had gotten up to get a baby bottle in the kitchen when from behind her she heard a woman softly humming. Mara was tired and fixated on feeding her baby so the suddenness of it all surprised her. She said she "kind of blew it off."

One evening shortly after that, the family was watching television when Danny went upstairs for a few minutes. He came back down "white as a ghost," Mara remembered. Her husband is a sturdy, well-built man who is anything but "wimpy," Mara said with a laugh. He blurted out that he had just watched as a "black shadow" walked down their upstairs hallway, turned to look at him as if wanting to make certain Danny had seen it, and then vanished into a bedroom. Danny said he could pick out the shape of its head and a body below it, both misty and deeply black. It had no other features. What scared him the most is that it had turned around toward him.

Mara's son Gage had been listening. "Good, I'm glad someone else saw it!" he exclaimed. He'd also seen a shadowlike object moving around in the house.

Mara eventually made friends with the Fenskes next door because she knew the houses had been in the same family at one time, and because she wanted to know if they had ever experienced "oddities" in their house as well.

One bit of information Deb shared with her new neighbor might have helped solve the problem of the humming woman. When they had moved in a decade earlier, one of the first people they met was Shirley, who lived at that time with her husband in the house that Mara and Danny now occupied. What Deb remembered most about her was that she loved little children—she had twin granddaughters—and that she was always humming while doing housework and while tending her spacious gardens.

Mara wasn't too surprised. When they moved in there was still a small plaque on a wall that read "Oma and Opa's House." Oma and Opa are Dutch/German terms of endearment for grandmother and grandfather.

Shirley passed away while living there.

Other incidents had Mara and her family on edge for a time, not certain what might happen next. Their pug dog Chloe acted peculiarly at times—not unlike the Fenskes' Dalmatians—suddenly growling at something that seemed to be at the far end of the upstairs hallway, or quickly popping her head up as she lay on Mara and Danny's bed, growling and jumping to her feet, fixated, it seemed to Mara, on something invisible moving between the door and the bed.

Once Mara tried to melt a bowl of chocolate in the microwave but over-heated it and ended up throwing it away. A few minutes later, she found a gob of the gooey chocolate on the kitchen floor. She assumed it had dropped off the bowl, wiped it up, and threw the paper towel in the garbage. Twenty minutes later she found another lump of melted chocolate in the same place.

"That was the first time I thought something definitely was going on here. I know I wiped it up because it was all in the garbage can. I don't know where [the second chunk] came from, but it was in the same place and I was the only one home."

Today, Mara, Danny, and the children all feel very "comfortable" in the house and haven't wanted to make a "big deal" out of the mischievous nature of most of what has transpired. Other than the passing shadows Danny and Gage witnessed, no one has actually seen an apparition.

"If I ever *did* see anything," Mara acknowledged, "I think that would change my tune. I'm still kind of light about it. It's not scary to me."

Across West Fulton Street and half a block down is a tall, attractive, light blue Victorian with white trim and blue shutters, surrounded by a pretty white picket fence. At one side a second floor room covers an unusual open carport. Steve and LaDonna Nieland live there . . . and appear to be residing in another of this trio of haunted Waupaca homes, all within shouting distance of one another.

The Nielands describe their home as "Victorian transition" similar to Mara and Danny's home, but with many American Craftsmen features, and built by noted commercial designer Hans Knutson between 1896 and 1902 for the commandant of the nearby Wisconsin Veteran's Home. It was a gift for one of his two adult daughters. The other daughter lived in a "mirror" house right next door that Knutson also built.

The Nielands give the impression of being a couple comfortable with paranormal encounters . . . even when such occurrences take place a long way from home. Two years after the couple moved into the house, they were vacationing in Maine when their most "profound" paranormal experience unfolded at the elegant Captain Lord Mansion Inn, in Kennebunkport. After a day of sightseeing, the couple returned to their room in the late afternoon. Steve laid down on the bed for a quick nap; LaDonna curled up in a chair to read. But not long after he shut his eyes, Steve suddenly awoke to the pressure of LaDonna's hand holding his own. He thought that was nice and turned to give her a hug. But she was still sitting in the chair across the room. Whatever held his hand in its warm grasp gradually lessened the grip and finally let go. Later that night, someone tromping across the room awakened both Steve and LaDonna. Whoever it was seemed to sit down for a short time in a rocking chair that then began to squeak. The visitor then walked over to a closet and opened the door. Neither of the couple saw anybody connected to the footfalls, but they both heard the soft *skreek* of the rocker and the squeaky closet door swing open.

After breakfast the next morning, the Nielands quietly told a front desk clerk that "really weird things happened" in their room the previous night. Discretely and cautiously they related their experience to the clerk, who then revealed that the ghost of a woman—possibly one of the elderly women who roomed at the inn prior to 1978—had been seen in their room by others too. She was an earthbound spirit, the clerk explained, and not mean or malicious in the least. The closet door she seemed to open and walk through was formerly a connecting door into the next room.

Their interesting encounters in Maine were but a prelude to the intermittent mysteries at their charming Fulton Street home, where they have joined the Fenskes, Mara Westerhouse, and Danny Tamburrino in wondering why it is that so many odd phenomena seem to be centered at their three closely situated homes.

When they bought their house in 1983, the Nielands thought the rough-finished room over the open carport was "novel." It looked like it had been used for attic storage or perhaps a home studio or office. Later they discovered that the room had been added because an earlier family had a son with tuberculosis who was kept isolated there. At that time in the early twentieth century, it was thought TB patients could be cured with "fresh air," so keeping open the room's numerous windows had been part of the treatment. When LaDonna, a former elementary school teacher, worked as curator at the historic Hutchinson House Museum, she met a woman in her eighties who told her that as a young woman she often noticed the sickly boy staring out of his isolated bedroom window. The Nielands surmise that he may have died young there because a grandson of the builder Hans Knutson told them he had seen his first "dead body" during a visit to the home many years earlier. At that time it wasn't unusual to have viewings of the deceased take place in the family home.

That boy may be one of the house ghosts. Deb Fenske thought she saw him looking out of a window in that room when the Nielands were away on vacation and she was taking care of their outdoor plantings. She didn't have a key to get inside, but did check to make sure the doors and windows were locked, which they were.

The house had fallen into disrepair when Steve and LaDonna bought it. They refinished the room over the garage and transformed it into their daughter's playroom. LaDonna said that by doing that they turned a sad room into a happy one. Their daughter never said anything about any unusual encounters there.

The grounds also had been poorly maintained; the family spent their first couple of years rebuilding and replanting the yard and gardens, which led to Steve's disconcerting encounter with their first ghostly visitor.

It happened during the second year after they moved in on an afternoon when he was mowing the lawn. He had spent months restoring the once-extensive gardens, including a spacious herb garden. He passed about ten feet away from it with the mower when suddenly standing within its boundary was a slightly built woman wearing a long-sleeved brown "work dress," her hair pinned up in a bun. She looked over at him with a warm, welcoming smile and then was gone.

"That was it," Steve said of the brief encounter. "Was it the commandant's daughter showing that she liked what we were doing? I don't know. She was solid, perfectly clear, and about medium height."

He ran back into the house and told his wife what he had just seen.

"It scared the crap out of me," he admitted.

For Steve Nieland, who is in the research and development department at the same company where Deb Fenske works, the most astonishing episodes took place on two consecutive Christmases in a family room addition he built onto the back of the house. Below that and reached by a staircase was a basement room used as their family's media room. He designed the airy addition so the existing kitchen would merge with the new space. A large dining table was a favorite place for the family to gather or to do things like frost freshly baked cookies—which is precisely what Steve was doing that Christmas eve.

His wife and daughter had gone off to do something else so he was alone finishing up. "Andy Williams [Christmas music] was on the radio. It was nice. Now, we had a black-and-white tomcat. So when I saw . . . a black shape walk up to me I looked down to say hi . . . but it wasn't him."

Instead, a small black dog that he'd never seen before was standing at his feet, looking up and panting.

"I'm wondering, how did this dog get in here?"

Then—*SNAP!*—the dog was gone, just like the woman in the garden.

A year went by and Steve found himself again at the table frosting Christmas cookies. He saw what he thought was their cat saunter up, but again it was the same dog, happy and panting and gone within a few seconds.

"Apparently he liked Christmas cookies because he was back. It became a running joke in the family. I said I didn't want to be in the room alone making . . . cookies because I'm going to start seeing things," Steve said with a laugh, while at the same time knowing full well that there was no way he could mistake their cat for a dog, or "create" this four-legged phantom with his imagination.

"I kept asking, how could that dog have gotten into the house? Where did he come from? I saw him, he's sitting there panting, looking up at me and then . . ." He finishes the sentence with a snap of his fingers.

The little dog made itself known once more several years later. Again it was at Christmas, but this time it came in the form of a sharp *YIP!*—a small bark from the doorway leading to the basement media room. Steve looked over in that direction, as did their cat, who had been curled up in a chair. He later told LaDonna, "Well, I didn't see my dog this year, but I heard him bark."

Steve noted that the house addition he built would have covered part of the backyard in earlier years, so he speculates the ghost dog may have belonged to some earlier homeowners who kept him in the backyard. Or perhaps he had been buried there after he died.

The Nielands haven't done enough research into their home's history to pin names on any of their household apparitions, or to know whether the young boy died of his tuberculosis. They're also perplexed that their house seems to be a center of some paranormal activity. In that, they are in good company with their neighbors—the Fenskes, Mara Westerhouse, and Danny Tamburrino—all of whom find it rather extraordinary to be living in a haunted neighborhood in this small Wisconsin city.

Another Voice

The frantic call came into the police dispatcher at about six thirty on an April evening. A couple was making the call. The man quickly explained that a violent argument had broken out in an apartment on the floor directly above their own; a female voice on the same line described a loud, obscenity-strewn quarrel punctuated with blood-curdling screams. It appeared to be between two people, and one of them involved—perhaps a woman—was in imminent danger of being injured or worse.

Within minutes, the first patrol officer arrived on the scene. He was Charles "Chuck" Golden, a relatively new member of the River Falls Police Department. The address was an older, foursquare-style house that had been painted a garish pink and subdivided into apartments. The couple making the emergency call lived in a first-floor apartment. They went over what they had told the dispatcher and added that someone sounded like they were being gagged or choked.

At first Golden didn't hear anything. But then all three of them were jarred by "a violent, horrific scream," as Golden described it, from the apartment above them. He was certain someone was in a potentially life-threatening situation.

All cops know a domestic disturbance call can be one of the most dangerous they face. In the heat of the moment, the people involved could turn on each other or on the officers, or the latter might have to use their weapons to stop a violent assailant.

Golden's backup arrived and together the two officers rapidly climbed a rear, outside staircase to an inside hallway by the apartment in which the brutal argument was taking place. As they turned a corner, the officers heard a man's hysterical screams punctuated with coarse expletives.

Interlaced with the man's tirade, Golden heard a woman suddenly cry out from inside the apartment: "Oh, God! Oh, God! Oh, God!"

"She was in distress," Golden explained.

That was enough for the rookie cop. A woman inside was being injured or, worse, at risk of death.

"The door was open, but I would have kicked it in if it wasn't," he later admitted.

With his gun drawn, Golden barged in, his partner close behind, and announced they were police officers, scanning the untidy room to confront what they had every reason to believe would be a horrific scene.

A blast of pungent smoke told them heavy marijuana use had been going on not long before. A naked man staggered from the bathroom. Golden ordered him to raise his hands, still quickly looking around for the woman whose cries he had heard moments before.

"Were you yelling in here?" Golden demanded.

Yes, the suspect admitted, but only at the bathtub because he couldn't get hot water out of the faucet. The cops were incredulous.

"Where's the woman?" Golden yelled.

The young man said there wasn't any woman in the apartment. He was the only one there. Golden figured that's what anyone would say.

Again Golden demanded to know what he had done with the other person, the woman, and again he was met with a denial that anyone else was in the apartment.

By this time, other officers had arrived. The cops eventually let the man get dressed but at the same time launched a search. While Golden continued to question the man, the other officers fanned out.

"I told him I'd heard a second voice that I thought was female, but he denied there was anyone in the apartment with him," Golden said. As improbable as the story seemed to the officers, it seemed to be confirmed by what the police search turned up over the next few minutes—absolutely nothing.

The officers looked under beds, opened closet doors, and checked the windows. They even searched inside a distinctive cupola that perched on the center roofline. Not only was there no other person in the apartment, but there was no indication that any sort of physical confrontation had taken place: no blood, no overturned furniture, no sign of a struggle anywhere. Nothing, Golden said, that would indicate someone had been harmed.

Golden asked the man if he had a girlfriend. Sounding puzzled by both the police presence and the questions, he confirmed that he had a girlfriend and that she was at work. He agreed to have her call the department when she got home.

"I know that I heard what I believed to be a woman in distress," Golden said. He reacted as he had been trained, to take necessary action to prevent an innocent person from being harmed or killed. Although that training turned out not to have been needed that evening, the episode left him with perplexing questions.

The officers took down the man's identifying information and again asked that he have his girlfriend call the department when she got home. They did not issue any drug citations against the man.

Back downstairs, they updated the couple that had reported the disturbance and instructed them that if they heard any more disturbances to call the police. And that's where they left it.

"All I know is that after we searched [no woman] was there. We cleared and left . . . scratching our heads."

Officer Chuck Golden didn't know what to think.

"Afterward," he recalled, "I was thinking maybe I did hear things, maybe it was the guy altering his voice. Certainly you're going to question yourself, rationalize it. But I know what I heard."

A few days later, Golden's partner showed him an earlier edition of *Haunted Wisconsin*, which prominently featured the same house where they'd taken the "weird" call—locals know it as the Parker mansion—and a haunting there described by earlier owners.

Golden knew nothing of the house's history or its earlier tenants, but upon learning the house's reputation, he wondered if perhaps the woman's cries might have been somehow connected to the mansion's supernatural past.

"I probably shrugged it off until I saw the book . . . I was shocked," he added.

That century-old Parker house—now painted grey—stands prominently a few blocks off Main Street on the east side of River Falls. Although today rather unkempt, the once gracious appearance of this mansion can still be seen in its grandiose, classic foursquare-type design and in the open cupola (known as a "widow's walk") sitting like a steamboat lookout atop its roofline.

Charles D. Parker, Wisconsin's lieutenant governor from 1874 to 1878, built the home for his family. Through the decades the house has undergone numerous renovations and several additions—a small, open, side porch and enclosed front entryway were added on years ago. It's been variously a single-family home, a duplex, and, more recently, small apartments and sleeping rooms carved out of its high-ceilinged rooms. When the police were called to answer the disturbance, it was serving as a rooming house.

However, years before Officer Chuck Golden's encounter, Tim and Alice Early lived there and might have had some insight into what Officer Golden experienced.

The young married couple planned to rent out the second floor and remodel the downstairs portion for their growing family. Their idea was to restore the home to its former grandeur. The Earlys were prominent business owners in River Falls; Tim's late father was once a Wisconsin state senator.

For the first few months after the Earlys moved in, "it was like someone was with us," Tim recalled. "You know how someone can sneak up on you and, although you don't hear them or see them, you know that someone is there? Well, it was that kind of an experience."

In time, the couple began to think it might be something they hadn't wanted to consider—a ghostly presence—though neither of them ever saw any sort of apparition. Along with that sense of someone always nearby, the couple said there was enough mischievous business to add eerie details to their general impression—doors swinging open for no apparent reason, lights suddenly blinking on, their little daughter Jessica's rubber ball inexplicably rolling across the room, the volume of a stereo suddenly increasing.

Neither parent ever discussed the odd events with Jessica, then two years old, yet on more than one occasion the child came toddling out of her bedroom at night because something had frightened her. She could never, of course, put into words what had scared her, but her parents didn't think it was her imagination at play. Later, Tim learned that a friend of his had sensed a presence in the same room when he had been a tenant there as a college student some years before. The entire house had been subdivided into several apartments and sleeping rooms. The man often joked with his friends about his "third roommate."

The unexplained incidents increased when the Earlys started a major remodeling project on the first floor. The two largest rooms had been a living room and dining room separated by a pair of the mansion's original French doors. Curtains also had been draped over the wide doorway since earlier tenants had once used both rooms as sleeping quarters.

Tim Early remembers one day in particular:

> We were remodeling what was going to be our living room. The evening we completed the work I was sitting in the dining room with my daughter. Alice

was in the kitchen. At the same time the light went off in the empty living room and the French doors between the rooms swung open. I called [out to] Alice and about the same time, the screen door on the front porch opened and slammed shut.

There was no breeze that night. Alice assumed that their "friend" had left the house and perhaps for a very specific reason. She thought it was because they had remodeled the main room and were going to make use of it. This otherworldly dweller would simply have made the place too crowded.

Any old house has a varied and sometimes obscure history. The Earlys researched the history of their home but couldn't establish any link between the haunting and former owners or occupants. Their experiences did, however, prompt a continuing interest in psychic phenomena for the couple: living in a haunted house can do that for people. On one occasion, an English exchange student told them the rounded walls found in some parts of the house were designed to foil evil spirits—they couldn't find a corner to hide in.

The Earlys tried to find out more about the source of the mysterious happenings when they asked a psychic friend from southern Wisconsin to hold a séance in the house.

The woman found two presences in the house, a negative entity and a "friendly" spirit, which is the one Tim and Alice had encountered. The psychic did not want to dwell on the negative presence but described the pleasant spirit she could "see" as a gentleman sitting in a rocker on the long-vanished side porch, stroking a cat and gazing off into the distance. He seemed to be very fond of the cat, the psychic said. Tim Early thought the man was probably looking off toward a side street that has since been blocked from view by several large houses. The psychic could not get any better mental picture of the negative specter and they all left it at that.

"There is definitely a [friendly] spirit in that house," the psychic said. "This was his house at one time. I don't think he'd do anything negative. If the spirits [who live in a house] are friendly, they were very happy."

The Early family eventually moved away from the Parker mansion, but neither Tim nor Alice would be surprised to hear of the police officer's peculiar experience. They've certainly never forgotten their years in the Parker mansion.

Is it possible Officer Chuck Golden heard a cry from that second, more negative presence?

Golden, now an investigator with the River Falls Police Department's Youth Services Division, isn't willing to go that far, but he maintained, "I heard what I heard, yet I couldn't substantiate it by finding a woman in the apartment. I believe to this day I heard two voices."

Is it possible the apartment's occupant was arguing with himself or somehow changing his voice throughout the episode? Maybe the "gagging" the woman in the apartment below heard from upstairs was the pot-smoker choking when he inhaled.

Golden won't rule out the possibility, but he is clearly skeptical about it:

> What I heard from [the woman's voice] was substantially different in style and tone from what the guy was saying. It was just different. It was a plea for help. The guy sounded like the aggressor. The other voice . . . was a plea like "oh God, something bad is going to happen."

And that was what led the officers through the doorway, knowing full well the legal implications of going into a private residence without a search warrant.

The veteran River Falls police investigator has gone on to handle hundreds of other cases during his seventeen-year career. Yet this "weird" and "odd" case from Chuck Golden's earliest months on the force has stayed with him, and comes back as clearly as if it took place yesterday.

Although he doesn't know how it could be possible, Golden remains certain of one thing: it is his absolute conviction that he *heard* a violent domestic altercation underway in that second-floor apartment, that he *heard* a female being attacked, crying out to God in obvious agony. The only question is, *to whom* or *to what* did that voice belong?

Ghost Island

The heavily overcast sky draped the fabled seventeen thousand-acre Chippewa Flowage wilderness waterways in a gloom that seemed unusually appropriate for this brisk October afternoon. A cold front had slipped through the region, bringing with it a hard breeze rustling through the lofty second-growth birch and pines. A fine mist roiling across the open water washed against the shores of the 140 islands in the Flowage. Off a spit of land called Sliver's Point, two fishermen bundled against the cold sat in their open boat debating the best way to find a few of the water's fabled muskies.

The two men included veteran fishing guide Al Denninger. He'd been hired to take the other man in the boat on a daylong outing. Denninger said they'd pull up to shore on the closer island, near Sliver's Point, lay out their lines with hook-rigged suckers, set them up along the water's edge, and open their spools. They'd then sit back and let the suckers do the hard work, luring the elusive muskies. Denninger joked that it was angling the "lazy way."

The men pulled their boat up on the sandy shore, put out the rods and lines, and unfolded a couple of lawn chairs. Then it was just sit and wait.

The men checked their lines every so often and listened for the "clickers." A lot of time to kill until something happens.

Directly across the water from the men was an island whose southernmost point, where the channel narrows, was only some eight to ten yards from the tip of the island on which they now sat. The channel is so shallow off the isles' points that during dry spells a sand bar is only a foot or two beneath the water's surface.

As the men quietly talked fishing and listened for a hit on their lines, their gazes ranged across the pristine waters. Only nature interrupted their reverie, the occasional cry of a loon or gull and the gently lapping waves of the clear waters against the shore.

Suddenly, Denninger saw his friend's face go pasty white and his eyes widen. He was looking off toward the island across the channel.

"What's that?" his friend stammered.

Denninger turned to look, expecting to see an animal swimming in the water, or maybe a loon.

"No, no! That, up there!" the man said, pointing down the distant shore, about a hundred yards away.

Denninger followed the man's gaze.

Against the island's tree line and about ten feet in the air, a floating, white, bulbous form was clearly visible. It had emerged through the trees yet did not change its form or shape as it moved. The solid object hovered at the water's edge.

It had been misting off and on during the day and that's what Denninger thought it was at first, some sort of haze or vapor cloud. But then again it didn't dissipate or change in any way. No darkness to it, nor any shadow.

Denninger, immediately aware of its human shape, later explained, "It looked like it had shoulders and it tapered on both ends." A yawning gap was at the place where its right shoulder should have been.

As an outdoorsman, he noticed more than anything else that the mysterious shape moved . . . *against the wind.*

What Al Denninger didn't know at the time is that the island on which the strange apparition materialized has something of a history of peculiar and unexplainable phenomena. The owners of a nearby lodge had even given it a name bespeaking its unsettling legacy:

Ghost Island.

Barb and Bill McMahon have owned Golden Fawn Lodge on the Chippewa Flowage for more than thirty years. It's within eyesight of Ghost Island a few hundred yards across the water.

From its earliest years, lodge guests would make discreet inquiries about the island across the channel. Did someone live on that island? Why would there be noises over there at night?

"No one would ever tell me *what* they heard, though, just odd sounds," Barb McMahon said.

The name Ghost Island cannot be found on any official map because very few of the seven score islands in the Flowage have official names. Locals know them by geographical or historical landmarks, such as Big Timber Island or Darrow Island. Resort owners have their own maps with hand-lettered names to help vacationers navigate the waterways.

The islands are what remain after Northern States Power Company dammed the Chippewa River back in 1923. The river merged with ten existing lakes in the overflow to form the thousands of acres of interconnected waterways and island wildernesses known today as one of the nation's premier vacation and fishing destinations.

When their guests' reports about the nearby island started surfacing in the early 1970s, the McMahons first attributed their uneasiness to the sounds of nature perhaps unfamiliar to "city people." The McMahons knew the island had no cabins or camping sites. The odd fall deer hunter perhaps, or a fisherman, might arrive to spend some daylight hours, but no one would have any business on the island after dark.

That's what made reports by the Golden Fawn Resort guests about nighttime activity on that island so unusual. There are fewer than two dozen camping areas on the entire flowage. Otherwise island visits are limited to daytime hikes or shore lunches.

Could it simply be that natural causes were at play, or that hikers or campers were on the island against regulation? It's possible, but Barb eventually concluded that maybe, just maybe, something more disturbing was at play here.

The McMahons first labeled the place Ghost Island on their resort brochure in the 1970s as a kind of joke. But then the teasing tones faded. She could understand questions from an occasional puzzled guest or two; after all, the sudden cry of a loon can startle almost anyone. But when it became a half dozen or dozen times each season that vacationers tracked her down to ask if someone lived on that island, well, Barb started seeking more detailed information.

"They just heard odd, strange noises. I always thought it was unusual that people would *not* describe for me what they heard, but then again people perhaps don't like to because they don't want someone to think they're peculiar or hearing things or to be told it was all in their imagination."

The McMahons' resort stretches across several hundred yards of water-front acreage on a wide, quiet bay. Vacationers staying in the cabins farthest away from the main lodge, at the tips of the bay's "arms," and thus closest to Ghost Island, most frequently asked about the island.

Ghost Island and its ominous atmosphere was experienced firsthand by Barb's husband.

Bill McMahon loved to fish an inlet on that island, but he was uncomfortable there and didn't know why. He stayed for only short periods of time and then left for another site.

Bill is a veteran outdoorsman who knows the Flowage well; he is not easily intimidated by the loneliness inherent in wilderness living, nor has he any similar feeling about any other location in the Flowage. He didn't fish near Ghost Island for years.

He said the hairs on the back of his neck would rise right up when he was by that island . . . like *someone* is up there watching him . . .

Or some *thing*?

But Al Denninger and his client didn't know any of that history as they sat transfixed at what they were watching. Nothing in Denninger's experience had prepared him for this, and from his background it's safe to say that he is a man prepared for almost anything.

Although he was an old hand at the Flowage, guiding had been a sideline. Until his retirement in 2001, Denninger was a professional Milwaukee firefighter. He had seen nearly everything a firefighter could witness in his three decades in one of the world's most dangerous occupations. He is not a man to be trifled with, nor someone who seems even remotely capable of being frightened.

Denninger called the Ghost Island experience "interesting."

"I knew that it was something that didn't belong there. It was totally foreign, strange; I've never seen anything like that. I wasn't scared, but I did get more excited as I wondered what it was."

His client was clearly upset. He wanted to pull up their lines and get away from the area as soon as possible. Yet as the object continued to hover on the shoreline across the channel, Denninger characteristically kept his wits about him and grabbed a Polaroid instant camera he kept on his fishing boat. Those who know him best joke that he is rarely without his cameras, and takes photographs of anything and everything.

He steadied the camera and shot off one picture, but when he tried to take a second the shutter failed to operate. Assuming the Polaroid was out of film, he pulled the developing print out and put the camera back down in the boat as he kept an eye on the white orb still lingering along the shoreline. In retrospect, Denninger wished he had taken out either the video camera or the 35mm camera he kept onboard to fire off more shots, but he wasn't thinking of that at the time.

The picture Denninger captured on that day was of this extraordinary floating form that looks more than a little human. The soaring birch and pine trees in their fall foliage along the shoreline are clearly visible behind the figure.

The orb sat there for a couple of minutes before it slowly made its way down the shoreline about fifty yards, paused there for a second or so, and then lifted slowly in the air. Denninger said it blended into the sky and he lost track of it.

Denninger estimated the object's height at anywhere from twelve to fifteen feet, based on the distance he was from the object. "It was big. You found yourself stepping back mentally" to keep it in perspective, he said. "You knew it wasn't right."

He even climbed in his boat and motored over to where the object had first appeared. There was no evidence that anything had disturbed the shoreline.

Despite his companion's unease, the two fished a short while longer before leaving the island for another spot some distance away, but neither place proved very good for fishing and so they headed back to Indian Trails Resort, a few miles down the Flowage, where Denninger was headquartered.

Then there is the matter of the Polaroid camera.

It was *not* out of film.

Once they got away from the island, he looked again at the camera. It indicated three exposures remained. He aimed it at his client and it worked. And continued to work for as long as he owned it.

"Now, I'm not an idiot. I wasn't so excited or scared that I was too stupid to push the button. So I've always wondered if that [orb] had anything to do with what we saw."

Sawyer County historian and author John Dettloff owns Indian Trails Resort, one of the oldest in the region. Denninger showed him the picture.

"He said this thing kind of rose up and disappeared," Dettloff recalled. "We were all baffled. It has very defined edges on the sides and the top. It almost looks like the shoulders, the torso of a figure. But it was huge, about ten feet tall when you compare it to the trees. For quite awhile we just talked about the picture as odd."

Dettloff later took a boat down to look at Ghost Island himself, walking through the brush and thick woods. He didn't find anything unusual that might pinpoint the source of the mysterious object.

Dettloff said that everyone who lives, works, or vacations on the Flowage is used to seeing fog, smoke, or low-lying clouds. But he didn't think the photograph was any of those natural phenomena.

"You might see . . . on a distant shoreline a bunch of vapory clouds or fog, but it has a different type of look to it" than what's in the picture, he explained.

Dettloff has known Denninger for decades and believes in the photograph's authenticity. Besides, both men in the fishing boat that day saw the object *before* the photo was taken.

"It's something we can't explain. What would cause Al's client to have his blood run cold and for Al to even take the time to photograph it?" Dettloff wondered.

The photograph and Denninger's experience were topics of conversation around Indian Trails Resort for weeks but didn't spread much farther until John Dettloff visited the McMahons at Golden Fawn Lodge sometime later. He took the mysterious photograph with him.

But before he showed it to Barb McMahon, he asked if she knew anything about the island across the bay from their resort.

Dettloff pointed on a map of the Flowage to an island that they could also see from their main lodge.

"Oh," Barb answered. "You mean Ghost Island."

Dettloff could barely conceal his surprise. Although he had lived in the region nearly his entire life and had closely studied its history, he had never heard that name applied to this or any other island.

"Why do you call it that?"

Barb McMahon said guests had been reporting strange sounds and lights coming from that island since they bought it a quarter of a century earlier. It seems like a "haunted place," she told Dettloff. She showed him a notebook the family kept of the reports of unusual activity on the island. A ghostly guestbook.

"When I heard the story, I was pretty skeptical," Barb admitted. "But when I saw the picture, well . . ."

Al Denninger later visited with the McMahons, whom he had never met, to learn of the stories vacationers had passed along.

Dettloff said there is little exceptional in the history of the high ground now called Ghost Island. Before the 1923 flooding, it was actually just another wilderness tract close by the Chippewa River as it flowed through Sawyer County. As far as he can determine, Dettloff said, there had never been any permanent settlements at that particular locale, but he did point to two interesting historical facts that make the argument for a haunting more intriguing.

A pioneer trail known as the Chippewa River Road between Eau Claire and Chippewa Falls to the south and Hayward to the north was built in 1884, and followed, as its name suggests, the river nearly all the way. Dettloff found that a section of the road cut directly across what is now Ghost Island.

Although the highway was rerouted when the Flowage was created, for nearly forty years, travelers on foot, horse, wagons, and finally in automobiles traveled that historic route.

Could some foul event on that old roadway have released the ghosts of today?

A second possibility links Ghost Island with the Ojibwe people, the historic Native American inhabitants of the region. The vast Lac Courte Oreilles Reservation is intertwined with the Flowage on its western and southern borders.

Dettloff said it's not inconceivable that there could be Native American burial grounds on the island.

High ground, now the islands of the Flowage, would have been used for Native American interments in centuries past. To protect the sites from encroaching white settlers or even other tribes, the Ojibwe seldom marked burial sites or disclosed their locations.

Despite all the speculation and discussion, only one firm conclusion about Al Denninger's photograph and Ghost Island has been established: there was *something* hanging in the air on that foggy day, and the Polaroid photograph establishes that fact, but what it was and why it was there continues to puzzle.

The newspaper journalist and photographer who initially broke the story kept her reportorial neutrality yet said the photograph and Denninger himself provided rather convincing evidence of something at least . . . *unnatural.*

"Skeptics will say it was a cloud formation or fog and I will never convince them otherwise," Kathy Olson said. "But I think there are a lot of things that can't be explained away. This may be one of them. A ghost? I don't know. A presence? An entity from another dimension? I don't know how to explain it."

Historian John Dettloff took a matter-of-fact approach.

"The picture tells the whole story. It's a Polaroid. Whatever is on that picture was there. It's something we can't explain. It has nothing to do with Al's character. Where did the picture come from?"

As for Al Denninger, he doesn't talk much about the story anymore. He has the photograph to prove what he saw. A psychic who hired Denninger to take him to the island after the story was publicized "felt nothing," Denninger said. The psychic did say the object in the photograph was "something from beyond."

Denninger, who lives in Rhinelander, remains puzzled and "overwhelmed" by what he saw. "I do believe in ghosts. But I never gave it much thought before that. I was . . . totally in awe of what I was seeing."

He's never seen anything similar in the years since.

The years have not changed Ghost Island, or the nearby resort still owned by the McMahons. They have more people interested in talking with them about the story of Ghost Island, or sometimes exploring it themselves. Perhaps those visitors are looking for . . . what? A glimpse into the hereafter? An encounter with their own globular apparition? Some evidence that not long ago two ordinary men encountered a mystery that lingers still, unsolved, in that corner of the North Woods?

"It surprises me," Barb McMahon admitted of the continuing fascination with the story of Ghost Island. From entire families to college-age "ghost hunters" to university paranormal study groups, McMahon regularly fields questions about the haunted island just across the bay from her home, handles requests to rent boats so that visitors can row out to see it for themselves, or sometimes even poses for photographs or autographs earlier copies of this book.

Perhaps Barb has the most interesting perspective on Ghost Island and its reputation for unnerving resort guests or veteran anglers looking for the elusive muskie.

"Sometimes you talk yourself out of something. You think that it must have been your imagination. That's why people . . . won't tell you what they've heard, or what they've felt."

Like a fisherman who suddenly weighs anchor because of that gnawing discomfort, that eerie, unexplained sensation that someone is watching him, someone he can't see.

It is, she said, a fear of . . . the unknown.

The Lynch Affair

The time is shortly before noon on a sunny day in early December 1871. The place is the 160-acre homestead of Richard Lynch, near Hatchville in southeastern St. Croix County. One of the hired men, young Jim Snodie, is raising his broadax for another swing at a chunk of downed timber that he will shape into one more railroad tie his boss will sell to the railway companies for their burgeoning passenger and freight system connecting Chicago and the Northwest.

Although he is still a teenager, Snodie is a powerfully built young man with considerable experience in cutting and shaping ties for other farmers in the area. The ties are made from the trees clear-cut to make way for settlers' cabins and farm fields. They are a good source of quick income for the farmers and local woodsmen.

Richard Lynch has hired Snodie and several other men to clear a portion of the heavy stand of timber on his farm. He is working in a clearing some forty yards behind Lynch's two-story log house.

On this swing, however, he stops abruptly when he hears the welcoming clang of Mrs. Lynch's dinner bell coming from the back porch. Snodie drives the broadax's blade deep into a white pine stump, turns and runs for the kitchen door, his thoughts fastening around the pleasure of a few minutes of rest and a hot meal.

But as he reaches for the door latch, *Thwack!*

His broadax embeds itself in the doorframe just inches from his outstretched hand.

He whirls around to confront whoever has thrown the ax with such powerful force and accuracy. Everyone else appears to be either already in the house or working elsewhere on the spread.

Snodie frowns as he grabs the ax with both hands and pulls it out. A few feet away from the porch is another pine stump into which he sinks the ax with all his strength. He pulls a bit on the handle to make sure the blade is firmly embedded before he turns and heads again for the kitchen door.

Whooshh! Thump!!

The lethal ax flies past his left ear and bites deeply into the doorjamb. Again the young woodsman looks around for the perpetrator but no one is within sight.

Thoroughly perplexed, and not a little frightened, the brawny teenager yanks the ax from the frame, which it has nearly split in half, hefts it over his shoulder, and treads warily back to the clearing. He doesn't know what is going on or why he's being attacked, but clearly it seems to him that some force does not want him to go inside that house. And he's not about to push his luck.

The flying broadax that nearly ended Jim Snodie's young life on that day proved to be among the first in a series of bizarre ordeals that some called the work of poltergeists or spirits, and which would continue through most of the 1870s at the Lynch farm, about thirteen miles west of Menomonie, in St. Croix County's Cady Township. So notorious and widespread became the reports that newspaper reporters and curious visitors by the hundreds from the United States and abroad descended on the little homestead tucked away in the Big Woods of Wisconsin.

And what exactly did the sightseers and journalists witness?

A Menomonie newspaper editor, R. J. "Rock" Flint, found "chairs jumping to the ceiling and then falling to the floor with terrible force, crockery and tinware flying across the room like lightning, propelled by some invisible agency. Bullets of wood, pieces of board, axes, handspikes, etc., etc., hurled through the air by unseen hands."

Cooking utensils were said to have hurtled across the kitchen, furniture rearranged itself into piles, and bolts of cloth mysteriously cut into patterns . . . or slashed to shreds. On another occasion a pair of shears hovered in midair above a quilt before veering downward to cut it to pieces.

Whatever—or whoever—was responsible for the events created one of the most sensational "hauntings" ever reported in Wisconsin.

One visiting member of a Spiritualist church believed as many as seven spirits were loose on the place, while editor Flint wrote in the *Dunn County News* that some people thought it was the work of "Auld Cloatie," an archaic term for the devil.

Flint wrote on September 13, 1873, that the problem was "a conundrum we cannot answer. It may be a spirit, animal magnetism, an 'odylic force,' witchcraft, or the devil, for naught we know. We believe the Lynches are honest and are not practicing deception."

Were the Lynches honest and guileless victims of some demonic force, or were family members, as some observers suggested, at least partly responsible for the widespread commotion?

Not much was or is known about the family's background, so such a question is difficult to answer—and especially now from a distance of nearly a century and a half.

What is known is that Richard Lynch, his second wife, Elizabeth, and five children—three boys and two girls—moved to Cady Township in May 1871 from Marshall County, Indiana. By August of that year, Richard had built, with the help of several area neighbors, a two-story log house in the midst of what was called the Big Woods, a wilderness tract stretching for miles in all directions, broken only here and there by settlers' cabins with their few acres of planted crops. The Lynch homestead was in Section 36 of Cady Township.

Rumors about the first Mrs. Lynch circulated soon after their arrival. Some said she had lost the thumb and forefinger of her right hand in an accident and died from the infection. Another tale had it that she'd been murdered, but details were sketchy.

When the family arrived in Wisconsin, Elizabeth Lynch was barely out of her twenties, scarcely a decade older than her stepson, twenty-year-old Alfred, who was away working on another neighborhood farm during most of the "troubles," as it was called at his family's farm. The children who lived at home included David, age seventeen; Mary, ten; Georgie, seven; and Lucinda, nicknamed Rena, two. Rena was Richard and Elizabeth's only child together.

Most contemporary reports about the Lynch haunting assert that all was serene in the relatively spacious cabin for their first six months. Later, however, a Minnesota newspaper reporter would claim Elizabeth Lynch had grown unhappier by the month on the Wisconsin frontier, and that the alleged ghosts or spirits were nothing more than pranks instigated by her and ten-year-old Mary to convince Richard to move back to Indiana.

Whatever the case may be, the series of intriguing, albeit sporadic, episodes eventually touched the lives of not only the Lynch family but also neighbors, volunteer "investigators" of the paranormal, newspaper reporters, and the simply curious.

It is not entirely clear at what point the family problems became public, nor is it fully possible to piece together a consistent chronology of what is alleged to have occurred. The public record is sparse and, of course, no one is alive today who remembers the events.

Apparently, Richard and perhaps Elizabeth first thought it was nothing more than prankish behavior by one or more of the children. All of them denied knowledge of the mischief, but Georgie, who had been caught in a number of typical childish high jinks, was sometimes spanked when household items went missing. For instance, when Mrs. Lynch put down a utensil while preparing a meal, she'd find it had vanished if she became occupied with another chore. Her dresses also began to go missing. Some were found rolled up and stuffed into odd nooks and crannies; others had been cut to shreds, suitable only for the ragbag. Two holes were cut in a feather bed. Dishes and pans disappeared.

The month of December 1871 seems to be close to the beginning of the Lynch family troubles, although much of what happened before stories began appearing in the newspapers is conjecture and second-hand information.

One of the few eyewitnesses who left a record was that young hired man, Jim Snodie, who spoke in detail sixty years later to his grandnephew, Dick Owens, about what he termed the "happenings." Much of what he relates, though quite detailed, is astonishing in retrospect.

On the same day Snodie was attacked by the broadax, he told Owens, Elizabeth Lynch hosted a quilting bee for several local farmwomen. The women were sitting in a circle admiring their handiwork when a pair of shears, which had been used to cut the cloth squares, leaped into the air and slashed the quilt to pieces.

As the other women watched in disbelief, Elizabeth screamed, prompting her husband to come running. He got to the room in time to see the cutting shears ripping up the last of the quilt before falling to the floor. Understandably, the women quickly gathered up their belongings and left.

Snodie said the Lynches were "highly disturbed" as they grimly picked up the pieces of quilt and put them in an old carpetbag.

Many of those early episodes in late 1871 and early 1872 seemed to center upon cloth, quilts, or clothing.

Once after Richard Lynch had returned home from town with dress fabric for his wife, she put the material away in the bedroom. Several days later when she went to fetch it, the cloth was gone. They found it in the barn, rolled into a bundle with the cutting shears inside. From the cloth had been cut the skirt and sleeves for a dress to fit ten-year-old Mary.

A second bolt of fabric also vanished, only to be discovered weeks later rolled inside a hanging wall map Richard had in the house. A perfect bib-type apron had been cut out.

The family was successful for quite some time in confining knowledge of the events to family, a few hired men such as Jim Snodie, and some neighbors. However, an afternoon of hay cutting in August 1873, some eighteen months after Jim Snodie's run-in with the broadax, ended in several disturbances so astounding that they eventually attracted the attention of the regional press.

A neighbor, Frank Duffie, had volunteered to help Richard Lynch cut the hay. Side by side the men worked, swinging their scythes in the sun-washed field at the hem of the forest.

At about four o'clock, Mrs. Lynch screamed from the house. The men raced into the cabin in time to see chairs jumping to the ceiling and crashing to the floor, tinware and cooking utensils flying across the kitchen, and then, just through the open doorway, slabs of boards and scraps of iron sailing through the air.

Lynch and Duffie thought that somehow they could catch the culprit if they stationed themselves at two corners of the house so that together they had a full view of all sides of the house. Mrs. Lynch stood nearby.

They waited.

Suddenly, a large pine box leaped into the air and landed ten feet away on the porch. An old horseshoe that had been hanging on a peg in the milk house arced through the air and came to rest beside the box. Instantly, a commotion rocked the empty house. Duffie and the Lynches ran back inside, but everything movable had been piled high into one corner.

Later that day, an ax that had been rammed into the end of a log struck the side of the cabin's doorway and bounced several feet into the front room. Mrs. Lynch took it to the milk house, wedged it inside a wooden crate, and then piled wood planks and a bag of salt on top. But no sooner had she returned to the house than the ax reappeared, this time clattering onto the porch. Her husband grabbed it, took it a short distance into the yard, and pushed it inside a hollow log. There it remained—at least for the rest of *that* day.

Although a few neighbors had known of some of the earlier incidents and kept the news relatively quiet, gossip about the flying furniture and farm implements spread like wildfire. Area newsmen began showing up on the Lynches' doorstep to witness the supposed poltergeist's activities, then vied with one another in sensationally recounting what one reporter called "the most absurd capering of some supernatural agency."

Strangers' imaginations were then sparked by what they read. They converged by foot, horse, or wagon, winding their way along narrow forest trails.

By one estimate more than three hundred visitors descended on the Lynch family within a six-week period; by another, closer to a thousand.

Meanwhile, Elizabeth Lynch had begun binding Georgie's hands and feet and tying him into a chair or to a cradle, still believing that he was somehow partly to blame. Even that didn't work. One day while Mrs. Lynch was washing clothes, Georgie sat tied to his cradle. His sister Mary watched him. Their mother turned from the washboard to put some wood into the stove. Turning back to the tub, she found her bowl of soft soap gone. She went after more, and, upon her return, Georgie told her that the soap could be found under his head. Sure enough, when Elizabeth raised the child's head she found the soap. Georgie and Mary denied any responsibility.

It didn't seem to matter whether Georgie was bound or not. Often, while the child was confined, a teacup might fly to the floor and shatter, or a saucer would leap from the sideboard and land undamaged on the floor.

"There, Mother! You see I didn't do that!" Georgie would shout.

On another day, Mrs. Lynch cooked a kettle of fresh squirrels for the family's hot midday meal. After cautioning Mary to watch the boiling pot, she took a pan to the milk house to get flour to make bread. She got the flour, sprinkled salt over it, and then returned to the house. As she stepped through the doorway, she saw that the pot of squirrel stew had disappeared from the stove. Mary professed her innocence. Mrs. Lynch put the pan of flour on the table; then she, Mary, and Georgie searched for the missing kettle.

After she had rummaged around a bedroom, Mrs. Lynch saw that the flour was gone. In a few moments, it was discovered under the stairway; again it was placed on the table. Mother and children then went up to the garret, where they found the pot of squirrels sitting in the middle of the bed, a corner of a bedspread thrown over it. As Mrs. Lynch took off the spread, the contents steamed and bubbled as if it were being lifted off a hot stove.

Little Rena's beautiful hair was at the center of another incident that spread the family's notoriety to the farthest reaches of North America.

Elizabeth Lynch had called her children to an early lunch before she fed
the hired men. Georgie and Mary showed up, but not Rena. She was sitting in
the front yard with her hands in her lap. Her long hair, which had hung in
golden ringlets, had been shorn from her head; chopped tufts of hair were all
that remained of her waist-length tresses. A pair of scissors lay nearby, but not
a strand of her hair was ever found. Understandably, two-year-old Rena could
not explain what had happened.

Dunn County News publishers Flint and E. M. Weber visited the Lynch home in
September 1873 and reported on their "investigation" in several articles reprinted
in newspapers from coast to coast.

The men arrived on a Saturday night that apparently passed uneventfully.
On Sunday morning after breakfast, Flint and Weber went outside in order to
smoke cigars and to give the family a chance to finish up their housework.
Several clerks from the nearby Knapp, Stout & Company store joined them in
the yard. The morning air was cool and the men built a fire at the edge of the
woods, about forty feet from the house.

Suddenly, they heard a commotion in the house. Someone shouted that
teacups were falling to the floor but not breaking.

Flint said one man "who was near the door, stepped forward and picked up
the cup, placed it on the table, took Georgie, who was in the room, by the
hand, and started for the door. In a moment another cup sped to the floor and
lay on its side, whirling with great rapidity. Thompson started for this one, also,
and as he grabbed it, the cup moved away from him and passed under the
table. He went around to the other side and caught it while it was whirling.
This transpired while we were at the fire, and we relate it substantially as it was
told us by several eyewitnesses."

Flint and Weber raced to the house hoping to watch this "spirit" at work.
They stood in the doorway when, as they wrote,

> with almost lightning swiftness an egg darted across the room, struck the corner
> of a box, and was smashed. Shortly after, the potato masher, which stood on
> the dresser, went the same way with incredible speed, and landed in the corner
> "kerslap." In a little while a couple of pieces of broken crockery lying on the
> stove made a sudden movement and landed in the corner.
>
> These three things we saw distinctly, and others in the room saw them.
> Perhaps we were fooled by some trick of legerdemain. If so, who did it? The
> boy seven years old who sat at the table quietly eating his breakfast? The girl,
> ten years old, who stood nearby, wiping a dish? Mrs. Lynch, who was busy at

work? Or Mr. Lynch, who was not in the house? It seems to us improbable, if not impossible.

Shortly after Flint and Weber's visit, the Lynches hosted one A. B. Finley, the Barron County school superintendent. Why he decided to "investigate" the mystery is not known. He, too, stayed the night and, as was not uncommon in simple frontier dwellings, family and guest stayed in one large room: Richard, Elizabeth, and Rena in one bed; Finley in a single bed across the room; and Mary and Georgie on a straw mattress laid out on the floor between the other beds.

Soon after everyone retired for the night, Georgie complained of something pinching and scratching him. Finley took Georgie into his own bed, but still the child complained. He clamped the boy's hands in one of his own and put his other arm so tightly around him that Georgie could not move a muscle without detection. The night passed uneventfully and Finley left the next morning without issuing a "report" of any kind.

A skeptical reporter from the *St. Paul Dispatch* visited the Lynches on November 3–4, 1873, and stayed through the night. When a curious scratching sound began to come from the bed shared by Mary and Georgie, he got up and held the hands of both children. The noises stopped immediately. The reporter spent twenty hours in the house. He went away persuaded that Mrs. Lynch and ten-year-old Mary, whom he called "strange and precocious," had duped people. He felt that Mrs. Lynch was bored and unhappy in her dreary, backwoods home and that, after her husband's refusal to sell the farm and move back east, she created her own excitement. And since the remote location of the house meant most visitors had to spend the night, the newsman said the Lynches were paid much more than a commercial hostelry would have been. It was a money-making scheme, he sniffed in print, nothing more, nothing less.

The majority of observers, however, continued to believe that the Lynches would have relinquished almost anything to be rid of the manifestations, that they were victims rather than perpetrators.

Certainly there were enough outside observers that it seems unreasonable to assume family members, including a girl not yet in her teens, could have tricked everyone. For instance, a Mr. Knight, who lived near Wilson, recorded more than forty different occurrences during the few hours he was there.

One Ambrose Evans visited the Lynches. When breakfast was ready, he sat down at the table. Soon, the distinctive odor of kerosene filled the air. It seemed to be coming through an open bedroom door. Evans followed Mrs.

Lynch into the room, where, in the middle of the bed, lay an uncorked jug of kerosene. Nearly a gallon of it had spilled onto the bed, saturating the feather mattress and ruining the quilts.

Meanwhile, newspaper reporters flocked to the isolated farm. When *Milwaukee News* reporter J. D. Goodrich arrived at the house for his own investigation, David and his father were working in a field while the younger children played in the yard. Goodrich was standing by the outside cellar door talking to Mrs. Lynch when a noise erupted from inside the house.

"There," Mrs. Lynch told the reporter, "you hear that, and you also see that none of the family are in the house."

Hurrying inside, Goodrich and his hostess found a dining room table tipped over.

By eight-thirty the next morning, Goodrich was observing some very lively activity:

> One thing peculiar is that you never see a thing start, but the minute you turn your eyes the thing gets up and gets. Another peculiar feature is that where a thing strikes, there it lays, neither rolls nor bounds. We took some of the same things and threw them a number of times, but they would bound or roll every time. We saw a piece of broken cup hit a little two-year-old girl on the back so hard she nearly cried. A raw potato hopped out of a dish near where we were and lit on the floor; and while we were watching a stove handle light in one place, a tin plate whisked by our head in another direction.

Newspapermen were not the only ones who wanted to discover the causes of the family's troubles. Ministers, spiritualists, and mediums were also unsuccessful, but they did offer some astonishing ideas.

The Rev. John Barker, who lived on Cady Creek in Pierce County, said the devil himself was at work in the Lynch household. Intent upon exorcising the demon, he approached the Lynch house, Bible and prayer book in hand. He put the books in a handkerchief, tied its ends together, and placed the little package on the staircase. The Rev. Barker then challenged the demons to remove it.

They did . . . when Rev. Barker wasn't looking. Both books were later discovered on a bed with every page torn out. The handkerchief was located in a barrel of feathers.

The purported psychics and clairvoyants weren't any more successful than the Rev. Barker.

One Saturday afternoon a self-described seer named Mellon, from the tiny community of Rock Elm, visited the Lynches. He saw nothing that day of an

otherworldly nature. The next day he had better luck. He said the spirit of
Richard Lynch's first wife was in the house . . . with six other spirits! Those
were the spirits responsible for all the turmoil.

When Lynch asked why so many household items had been destroyed,
Mellon said that it was to open the minds of the Lynch family and others in the
community to "the truth of Spiritualism."

Richard Lynch grumbled that it seemed a needlessly disruptive and
expensive way to gain converts.

One man asked Mellon if the spirits could throw things around as they had
done previously. Yes, he said. Lynch then asked the spirits to move a cup from
a shelf to the floor. The cup didn't move. The spirit, speaking through Mellon,
apologized by saying it was alone and could not perform without the assistance
of the other spirits.

And where *were* the other spirits? someone asked.

Gone to Knapp Station, the solitary spirit said, to attend a camp meeting.
He could not predict when they'd return; he grudgingly agreed to go after
them.

Mellon then announced that the "spirit" had departed, presumably for
Knapp Station.

"Humbug," muttered some in the crowd, disappointed at not seeing an
example of unearthly tomfoolery.

A few weeks later, another visiting clairvoyant, a Mrs. Carlton from River
Falls, said she, too, saw seven spirits. However, she told the family to bar any
more visitors and to hold séances among themselves, during which the mystery
would be solved through the mediumship of someone in the family.

Though skeptical, Richard Lynch gave it a try. It was reported that during
several family circles the table around which they sat moved about, but all
attempts at questioning the circling "spirits" were fruitless. The family gave up
spiritualism in disgust.

The personal recollections of Jim Snodie include two quite astonishing episodes
that, if they are to be believed, make the Lynch affair far more sinister than the
relatively innocuous tricks perpetrated by a frustrated housewife in complicity
with one or more of her children.

The Lynches almost lost their house in a deadly roof fire. The incident
began one midday shortly after Snodie had seated himself at the Lynch's table
for dinner.

"We heard an eerie, high-pitched noise, similar to a pig's squeal, coming
from somewhere upstairs," Snodie recalled in a 1937 interview. "Mr. Lynch left
the table in a hurry and ran for the stairs. We could hear him walking around

from room to room, asking in a loud voice, 'Who is there?' The house was otherwise quiet. He returned to the table, shaking his head but saying nothing."

Lynch and the hired men resumed eating. The squeal again came from upstairs.

"Naturally, we all looked upward. It was then we saw a piece of white paper floating down from the ceiling. The boss made a grab for it and caught it before it could hit the floor. He read it out loud to all of us."

Snodie remembered the words Lynch read aloud:

Everybody leave the house at once. All the women line up on the west side of the house and all the men line up on the east side. Hurry, for if you don't, the house will burn down.

Richard Lynch told the group to settle down, finish their meals, and get back to work. Just then there was a loud noise from the roof.

"The smell of wood smoke drifted into the room from a partly opened window," Snodie said. Mr. Lynch "rushed outside and then hollered that there was a fire on the roof. We all jumped up and ran out. Sure enough, the shake roof was blazing away, the flames at least two or three feet high. Mr. Lynch lined all of us men up on the east side of the house and the women folk on the west side. He was trembling with fear when he joined us on the east side. At that time, the whole roof was covered with flames."

The fire quickly went out. A few wisps of smoke drifted skyward, but they soon dissipated.

"The boss got a ladder from somewhere. He climbed onto the roof, examining the shakes as he went along. He said there wasn't one shake that was charred. No evidence of a fire was found anywhere on the roof. We were all pretty well spooked by then, I'll tell you."

The news accounts of the Lynch haunting brought strangers from as far away as Norway, Sweden, France, Germany, and England; all were attracted by the prospect of seeing "spirits" at work. But many of them were far from welcome, as may be seen in a shocking incident involving two men from Albany, New York, witnessed by Jim Snodie.

"We were getting ready to go back to work after lunch," Snodie recounted. "A loud knocking came at the door. Mr. Lynch jerked the door open. Two men appeared in the doorway. One asked if they could come in. He said he and his friend had come all the way from Albany, New York, to watch the 'spooks' at work."

Lynch refused because the hired men were going back to work and nobody would be home. But both men crowded into the room and slammed the door shut.

"Almost simultaneously," reported Snodie,

someone shouted, "Here comes a note!" And, sure enough, down from the ceiling fluttered a piece of white paper. Mr. Lynch ignored the note and grabbed the door latch intending to physically eject the men. He tugged and tugged at the door but could not get it to budge. He then stooped and picked up the note. It stated that the men were not welcome, and should state their business immediately.

One of the men, referred to by Snodie as "Mr. Loudmouth" because he did all the talking, said they'd come to identify the culprit behind the "foolishness" and report that person to the "authorities." He boasted that neither of them was afraid of any unseen force and that whatever was responsible should show itself.

At that moment, another note floated down from the ceiling. This one said the men should go up to the bedroom at the top of the stairs at one fifteen that afternoon. Everyone else was to remain downstairs.

At the appointed time, the visitor who'd been doing all the boasting headed for the steps. His friend declined to accompany him. With a nervous laugh, Mr. Loudmouth headed for the bedroom. The men downstairs heard him slam the door.

Minutes passed. Finally, Richard Lynch said he would see what was going on. He didn't appear to be in any hurry as he climbed the steps to investigate the problem.

Lynch opened the door. He didn't go in.

"He's dead," Lynch called down to the men.

Just inside the bedroom door was the body of the boastful visitor.

"I think he died of pure fright," Snodie said.

The hired men filed out to their jobs. The Albany man's body was loaded onto the light livery wagon in which the visitors had arrived, and was taken to Menomonie.

Richard Lynch came to regret his decision to leave Indiana. Whether it was the death of the visitor from Albany, the roof fire, a survey of his property losses—smashed furniture, broken dishes, mangled silverware, shattered mirrors and clocks, shredded clothing—or the continual disruption of strangers and nosy newsmen banging on his door that motivated Lynch to make a bold decision, we will never know, but he decided to split up his family.

Young Georgie and Mary were bundled off to live with neighbors a mile away, though it is unclear why Elizabeth Lynch would have agreed to let two of her stepchildren be sent to a neighbor's house. Peace apparently then settled upon the Lynch household and all of Cady Township.

What are we to make of all this?

According to Jim Snodie, Richard Lynch was a stern and formal employer who insisted upon being called "Mr. Lynch."

"He commanded respect and since he was a big man, nobody argued with him about his request," Snodie said. "He seemed to lack a sense of humor."

If that is the case, perhaps reporters were right when they speculated that Elizabeth Lynch was retaliating against her strong-willed and much older husband for his refusal to sell the farm and move back to Indiana. She could easily have enlisted Mary's help in performing some of the "mysterious" feats. Much of what was reported was simply missing household items or petty mischief. She could have encouraged the children to hide the utensils, pots, and pans, to throw objects when adults weren't looking, or to cut up clothing material.

Yet, there are the other, far more disturbing events—the cruel shearing of little Rena's beautiful hair, the roof fire, the near fatal ax attacks, and the death of the visitor from Albany. Unless we are to dismiss Jim Snodie's recollections of those years or question his honesty or memory in reporting this episode, or to assume that Elizabeth Lynch conspired with her children to brutalize her own daughter, to commit arson, and to murder, the Lynch affair leaves many unanswered questions.

The fact that all disturbances ceased after the two youngest children were removed doesn't necessarily prove they had anything to do with it, at least not on a conscious level. Parapsychologists say that moving objects are often associated with the presence of young children and, more frequently, teenagers. The only teenager, seventeen-year-old David Lynch, is rarely mentioned in contemporary accounts; he had possibly been "hired out" to nearby farmers. Eventually, the Lynch family left the region, presumably headed back to Indiana and a quieter lifestyle.

Most of the Big Woods were cleared long ago. A county road crosses about where the Lynch house once stood. Lush farm fields stretch to the horizon, while silos dwarf the scattered farmhouses. The once-thriving village of Hatchville is a forgotten memory. There is little to remind the visitor of those years when this little corner of Wisconsin drew international attention to events that still tantalize and mystify.

Confirmation

All the young teen was thinking about was that he had to go to the bathroom. He jumped out of bed and headed toward his bedroom door. But the boy never made it to the bathroom. Instead, he got the shock of his life.

An apparition hovered in the hallway less than ten feet away from the doorway where he had stopped cold in his tracks.

The transparent object hovered in the air a couple of feet off the ground. He could see that it had a head with some hair, perhaps even a pair of glasses. The face itself was featureless. As much as he could see led him to believe it was female. It had, he said, a maternal bliss, a kindness about it.

The pale, billowing mass seemed to undulate as if a gentle breeze swept down the hallway. There were no discernible legs or feet. It filled the space between the two walls.

"Where the arms would be there was a bit of a bulge, like its arms were crossed or it was holding flowers or something. But I couldn't *see* its arms. It seemed to be turned in my direction, looking at me. I didn't sense any hostility. It didn't move toward me or away from me, it just stayed where it was," the boy, now an adult, remembers.

The boy could not think of what to do. What he *wanted to do*, of course, was get to the bathroom, but to do that he needed to get past this *thing*. The boy really, really did *not* want to go down there.

"I remember seeing moonlight coming in from one side of the hallway, and I remember wondering if that could be moonlight bouncing off the mirror at the end of the hallway and coming back and creating a reflection. But I looked at it and decided that no, that was not possible. It couldn't be a reflection off the mirror because it wouldn't look like that. That's when I decided I'd have to stay in the bedroom for the night. I dropped to the floor, stretched my arm out, and closed the door. I went back to bed and stayed there."

Suddenly a young boy's physiological needs were of far less urgency than trying to figure out what in heaven's name loitered in the hallway just beyond his now firmly closed bedroom door.

It wouldn't be until much, much later that an answer came. Long after he'd left that house in which he grew up, long after he had left the town of his youth and gone on to make his way in the world—it would only be then, decades later, that he would realize the figure he saw on that night had probably been his own grandmother comforting him, saying *good-bye* to him.

The young boy's name is Tom Blair* and the small Wisconsin community in which he grew up and where his parents still live in that split-level house provided him with a fairly typical childhood. He went to public schools and then attended UW–Madison, where he was elected to Phi Beta Kappa and graduated with a double major in German and geography.

That youthful encounter with what some would dismiss as a figment of teenage imagination or a particularly disturbing dream might be expected to be forgotten or even laughed at as young Tom entered adulthood and put away the fantasies and nightmares of childhood. That would be the natural reaction to a story like this, but Tom Blair is no ordinary witness to ghostly encounters, nor did he ever forget what he saw on that night so long ago.

Dr. Tom Blair is a scientist—specifically, a soil biochemist, with a master's degree in geography and a PhD in soil science from the University of California. His curriculum vitae lists nineteen refereed journal articles, seventeen book chapters and published proceedings, and five manuscripts either submitted for publication or in preparation.

He worked for eight years as a consultant and visiting scientist for an international rice research institute in the Philippines before taking his current position in Iowa as a soil scientist for the federal government. Blair's formal education and fidelity to the scientific method make him a particularly credible observer of matters supernatural. But that doesn't mean he entirely understands, even now, his experience of three decades ago. It is an event that will stay with him for the rest of his days.

"I didn't tell anybody about this," he said of that floating figure in the familiar hallway of his comfortable home. "Being a bit of a scientist even then, I suppose, I knew I couldn't explain it. I wasn't sure what it was. And of course you don't want to be laughed at for seeing something that other people wouldn't understand. So I filed the experience away, sort of put it under my 'not explained' file hoping that someday I would be able to explain it first to my own satisfaction, and then to other people."

He knew full well that he had not imagined the entire incident, and yet didn't know what it was he had seen.

"When I woke up in the middle of the night, I wasn't having bad dreams. Nor had I ever had any ghostly experiences; I hadn't seen a scary movie the night before. I just needed to get to the bathroom. That's *all* I was thinking about."

What he eventually yearned for, Blair said, was some outside corroboration that this sort of vision was possible. Even though he trusted his own eyesight, the doubter in him kept pecking away at his subconscious.

"I needed confirmation and replication before I would believe it myself. And I didn't want to discuss it unless I had adequate confidence in it," he noted.

Blair didn't know that the vaporous woman in white would linger in his mind's "unexplained file" for so long, tugging at the back of his mind, and that it wouldn't be until he took a research position on the other side of the globe that he found that what he saw in a small Wisconsin town was remarkably similar to experiences people had in the Philippines and throughout Asia.

In Asia, she is known as the white lady, and stories of her appearances, according to Blair, are amazingly similar to what he saw: billowing figures with absent or indistinct arms and legs who dwell within a limited geographic area.

"Shortly after I moved to the Philippines, I began meeting people who would tell me stories about the white ladies they encountered. I asked what these ladies looked like and my friends gave me the exact same vision, the same description—of something floating off the ground, a white, transparent being, usually a female."

They had heads but no distinct faces. The more Blair heard, the more he thought they were describing the same being, the same type of experience he had years before.

Blair told the story of a Filipina friend who attended a school in which a stairwell was reputedly haunted. Several teachers were said to have died there. Blair's friend was running up those stairs one morning when she saw a white lady hovering near a landing.

"As in my case," he said, "the white lady there seemed to be looking at my friend with a benevolent air, maybe 'kind' is the right word. Like an older lady would have for a younger child."

The idea of a warm, caring, *motherly* being keeping watch over a family or a place she loved also helped Blair identify who his "own" white lady might have been:

I hadn't thought about that [the identify of the ghost] for many years, but then in the last couple of years I began to . . . I realized that the figure matched quite closely my grandmother. She was a relatively large lady and this figure I saw in the hallway was not a thin being at all. My memories of my grandmother are quite distant, but she had hair like the figure did and she wore glasses. My grandmother died when I would have been about twelve years old.

I don't really remember her well. My memories of her are as an older lady, but I hear from older relatives that she was a very kind human being, very people oriented, very devoted to her family. My mother is the same way; her life really is her children.

While he was not unusually close to his grandmother, Blair said his family was quite close, usually spending any holidays with his mother's family rather than his father's. His grandmother spent her final years in a nursing home.

If indeed Tom Blair did see the ghost of his grandmother, why was he chosen for that singular experience and not his own mother or one of his siblings?

"I don't know," he conceded. "My mother was the baby of her family. I think she was quite close to my grandmother. It could have been that [my grandmother] was trying to get close to my mother, not necessarily to me, and I just happened to be there at the time."

But Blair believes it may be something more, something almost intangible — his willingness to look at the world in new and different ways:

Throughout my life I've had, every once in a while, a very brief experience that I think could be related to my mind being relatively active. Suddenly thinking of somebody while I'm walking down the street, for instance, and then a few seconds later that person drives past and honks his horn at me. I talk to anyone, I listen to anybody's opinion, and I don't assume anyone is wrong until they're proven wrong. So I guess I might have been a receptive audience for this vision on this occasion.

He has never told his parents about the apparition, although he related the story to his brother and sister. Both of his siblings said they had not had any similar sorts of experiences, yet they were quite accepting of their brother's experience.

While he worked for eight years in the Philippines, Tom Blair traveled widely throughout Asia and came to some conclusions about the appearance of ghosts or apparitions in the United States and other cultures:

The countries I've lived in and traveled through are slower than our culture is. We're by far the fastest paced country I've ever lived in. We don't have time to slow down and open ourselves up, I would say. The thoughts of people in Asian culture are more toward people, their families, their relatives, their neighbors, whereas we spend more of our time focusing on work, [on] production, on buying things that we think we need for our lifestyles. We're more work- and progress-oriented. This would just be a guess, but maybe these [spirits] are more likely to appear to people who are more . . . receptive . . . you might say. These things do appear in our country, there are reports of them, but perhaps they are just not as common.

Blair cannot remember the precise date of his youthful ghostly encounter and thus doesn't know if his grandmother had passed on by then. That does not necessarily rule her out as the ghostly figure.

Blair cites Asian examples of appearances by people miles away from where they live. The spirits looks like the real people, let themselves be seen by people they know, and perhaps even speak; but usually they are seen far from where they would normally be expected. Perhaps the person is from a different part of one's life, childhood for instance, or lives in a different country or continent.

"If you see them in passing that's a sign that they are going to die soon," Blair said of this type of apparition. "Two Nepalese friends told me in separate conversations that that's quite well-known in Nepal, that if you see somebody out of place, that means they're going to die soon."

A close Filipina friend told Blair an unsettling personal experience of this very sort. Blair recalled:

On the same day her brother died he appeared to a very close friend on the street in a different city. He also appeared to his aunt in the town where their family lived. The aunt reportedly saw him walking down the street. He looked completely normal. They even stopped and talked. My friend's brother told his aunt he was staying with his grandmother. It was a normal conversation. Then later that day, the aunt went to the grandmother's house to look for that young man. The grandmother said he wasn't staying there and then they got into a big argument. My friend then arrived on the bus to tell her aunt and her grandmother that her brother had died earlier that day in another city.

Tom Blair the scientist doesn't hesitate if he is called upon to defend his role looking into paranormal experiences skeptics say are impossible:

One has to recognize what we understand and what we don't understand. Just because we don't understand something doesn't mean it's wrong. That's a common mistake even among scientists who say that if you can't prove something conclusively then your whole idea is wrong. That's simply not true.

Blair said that we must recognize the limits of technology, the limits of our understanding:

Something happened, I saw it, I know it happened, and if I can't explain it, that doesn't mean it didn't happen. That means we need to learn more, that there are parts of our universe we may never understand. These beings we see, ghosts, fit into the idea that we have spirits inside of ourselves, that we have a soul. When you die, your soul may linger on and perhaps that becomes what we call a ghost. I think when you consider the fact that so many countries around the world with so many religions all report ghosts that [the soul] may be part of us. When you're born you have a spirit inside of you. Who knows where it comes from or what it is or what happens to it after you die, but given the fact that these same experiences happen to people all around the world means that it's a part of us.

The Paulding Light Mystery

Ezra Zeitler first heard about the Paulding Light when he was a high school student in Minocqua.

"On Monday mornings students would come back and say they had seen the Paulding Light over the weekend and it was real scary and mysterious," Zeitler recalled.

Despite the captivating stories, he didn't make the 120-mile round trip to the Paulding area, just over the Wisconsin border in the Upper Peninsula of Michigan, for several years.

Ezra's younger brother, Micah Zeitler, heard similar stories. He eventually made the trip because his friends "guaranteed" him that he would see the mystery light. He was impressed with what he saw and heard, including that the spirit of a dead trainman produced the light.

"I told everyone I'd seen a ghost."

Micah and Ezra, however, eventually went one step further once they got to college in River Falls. They shared the tale of the Paulding Light with their geography professor. The three of them set off to uncover the truth about the light. Their results may once and for all reveal the origins of this particular mystery light, at least for those willing to accept something less than a paranormal explanation.

The Zeitler brothers certainly are not alone in their interest in what has alternately been called the Paulding Light, the Watersmeet Light, the Dog Meadow

Light, or, simply, the Mystery Light. For decades, thousands of visitors have made the nightly trek north out of Eagle River, Wisconsin, on U.S. 45, through Watersmeet, Michigan, to a point about a dozen miles from the Wisconsin state line.

The visitor turns off on an old gravel road about four miles north of Watersmeet, drives up the hill, and parks. If it's a "good" night, a dim, glowing orb of white light will appear in the far distance. The light may vanish for a period of time, only to reappear moments later. Sometimes other lights appear with it. During winter and early spring, the light may appear only infrequently.

Theories abound as to what causes the light. Some believe it must be supernatural. To these folks, the light glows from the lantern of a long-dead trainman, or maybe a slain dogsled musher. Some have even attributed it to passing UFOs draining energy from some nearby power lines.

More earth-bound observers maintain the light might be produced by methane gas escaping from a fissure in the earth. Others say the phenomenon is nothing more than the reflection of lights from boats on Lake Superior or cars on a distant highway.

Tourism officials quickly recognized the allure of the light. One vacation brochure calls it the Watersmeet Mystery Light and includes it in the same sentence as a local trout hatchery. Another brochure listing "Things to Do" in the Watersmeet region gives the phenomenon its own paragraph:

> The "Light" appears almost every night after dark on a lonely old gravel road and has defied explanation for years. It appears to arise from the horizon, glows like a beacon, splits, changes color and mysteriously disappears as quickly as it came.

But how did the legend of the Paulding Light come to be, and what will one see in that pocket of wilderness?

Despite the insistence of some locals—and tourism promoters—the "mystery" of the light is usually traced no farther back than the mid-1960s, when a carload of teenagers stopped one clear evening on a gravel road near the swampy area known as Dog Meadow. Suddenly, the teens claimed, brightness filled the car's interior and lit the power lines parallel to the road. They were so frightened they fled back to town and reportedly told the sheriff what they had seen.

Another of the earliest documented sightings came from two Wisconsin men, Harold Nowak and Elmer Lenz, who told a newspaper reporter that they parked their car on the gravel road and the light appeared in the distance—a bright spotlight shining directly at them. The light moved closer, backed away, and even appeared at an angle from time to time. Lenz grew up near a rail yard and he said the light looked just like a locomotive headlamp.

The men said a smaller light appeared below and slightly to the right of the large, white light. "The two, at times, seemed to move together, then part, one or the other disappearing, then showing again," Lenz recalled. The smaller light was red, though they claim to have also seen a green light.

Their description fit with one of the legends of the origin of the Paulding Light, that one night in the early twentieth century a railroad switchman with lantern in hand was crushed to death between two rail cars while attempting to signal the train's engineers. Another account holds that a trainman was murdered along the old railroad grade where the light appears.

A third tale has it that a mail carrier and his sled dogs were mysteriously slain at Dog Meadow, below the vantage point from which the light can best be seen. The modern road through the region was built on the Civil War–era military road from Fort Howard in Green Bay to Fort Wilkins at Copper Harbor. Men driving dogsled teams delivered the mail to isolated communities along the old trail. The light, it is said, is the lantern held by the mail messenger looking for the men who murdered him.

Harold Nowak and Elmer Lenz were skeptical of supernatural explanations when they decided to investigate the phenomenon. They bravely got out of their car and walked toward the light. As they approached, it seemed to disappear down over the next rise but continued to cast a bright glow on the horizon.

The two men hiked for another half mile, finding nothing that might explain the mystery. As they walked back, the lights reappeared behind them over the rise. When they got back to their car, other observers at the site told them that in the men's absence they'd seen a large red light above a small white one in the middle of the road a short distance ahead of them. If the reports were accurate, the lights would have been *between* Lenz and Nowak and their car.

The men drove on for some distance, parked, and turned off the headlights. The mysterious light reappeared with a smaller one beneath it shining down the middle of the road. A minute later, the larger light vanished, and the smaller light, according to Lenz, "seemed to touch down and burst into three [orbs]." The outer two lights disappeared, but the third remained about two hundred feet away. Nowak snapped on the headlights but the light in the road didn't move. Minutes later, the men claimed this single light rose in the air four or five feet and vanished.

Later, *Milwaukee Journal Sentinel* reporter Harry S. Pease described what he saw for the newspaper's now-defunct *Insight Magazine*:

> We had chosen the hill above Dog Meadow because it's easiest to find in the
> dark. You just drive north from Watersmeet on [U.S.] 45 about four miles, turn

left onto the town road and stop on the high ground. Our eyes and ears sharpened with the passage of the minutes. We could hear cars a long way away on the highway. We could see a dimness . . . as we looked ahead down the road and the power line that ran beside it. Then we saw the light. Right ahead of us, it began as a diffuse glow and then condensed into a hard knot of brilliant white. You had the feeling that maybe it was moving, but you couldn't be sure you weren't moving your head instead. It could have been big and distant or small and close. There was no way to tell. The silence remained unbroken.

The appearance of so-called mystery lights is not an uncommon phenomenon. In states as diverse as North Carolina, Missouri, Texas, and Colorado, dancing, pulsating, or glowing spheres of light have been described by thousands of witnesses. While supernatural explanations are the most unusual reasons given for these lights' existence—and often involve murdered train engineers or mysterious UFOs—many scientists have also taken an interest in them.

Some research indicates, for instance, that mystery lights are more likely to occur in earthquake-prone regions, or where unidentified faults in the earth could trigger visible atmospheric lights when escaping gases, such as methane, mix with oxygen. Another scientific explanation holds that the shifting and grinding of rocks deep below the earth's crust generates electrical charges in the atmosphere. The shifting charges can make any light produced seem to act in an "intelligent" fashion. This explanation has been used to account for the Hornet Spook Light in Missouri, for instance, since it appears near the famous New Madrid, Missouri, fault line.

However, the Paulding Light may be the result of much more mundane activity. It's an explanation that has been offered by many observers, including reporter Harry Pease twenty years ago, but one that seems to be disregarded by those who want to believe there is some supernatural or extraterrestrial "intelligence" behind this light—or those who think unsolved mysteries are good for tourism.

At the University of Wisconsin–River Falls, Micah and Ezra Zeitler met geography professor Don Petzold and told him about the light. He became intrigued by the mystery.

Petzold recalled:

I was immediately skeptical. Were these lights seen before cars were around? Before the highway was built? When was the first viewing made? I found out someone said it dated back to Indian times, but of course it wouldn't be associated with the ghost of a wrecked train because there weren't any trains

then. And who could document that it dates back that long? I was determined
at some point to see the light.

So Petzold and the Zeitlers assembled a set of good topographic maps and
set off for the Upper Peninsula to see if they could solve the riddle of the Paulding
Light.

The three men drove to the site one Saturday night in summer. "When
we pulled up, there were about ten or fifteen other vehicles there," Ezra
remembered.

The three men took out a pair of binoculars and walked over to a fence,
near where the gravel road ended. Petzold and the Zeitlers noticed that a
power line right-of-way extends in the northerly direction from which the light
appears. Then they saw the light itself.

"It was in the right-of-way," Ezra said. "It did look like it was hovering
around. A red light appeared. I can't remember if I could identify them as
moving up and down, but it looked as if they were hovering."

Complete darkness had not fallen, so the men could detect the skyline in
the distance. It didn't take them long to realize what they were looking at.

Car lights.

"I could tell they were headlights of cars, taillights of cars," Ezra explained.
"After that we kept passing the binoculars among us. Each of us agreed."

It was not as easy to accurately pinpoint the distance of the light.

"We had a gazetteer with us," Ezra said. "We figured it was probably U.S.
45 that had the traffic on it because there aren't many other roads around that
would have so much traffic."

Because the lights were miles off in the distance, the highway itself was not
visible.

"There's a straight line of sight right down the cut for the power line,"
noted Petzold:

The highway is very straight, with one short exception. We thought the light
appearing must have had something to do with cars coming up and over a hill
that's about a mile beyond Paulding, but that's a distance of about seven miles
from the viewpoint. The white light does appear as one large light, but over a
seven-mile distance the headlights converge because of refraction and temper-
ature differences in the atmosphere to look like one large light. Then as the cars
come down the hill, it gives the appearance of coming closer to you, but then all
of a sudden it disappears at one point. But that's when the light dips below the
trees or some lower elevation. As a climatologist, I attribute the movement of
the lights to refraction in the lower part of the atmosphere. I think it would
really be quite different if the car lights producing this effect would be closer.

The red lights, Petzold said, are occasional taillights going north up the grade outside Paulding, known locally as Cemetery Hill. "Sometimes you can see the red lights when the white lights are there and approaching and other times you see the red lights alone. And there are two red lights. We looked through the binoculars and you could see the two red lights."

To confirm their theory, Petzold and the Zeitlers got back in their car and headed north on U.S. 45.

"On the other side of Paulding," Ezra Zeitler said, "the highway goes up a gradual incline on a long, straight hill. Toward the top of the hill I could see in my rearview mirror the headlights of the cars that were stopping at the viewing point. That's when we really knew that seeing the Paulding Light was not a real mystery."

Ezra even flashed an S-O-S with his lights, but didn't get anything in reply from drivers who had pulled off the gravel road to watch the "mystery" light, which at this point was being produced by three geographers.

The trio headed back to the viewing area to let people know of their discovery. The response was less than enthusiastic.

As Micah Zeitler recalled, "There was a local guy who said *Ripley's Believe It or Not* had been there and it's been on *Unsolved Mysteries*. I asked him if he'd ever gone seven miles up on U.S. 45, on that long, gradual hill. I told him those are car lights. He didn't believe me."

Petzold said the man was quite adamant. He said he saw them every night. Apparently he visited on a regular basis to check out the lights. Whatever the geographers said would not sway his beliefs.

Not everyone watching the lights that night was such a true believer. As Micah was telling the local man about their discovery, another observer leaned in to Ezra and asked, "Is that true?" When Ezra confirmed that it was, the tourist turned to his buddy and said, "You owe me ten bucks!"

For Petzold, an understanding of the Paulding Light was not difficult to arrive at: "I said we can't possibly be the first people to have looked at a scale map and said, 'Aha! This is a pretty straight road and there is this gradual incline . . . ' It would be neat to stop traffic for a period of time and go up there with headlights and flash a signal."

There is an equally simple explanation for the light's supposed irregularity—uneven traffic flow in one of the more isolated regions of the United States. Micah Zeitler first visited Paulding late on a Thursday night in early spring. "It took fifteen or twenty minutes for the light to come out," he said. "Now I know why." There's not much late-night traffic on any Upper Peninsula highway during the early spring. But it's a different story on a Saturday night during the height of tourist season.

Another reason people who have seen the lights may not consider U.S. 45 as part of the answer is that motorists must turn left off the highway, which seems to mean they would be looking *west* to the lights and into the wilderness. In reality, the gravel road veers around so that one is looking north toward U.S. 45. The long hill north of Paulding is at Maple Hill Cemetery, some seven miles from where the Zeitlers, Petzold, and countless others watch the lights. The cemetery is at 1,315 feet above sea level, while Paulding, south of it, is in a depression. Thus, observers pick up the lights going up or down Cemetery Hill and then lose them as cars descend into Paulding. The village itself emits a soft glow in the sky that may account for some reports that the bright lights are followed by radiance as they disappear from view.

The rational explanation Petzold offers does not diminish his fascination with the Paulding Light.

Since his visit, Petzold has tried to find a duplicate convergence of lights over a great distance at other locations. "I haven't seen it yet, but it's in my mind fairly constantly to check that out. It's not often that you can see traffic for seven miles."

Petzold found the light "mesmerizing," even during a second visit later on:

> It was right at the point of sunset and we were able to see it, but not as distinctly because there was still some daylight. It was also a rainy day. If you stare at [the light], you can imagine that, well, here comes the train and there's the conductor with his red lantern trying to flag it down before it crashes again. You can believe that if you want. Because that's exactly what you see . . . in a sense.

Rational explanations, however, will not deter those who prefer to believe otherwise. Even the government has gotten in on the act by erecting a sign on U.S. 45 giving the "history" of the Paulding Light. Tourism officials have found the light to be good for local businesses. On a warm weekend summer night it is not unusual for several dozen people, some sitting in lawn chairs, digital video cameras at the ready, to watch the lights dancing in the distance.

Ezra Zeitler takes friends to see the light. "If they want to go there, I'll take them. I won't tell them anything. I want to see their reaction."

Micah Zeitler noted that a campground is near the best viewing point. He said the camp was probably built because someone "saw the light."

But another observer pointed out that if one turns west on the county road *before* the mystery light, he passes another geographic landmark: Sucker Lake.

Do Not Disturb

Old Teddy King grunted and sweated as he dug into the Knapp cemetery plot that held his mother's coffin. With each swing of his shovel, Teddy slowly cleared away nearly thirty years of dirt and stone so that he could move his mother's remains to another graveyard nearby.

It was late August 1936. St. Croix County officials had ordered the graves moved: a new road was going to be built and the county needed the cemetery as part of the right-of-way. Most of the remains had been transferred earlier in the month. Mrs. King was the last one to leave.

The old man wrestled the moldy casket into a makeshift wheelbarrow and set off down the country road.

Watching all this was one Lloyd Owens, a young man who was working that summer at the Al Larson farm, just crossways from the cemetery. Curiosity is a compelling affliction of the young. That's what persuaded Lloyd to cross the road to Mrs. King's empty grave. He shivered as he looked down into the damp hole. As he poked around in the fresh dirt with the toe of his boot, something shiny caught his eye. Lloyd picked it up, cleaned it off, and held it up to the fading sunlight. It was a pink glass handle.

Maybe it came off Mrs. King's coffin, he thought. I'll just give it to Teddy next time I see him in town.

He stuffed the object in the pocket of his bib overalls and trotted back to the Larson house and on up to his room, where he put the handle on the top of his dresser.

Lloyd didn't sleep well that night. Although houses were often sweltering during those summers before air-conditioning, his room seemed cool, yet twice he found that he had kicked his sheets and bedspread to the floor.

Early the next morning, the boy got up quickly, dressed, and was about to leave the room when the dim morning light struck something on the floor. The pink glass handle was leaning upright against the bedroom door. He carefully picked it up, put it back on the dresser, and hurried out the door without so much as a backward glance.

The day passed, evening chores were completed, and Lloyd again climbed those stairs to his room, this time a little more slowly than usual. He couldn't get that odd morning incident out of his head.

Lloyd pushed the door open but, as it moved, something scraped across the floor. He struck a match and lit the carbide lamp on the wall just inside the doorway. The pink glass handle again lay on the floor, tight against the bottom of the door.

Lloyd snatched up the handle and again put it back on the dresser, just where he was certain he had left it that morning. A cold breeze blew through the room. The carbide lamp flickered. Lloyd did not close his eyes that night.

Just after dawn, Lloyd packed his small suitcase and left the Larson farm for his own home a few miles away.

He asked his older brother, Dick Owens, if he would take his place for a couple of days. He said he was very tired from the heavy work schedule and needed a break.

Dick was only too happy to oblige. Several times in the past, he had helped out at the Larsons', and even replaced his brother when the younger boy had wanted some time off. In those Depression years good jobs were hard to come by, and Al Larson was good to his hired help and his wife served wonderful meals. Lloyd did not tell his brother anything more than that he needed some "rest."

Dick moved into Lloyd's room that same morning. But he nearly stepped on something in the doorway. He bent down to pick it up—a small pink glass handle. Dick put it on the dresser and unpacked his clothes. A light breeze blew across his neck.

A full day of farm chores nearly erased Dick's memory of the morning's incident. By nightfall he was more than ready for a good night's sleep.

As he lit the carbide lamp, a sudden breeze blew through the window on the far side of his bed. It was strong enough to make the gas flame flicker. In the semi-darkness he stepped around the bed to close the window. It wasn't open.

The gas flame steadied and the coolness subsided. Dick relaxed.

But that's when he noticed the glass handle in the doorway. He must have stepped over it when he came in the room.

Dick again picked up the handle and put it back on top of the dresser. He climbed into bed and fell asleep, but awoke only a few hours later with a chill. He reached for the blanket but it wasn't there. He jumped out of bed and found his covers in a heap on the floor. He flung the covers back on the bed, jumped in and pulled them over his head.

He half-dozed for the rest of the night. Several times Dick woke up feeling an iciness swirling around him. His rising time of five o'clock did not come soon enough. But as he swung his feet out of bed, his right foot landed on the glass handle. It had again landed on the floor. He tossed it back onto the dresser and rushed out the door. Milking cows never seemed such a pleasant chore as it did on that morning. Dick Owens said he was the most frightened teenager in the entire county at that moment.

But it would be another two days—and nights—before Lloyd returned to resume his job. It was then that he explained to his brother the origin of the glass handle. Dick in turn told Lloyd about his own troubling nights. Lloyd apologized for keeping it all a secret, but that did little to relieve his brother's anxiety.

That's when the boys decided the wisest course of action was to return the glass handle to the graveyard. Lloyd ran up the staircase but stopped short at the top. Now the glass handle was on the floor *outside* his open bedroom door. He grabbed it and with his brother ran to the cemetery, stopped just inside the gate, and then pitched the casket handle as close as he could to Mrs. King's now-empty grave. They hightailed it back to the Larson farm, where Dick packed his clothes, wished his brother luck, and bolted for home.

Lloyd told his older brother he had no further troubles in that bedroom. Dick wasn't curious enough to go back and find out if he was telling the truth.

A Flame in the Window

Joan Lecher was afraid of the dark. She slept with the lights burning. But when Joan moved her family into a house she said was haunted, for the first time in her life she wasn't fearful.

Joan was content and at ease in that tall, white house on the north side of Wisconsin Rapids. Built before the Civil War, it is a sturdy, comfortable dwelling, spacious enough even for Joan's family of six children.

It was Christmas, Joan remembers, when the idea first presented itself that another boarder shared her house. Joan and her former husband were sitting on the living room couch when she caught sight of a shadow passing by. Out of the corner of her eye, she saw it go into the kitchen. Five minutes later a second shadow seemed to flit by. Her husband saw it, too. The couple got up and walked into the kitchen and then looked in the combination den and laundry room behind the kitchen. They checked the doors and windows: closed and locked. They had no idea what they had seen.

A few days later, Joan's daughter, Kathy, stood in the kitchen combing her hair in front of a large, old-fashioned mirror. An elderly man's face appeared as a reflection in the glass from just behind her shoulder, staring intently at her. She spun around but found herself quite alone in the room.

During that same holiday period, a young girl temporarily living with the Lechers was staying in a small bedroom off the kitchen. She was asleep one night when she awoke with a start. An old man stood in the doorway watching her. It was no one she had seen before. Too frightened to scream, she pulled the covers up over her face and hoped he'd go away. He did.

Later, when the two girls compared notes, they discovered striking similarities between the two figures.

In an attempt to discover the identity of the apparition, the Lecher children and several friends gathered around the kitchen table for a séance. Someone asked the "ghost," if present, to manifest itself in some way. A coffee cup slowly rose in the air. The amateur psychics scrambled from the room.

On another night, the intrepid gang gathered again. Nothing happened, though several of the youngsters claimed to have heard sounds like the sawing of wood coming from the attic. Joan had begun remodeling the old house. She thinks perhaps the ghost—whoever it was—might have been helping, although no evidence of its handiwork was ever found.

Sometimes months or years would pass by without any additional evidence of a haunting. Then, suddenly, there would be a new reminder that the family was not alone. That's what happened to Joan's son, Lance, one night as he babysat his younger brother. He heard distinct footsteps upstairs; someone was striding back and forth in the hallway and through the bedrooms. Lance was certain that someone, somehow, had broken into the house. When his older brother, Kim, arrived home shortly thereafter, he went upstairs to investigate. No one was there and nothing had been disturbed. Little Joe had slept downstairs all through the excitement.

The footsteps persisted. Joan heard them, too. On at least one occasion, the footsteps came from a room in which several mattresses covered the floorboards.

"Somebody's here keeping an eye on me," Joan remembers thinking, adding that the footfalls became such a routine in the house she no longer investigated the noises. She decided the spirit was friendly and was taking care of her. One winter's evening, Joan sat in an archway between the living room and the kitchen. She faced the tall living room windows that looked out upon the street. In the bottom left-hand corner of one window a small flame suddenly appeared; it was a bright, single image that glowed for several seconds. The flame was pure white.

Joan particularly sensed the mysterious resident when she was troubled. Her children took to calling the ghost H. B., the initials of a previous owner of the house, an old bachelor who had been found dead in bed, apparently of a heart attack. Yet Joan had first seen *two* shadows. H. B. had taken care of his invalid mother in the house before she entered a nursing home.

For her part, Joan Lecher believes her own senses and those of her children, yet she can offer no rational explanation. She is certain that whoever or whatever watched over her and her family was there for protection against the vagaries of life.

There Goes Mamie!

Grandmothers come in many shapes, sizes, and dispositions. But they all have one thing in common—grandmothers want to be remembered by their families. One way in which they can be certain they're not forgotten is by coming back in the afterlife to check up on their loved ones.

Grandma Mamie did that.

On a crisp fall night some years ago, Pat Orcutt, of Whiting, Wisconsin, curled up in bed with a good novel. At about ten o'clock she happened to glance up from the pages. Her grandmother was standing beside the bed. There would have been nothing odd about that, except that Grandma Mamie had been dead for many, many years and was buried in Elmira, New York.

Oddly enough, Pat recognized her immediately even though the apparition was that of a young woman dressed in turn-of-the-century attire. A "feeling of warmth and benevolence" filled the room as the ghost smiled down at Pat and nodded. Pat called out to her husband, but the ghost vanished before he came into the bedroom. He contended that she had been dreaming. She insisted she had not. Suddenly all the window shades in the room snapped up noisily.

"Well, there goes Mamie," her husband said with a chuckle, remembering that his wife's grandmother had been a bit mischievous with a colorful personality. Perhaps Pat had *not* been dreaming.

Pat believes her grandmother materialized at that moment to "see" her first great-grandson, Pat's baby, who had been born recently. An earlier miscarriage had caused her grandmother deep concern. She herself had cared for Pat as an infant and Mamie remained close to Pat's family through the years.

Grandma Mamie's ghost returned again several years later when the Orcutts lived in Wisconsin Rapids. Pat had painstakingly transformed a den wall into a sort of family museum, with old wedding licenses and ancestors' portraits in an assortment of frames. One day Pat found a frame—containing pictures of Mamie, her husband, and Pat's other grandparents—face down on the floor. The glass was not broken; the hanger was still attached to the plaster wall.

Pat re-hung the picture but several days later found it again face down on the floor. This time the hook had come out of the wall. She found a sturdier hanger and put the picture back up.

But the picture and its hanger continued to fall. Sometimes it was on the floor early in the morning; at other times, Pat found it there after coming home from shopping.

Pat's husband thought the picture either fell because of some vibrations or that one of the family's cats knocked it down. Yet that picture was the only one of the many wall hangings disturbed.

One of the Orcutt sons had a different opinion.

Shrugging his shoulders, he suggested to his mother that Grandma Mamie had come back because she didn't like being in the same frame as her in-laws! For a time the family joked about that possibility.

When Pat's parents came to visit, she told them about the falling picture. Her mother offered another explanation.

In her later years, perhaps due to dementia, Grandma Mamie set out to destroy all photographs of herself. She had thrown away every photograph that she could find, and even cut her own image out of all the group pictures in the family albums. Pat had never known about that.

Pat had no idea whether Grandma Mamie really was continuing her crusade to erase photographic proof of her existence even after death. Perhaps she was and perhaps she eventually gave up. Grandma Mamie was not heard from again.

Uncle Otto

A ghost can make itself known in a number of ways. The poltergeist, or "noisy ghost" to translate from the original German, allows its presence to be known through clamorous behavior—flying dishes, overturned furniture, clattering footfalls on the stairway.

The origin of the poltergeist can be similar to that of most supernatural beings. When a person dies, as many experts speculate, an imprint much like that of a photographic negative is left behind. That imprint may take on physical properties and become a force of its own. If that negative behavior is powerful enough, the poltergeist, or in some cases an apparition, manifests itself to onlookers. Thus, we might find ghosts haunting homes to which they had a strong emotional or physical attachment during life.

The ghost of Otto Wolf* in Prescott, Wisconsin, was just that sort of poltergeist. In life, Otto had been a kindly man, blind since childhood. He lived in a rambling two-story house on Walnut Street with his brother and sister-in-law, Carl and Marian Wolf, and their son, George.

Uncle Otto, as he was called by one and all, including his own brother, had attended college and traveled the world, but in his later years his blindness and frail health prevented him from venturing far from his modest room on the second floor of the house. His favorite pastime was to sit in an old wooden rocker as he quietly sang the German folk ballads he'd learned as a child.

Carl and Marian Wolf bought the house shortly after they'd married. Carl was a businessman and local politician. His wife worked as a registered nurse at the local hospital. Otto moved in with his brother two years later and remained with the family until his death.

After Otto Wolf passed away, the first in a series of bizarre events convinced the Wolfs that the kindly old man's ghost had returned to the family he had loved so much in life.

George Wolf was a young adult in that summer when Uncle Otto first let his presence be known. Late one humid August night, as George lay awake listening to the usual symphony of tree frogs and crickets coming through his open bedroom window, the nightly chorus was joined by a new sound. He listened intently. What he heard made the small hairs on the back of his neck prickle. Slippered feet scuffed back and forth over the creaking floorboards of Otto's old room directly next to George's. He had gotten used to the old man's nocturnal pacing when sleep eluded him. The shuffling pace he heard now was slow and steady just as it had always been.

George's curiosity got the best of him. He crept down to his uncle's old room. He paused briefly, swallowed hard, and opened the door. He need not have worried: nothing disturbed the gloomy quiet.

Maybe he imagined the entire episode, he thought. At breakfast the next morning, Marian Wolf scolded her son for walking around in Uncle Otto's room! George protested his innocence and insisted it wasn't his doing. At least he knew now that he hadn't imagined the whole episode.

Nearly every night for days on end the footfalls came and went. George knew that somehow the old man was still in the house. Even though Marian had heard the footsteps, she still thought George was pulling some sort of prank. His parents scoffed at the idea of a ghost, but later events would convince them otherwise.

Surprisingly, George was not at all upset with the nocturnal ramblings. His uncle had been a kind and gentle soul during life, so he reckoned that the ghost, if indeed it was one, meant no harm to the family.

Nothing in Uncle Otto's room had been disturbed or changed since his death, including the old cane-bottomed rocker that had been his favorite resting spot. A few months after the pacing was first heard, George was walking down the hallway and noticed the door to his uncle's room was ajar. To his bewilderment the rocker was moving slowly as if someone had just gotten up. For many nights thereafter George heard the pacing during the night, followed by the soft creaking of the rocker. And each time he looked in the room, the rocker would be slowly swaying back and forth, back and forth.

George thought perhaps an errant squirrel or mouse, or one of the family's cats, had jumped off the rocker but escaped detection. He decided to play detective by scattering white flour on the floor around the rocker, looking for small, telltale footprints. His theory collapsed, however, when he rushed into the room after hearing the familiar creak but found no signs of beast—or ghost—in the carpet of flour.

There are many cases of poltergeist activity in a home beset by crises such as an emotional trauma or sudden tragedy. The Wolf family soon discovered that Uncle Otto's appearance might have been a harbinger of sorrow.

Carl Wolf developed the arteriosclerosis and diabetes that would cause his death at an early age. Within only a few years of Otto's death, his cherished family was experiencing hard times as a result of the financial drain of a serious illness. When Marian Wolf subsequently developed rheumatoid arthritis and thus the family faced an even deeper crisis, the poltergeist activity increased.

A winter soon thereafter was particularly trying for the family financially, medically . . . and in the more erratic behavior of their nocturnal visitor. The nightly walks and the swaying rocker had become a part of the family's daily routine. Marian and George Wolf had long ago accepted the unnatural source of the activity.

As George looked back on the events of that time, he believed Uncle Otto was trying to register his concern over the family's unhappiness. He knew the family was in trouble.

George was out of college and looking for his first job when he noticed that Otto's activities were increasing in intensity and duration. The footfalls could be clearly heard at all times of the day and night, quite unlike earlier years. Even Carl Wolf, nearly an invalid by this time and the last one to accept the presence of a ghost, admitted to his son that he often heard the footfalls when he shaved in a bathroom next to the haunted bedroom.

Then early one morning George was shaken out of bed by what sounded like a giant handball being batted against the wall in Uncle Otto's room. His parents also heard it. Together they ran into the bedroom but as usual found nothing. Up until that time, the ghost had been almost gentle in his behavior, but this turn of events put the Wolfs somewhat on edge.

The following December the family's financial plight worsened. They were forced into bankruptcy and had to sell the house and many furnishings to pay debts. Uncle Otto's ghost was not pleased. The disturbances grew in severity, coming now from his old room and minutes later from other parts of the house.

Within a month, as the family prepared to move to a smaller house, Uncle Otto tried to convince them otherwise in a most spectacular way. The family returned home one evening to find every light on, with light even streaming through the window of a storage room from which all the electrical fixtures had been removed.

George quickly unlocked the front door and raced up the staircase. He opened the door to Uncle Otto's room. It was dark.

In that final winter, and frequently before that time, the Wolfs' Siamese cats acted strangely when they were anywhere on the second floor. One cat had even been accidentally locked in Uncle Otto's bedroom overnight. The next morning, Marian Wolf found the cat crouched in the middle of the room with its fur standing on end. With a screech, it raced out of the door and never again ventured up the staircase.

Two cold spots in the house also mystified the Wolfs. One was in Uncle Otto's room and the other on a rear stairway. Passing through them, George remembered, was like walking into a crypt.

George and his mother said that in early spring, a few weeks before the family moved out, they witnessed the most terrifying incident in their eight years of living with a ghost.

George was in his room reading. Midnight neared. The house, and most particularly Otto's bedroom, had been unusually quiet. Suddenly the roar of splintering wood shattered the stillness. George launched himself out of his chair and threw open his bedroom door. The solid oak door to the haunted bedroom was being pulled slowly from its hinges. George saw no one near it. Marian Wolf arrived at the top of the staircase in time to see the door being tossed into the middle of the hallway. Two large hinges hung limply from the shattered frame.

"My God! What's gone wrong?" George screamed.

His mother didn't answer.

Mother and son knew that nothing *human* could have pulled that door from its frame.

The next day George moved into a vacant downstairs bedroom.

Despite the terror of that night, no one in the family had ever been physically harmed or even touched by the ghost. That changed a few days after the door was torn away and shortly before the family moved away.

George awoke to a soft, gentle stroking of his face. It was the caress of a human hand on his cheek, reassuring in its touch. Then it was gone. In the dim light, he saw one of the cats sitting in an old chair, its back arched rigid. Its eyes followed the progress of someone moving slowly across the room.

George Wolf knew then that Uncle Otto was apologizing for his outlandish behavior. And saying good-bye.

Don't Mess with Elmer

In the hardscrabble Depression years of the 1930s, when a person's economic security was often determined by luck or resourcefulness, tempers sometimes flared over small injustices, whether real or imagined. At least that's how it was in northern Wisconsin between bachelor farmer Roy Nelson* of rural Cumberland and his neighbor Elmer Pederson*.

The men shared a hay crop on some jointly rented acreage. One day the men had an argument over the arrangement. No one today remembers what caused the disagreement, only that it led to a perplexing series of events between the two men.

Soon after the argument, Roy began complaining about a "ghost" on his property—a prankish sprite that left barn doors wide open day and night, filled feed troughs to overflowing with water, and pounded on the walls of Nelson's house all night long.

Roy named Elmer Pederson as the culprit. Neighbors were anxious to preserve harmony in the community. They didn't dare take sides. That and the pair's naturally ornery disposition led many to fear a lawsuit for slander should either one be publicly criticized. Secretly, they attributed Roy's wild tales to the eccentricities of living alone too long.

But the neutrality didn't last long. When the disturbances at Roy's farm continued, the neighbors got involved. After all, they reasoned, Roy was basically a good man always ready to welcome a visitor with a hot cup of coffee. He kept his Bible open on the kitchen table and paid his help well.

Roy called his unseen tormentor a "billy goat" for some reason. And he was determined to catch him—or it—in the act.

He persuaded a few nearby farmers to take turns hiding in his woodpile and watch from the windows of his modest farmhouse. Meanwhile, Roy would carry out his own surveillance. He ran a wire from his house to his barn and bought a German shepherd dog whose leash he looped around the wire. The dog was free to run back and forth in hot pursuit of any trespasser, seen or unseen.

Next, Roy borrowed a .38-caliber revolver from his brother-in-law and stood guard on the front porch. Whenever he heard a strange noise, he fired in the air, a sound that reportedly echoed three-quarters of a mile away in that quiet countryside.

Meanwhile, watchers inside the house usually congregated in the kitchen. If they heard pounding on the walls at the opposite side of the house they ran to that side. Then the thumping would jump back to the kitchen walls. But with men stationed at both ends of the house, the irritating noise would cease.

Even neighborhood children took their turns on the "ghost watch." A good friend of Roy's volunteered his son's services for a forty-eight-hour shift. Pete was a little boy of twelve years at the time.

"I shook from my belly button both ways," Pete recalled, "but I didn't dare say no."

He was given a chamber pot and instructed to go upstairs and remain there at all times. Roy carried food and water up to him. A horse blanket with a peephole cut through it had been tacked up over a window. On the first day, while the boy squinted through the hole watching Roy at work in a nearby field, he heard what sounded like someone moving an object around on the floor downstairs.

"That's when I quit growin'," claimed Pete.

Later that evening when Roy returned from the field, he discovered that the mail, which he had picked up at noon, was strewn all over the kitchen. Long after dark and still huddled upstairs, little Pete heard swats from a rolled-up newspaper. Roy was yelling at his "billy goat" to get away.

"After two days of Depression coffee, I went home," Pete recalled.

A day or so later the boy was helping Roy with the haying. As it happened, Elmer was haying at the same time.

As Pete recollected, "At one time we were all within fifteen feet of one another. The look they exchanged wasn't one of love, hope, or charity."

The ghostly disturbances ceased when Elmer died unexpectedly . . . of natural causes.

Now that could have been coincidence, or perhaps Elmer himself really was the "spook." Pete isn't sure today if anyone really wanted to catch the culprit. He said chasing after the ghost did cause a good deal of levity in that grim Depression-era year.

Pete doesn't really know who the ghost was.

It did turn out to be a good story, so maybe it never really mattered.

A Dream So Real

The Scots may not be the most superstitious people in the world, but some beliefs they hold to tenaciously. One such conviction is that the seventh son of a seventh son has precognitive powers, that is, the ability to foretell future events.

When Robert Laurie was born in Scotland the seventh son of a seventh son, news of his birth spread far and wide. His family learned when he was still a small boy that Robert had *the gift*, as many characterized precognition. Eventually, the Lauries immigrated to Sturgeon Bay, Wisconsin. As young Robert grew to manhood, his extraordinary, almost supernatural, powers flourished. His fame spread far and wide.

The problem with precognition is that one can "see" both good and evil. For Robert, his honesty dictated that he disclose whatever the future held.

He told a neighboring family with seven daughters that their eighth child would be a boy. It was and they were joyful.

On another occasion, Robert assured a woman that her fisherman husband would survive the roiling Lake Michigan waters after his boat capsized in a storm. Laurie had "seen" the man clinging to the cabin's hatch torn loose from the boat. Some time later, the hatch, bearing its human cargo, was indeed washed up on shore. The sailor was alive but barely conscious.

Not all of Robert's uncanny predictions were so welcome. Alex Laurie, Robert's older brother, along with another man set forth by boat for Green

Bay to buy supplies. Robert said they would never return. The boat must have capsized for neither it nor the two men were ever heard from again.

One night when he was in his sixties, Robert had a dream so vivid that in the morning he recounted it in precise detail to his wife, Catherine. He told her there would soon be a large funeral in Door County. People would attend from great distances, traveling by land and water to get to the service. He described the glistening horses pulling magnificent carriages, he named the minister, and he named the precise number of mourners.

The only thing he could not "see" was the name of the deceased. In his dream he saw only that the casket held a man's body.

A month later, a funeral was held, one of the largest in the history of Door County. People did travel from far and wide. Beautiful horses pulled the mourner's carriages. All of the details were unerringly like those Robert Laurie revealed to his wife. But among the mourners was one whose heart was the heaviest with sorrow—Catherine Laurie, now the widow of this seventh son of a seventh son.

The Summoning

The second-floor apartment of the private home in Manitowoc met the needs of the young couple Randolph and Esther Johnson*. Their elderly landlord lived downstairs.

The Johnsons' bedroom had two doors diagonally across from one another, leaving barely enough room for their double bed. A door near the foot of the bed led into a hallway, but that door was kept locked. An old-fashioned wardrobe blocked the way. A second door near the head of the bed opened into a rear room from which the tenants could reach the stairway leading to an outside door.

One night after they had lived there for some time and the couple had gone to bed, Esther was having trouble falling asleep. As she stared off into the inky darkness of the room, the startling apparition of a tall woman wearing a long gray dress and matching sweater floated out of the wardrobe. She moved with folded arms and bowed head around the bed and toward the door leading to the stairwell.

Esther nudged her husband awake. He looked over toward the ghost, grunted, and whispered to his wife, "Can't Mrs. Anderson walk around in her own house if she wants to?"

In the morning Esther and Randolph discovered that their landlord, Mason Anderson, had died in his sleep some hours before. His wife had come to get him by way of the Johnsons' apartment. She had been dead for nearly twenty years.

House of Chimes

When the George Websters moved into an old Green Bay house, everything went well—at first.

Until the kitchen screen door, equipped with a tight spring, began opening and then slamming shut for no apparent reason.

Until on one occasion the slamming was preceded by "a loud scraping, swirling noise," with George less than twenty feet away.

Until he rushed outside to investigate but found nothing that could account for the noise or the movement of the door.

On a late July afternoon, George was home alone doing paperwork for his job as district supervisor for a Chicago-based corporation. He had just started for the back bedroom when he heard the now-familiar slam. But this time, looking toward the door, he saw the apparition of a man attired in black who seemed to float rather than walk. It came straight toward him. George flattened himself against a wall. The ghost, as if sensing a head-on collision, veered to the right and edged by. It glanced toward him, glided into a bedroom, and vanished. The entire episode lasted about ten seconds.

Five days later the family left on a vacation. The house was locked up and empty—or so they thought. At about nine in the evening the neighbors, who were taking in the Websters' mail, saw the kitchen lights go on and through the windows dark apparitions move back and forth.

One day in August, Mrs. Webster watched two white-clad ghosts disappear into the master bedroom just off the kitchen.

Some time later, the family began hearing "scraping and screeching noises in between the walls." Playful mice? Hardly, according to George. The noises turned into chimes and bell-like sounds.

Lights also were being turned on and off by unseen forces both day and night, and neighbors often called the Websters to find out why they had left their basement lights on all night.

The family finally had enough and moved away. Although the electricity was shut off, neighbors reported that the lights continued to go on intermittently while the house stood vacant.

George Webster had the last word on the bizarre manifestations, a grand understatement to be certain. It was, he said, "most unusual."

The Girl in White

In the early days of the nineteenth century, few people in rural Wisconsin traveled by car or even by buggy. Those who owned horses rode them; those less fortunate walked. Young John Groat of Menomonie was among the latter. One hot summer evening, Groat and his neighbor Ed Forness* walked a mile and a half to town. On the way back they decided to visit their girlfriends, Carrie and Anna Chapman*, two sisters who lived with their parents in a farmhouse not far from the road on which the men traveled and quite near a small stream.

But as the men reached the wooden bridge that carried the roadway over the shallow stream, they stopped to reconsider their visit with the girls. After all, it was quite late and they weren't expected.

"Look, John!" Ed Forness suddenly called out, as he pointed off down the gloomy path. "Looks like there's a girl all in white coming down the road."

A girl about the age of Carrie and Anna walked directly toward them but then veered abruptly just before reaching the bridge, walked down into the stream—and vanished.

The two men dashed to where the girl had gone into the water. They waded back and forth, but found no trace of the girl.

John Groat feared that she must have been either Carrie or Anna, and he knew, too, without asking, that Ed shared the same trepidation. But why would either girl be out alone at night? And how could anyone simply disappear in such a shallow body of water?

"Ed, we've got to get to the Chapman place right away," Groat said, starting off at a fast pace. "I don't know how it could've been Anna or my Carrie, but we've gotta find out. And if it ain't one of them, well . . ." His voice trailed off.

At the farmhouse, the girls' parents were still on the porch, taking in the night air. Mrs. Chapman explained that they had had company earlier and that the girls were in the kitchen washing dishes.

"Carrie! Anna!" their father called into the house.

The girls came out. Vastly relieved, the boys told their amazing story. Both girls were as puzzled as their beaus. The description didn't sound like any girl they knew, and besides they had waded the stream many times and there were no deep holes anywhere in it.

More than a century has passed, yet no one ever offered a satisfactory explanation of who or what those two young men said they encountered. John Groat claimed he would never, ever have told the story if Ed Forness had not also witnessed the events on that remarkable summer night.

Spirits on the Land

In ancient days, when Native Americans roamed Wisconsin, game was plentiful in the dense forests, and hunters provided well for their families. One winter evening, a young Ojibwe wife, awaiting the return of her husband, became uneasy. He was always home earlier, tired but eager to sit by the fire and spin stories of the day's adventures for her and the child. But not on this day.

Suddenly someone approaching broke the evening's silence. The wife hurried to the doorway of the lodge. Two strange women stood before her, their thin figures wrapped in hooded garments that nearly concealed their long, sallow faces. The hunter's wife did not recognize them. These women were not of her tribe and she had no idea where they might have come from. Not wishing to appear inhospitable, she invited them in to warm up by the fire. They accepted her invitation, but instead of going to the fire, they huddled in a dark corner.

Suddenly a voice cried out, "Merciful spirit, there are two corpses clothed in garments!" The wife wheeled around. There was no one there, no one except the silent guests. Had she been dreaming? Hearing only the sound of a rising wind?

Then through the doorway her husband appeared, dragging the carcass of a large, fat deer. At that instant, the strangers rushed to the animal and began pulling off the choicest bits of white fat. The couple, although astonished by such impropriety, decided that their guests must be famished and so they said nothing.

On the next day when the hunter returned from the chase, the same thing occurred.

On the third day, the young man, deciding to cater to the whims of his peculiar visitors, tied a bundle of fat on the top of the carcass he brought home. The women seized it eagerly, and then ate the portion of fat that had been set aside for the wife. The hunter, although tempted to rebuke them, remained silent. For some mysterious reason he had had unaccountable good luck in felling game since the ghostly visitors had come into his home; he thought that perhaps somehow his good fortune had something to do with their presence. Besides, the women didn't cause any trouble; on the contrary, they were helpful. Each evening they gathered wood, stacked it by the fire, and returned all implements to the place where they had found them. During the daytime, they huddled unobtrusively in a corner. They never joined a family conversation, nor laughed or joked.

Finally, after many days of this, the hunter stayed out later than usual. When he did appear with a carcass, the visitors tore off the fat so rudely that the wife, who had become increasingly perturbed at their presence, nearly lashed out at them. Although she managed to hold her tongue, she was certain this time that the guests sensed her resentment.

After the family had gone to bed, the husband heard the women weeping. Recalling the looks exchanged between his wife and the guests, he worried that his mate had offended them. Had she spoken too sharply? Said something that he perhaps hadn't heard? He got up, went over to the women, and asked what was wrong. After assuring him that he had treated them kindly, they spoke further.

"We come from the land of the dead to test the sincerity of the living," one of them began. The living, bereaved by death in a family, say that if only the dead might be restored to life they would devote the rest of their lives to making them happy. The Master of Life had given them "three moons" in which to test the sincerity of those who, like the hunter and his wife, had lost a close relative.

"We have been here more than half that time," they said, "but now your wife is so angered by our presence that we have decided we must leave."

The hunter's wife, awakened by the voices, arose and stood at her husband's side. The ghosts went on to explain why they purposely had eaten the choicest parts of the hunter's kills.

The spirit went on: "That was the particular trial selected for you. We know, by your customs, that the white fat is reserved for the wife. In usurping that privilege we have put you both to a severe test of your tempers and feelings. But that is what we were sent to do."

Before the astonished hunter and his wife could respond, the ghosts blessed them, said good-bye, and vanished into the darkness. But their blessings were made manifest in the years to come. The hunter excelled in the chase, fathered many splendid children, and enjoyed health, happiness, and a long life. Such were the rewards of befriending two lonely ghosts who had come to test this family on a winter's night long ago.

In the time of the ancients there was a land called Moningwunakaunig, "place of the golden-breasted woodpecker." We call it Madeline, largest of the Apostle Islands scattered off Lake Superior's shore near Bayfield.

Madeline Island is a fourteen-thousand-acre refuge with white sand beaches hugging impenetrable forests of fir, spruce, pine, poplar, and birch, contrasting sharply with the rugged red granite cliffs on the island's windward side. It is an ancient place. For three thousand years Madeline has known human footsteps. The original peoples camped in the woods, taking from the waters and forest their diet of fish, meat, and berries at the time when Roman armies were conquering Europe.

Later, when the Ojibwe were forced from their ancestral home along the St. Lawrence River, they settled on the Apostle Islands. A great village was built on Madeline with a population, archaeologists say, of nearly twelve thousand. But the area became overpopulated and a terrible famine struck the community.

The men of the tribe could not kill enough fish and game to feed a population so large. In desperation, tribal elders and the medicine men resorted to cannibalism. Young maidens and children were chosen and offered as sacrifices on a primitive altar, their flesh consumed as food. But the population rebelled after a time and the old leadership was executed.

Tales began spreading of the victims' vengeful spirits haunting the island. They would rise from the earth near the sacrificial altar and wander over the island.

Legend has it that a great exodus took place and the entire village was evacuated to the mainland until eventually no Ojibwe remained. Various families migrated to locations in northern Wisconsin and Minnesota. Some accounts insist it was several centuries before native people would again camp on Madeline.

Now there are few Native Americans on the island, and few physical traces remain of the island's original inhabitants. Earlier in the twentieth century, it is said, some sacrificial tobacco was found scattered at the site of the ancient altar.

A modern yacht harbor and marina occupy the lagoon near which the sacrificial altar was located. Not far away, there is a lavish resort and a golf course created by the world-famous designer Robert Trent Jones. If the lagoon once harbored the ghosts of those butchered centuries ago, no one has reported any recent apparitions. Yet on a cool, foggy night in early fall, if you sit near enough to that lagoon along the edge of the old Indian burial ground, if you listen intently enough, you just might hear their plaintive cries.

The haunted house of legend is usually a stately old mansion perched atop a windswept knoll. One enters the grounds through a sagging iron gate attached by a single hinge to the decrepit fence winding around the property. The building is in a desperate state of disrepair—floorboards are missing from the veranda, windows boarded up or broken—and, for good measure, a few bats ought to flutter from one of the many gable windows. Of course, one visits the mansion on a cold and windy night where terror seems to wait just beyond that heavy and forbidding front door.

In fact, one of Wisconsin's more famous haunted houses fits only part of this description. In earlier days this house and property seemed to be cursed with evil. No fewer than ten people associated with it met unusual deaths. If any house can be haunted with grief and sorrow, it is the T. B. Scott mansion in Merrill.

In the early part of the nineteenth century, a Native American village occupied the west bank of the Wisconsin River in what is now the town of Merrill. French fur traders had often stopped at the village to barter for goods. The peaceful tribe had little fear from the white men. When lumbermen began traveling the river during the big timber drives in northern Wisconsin, they were welcomed as brothers by the Native inhabitants.

According to one legend, the village chief brought visitors to his dwelling where his only daughter would serve them meals. The beautiful, shy maiden, who soon became known as Jenny to her white guests, entranced the men. But the blissful life of the settlement soon turned to tragedy. A young lumberjack who was particularly fond of Jenny made love to her. The accounts differ as to what happened next. One version asserts that Jenny, ashamed of her actions, killed herself. Another tale holds that Jenny simply died soon thereafter, probably of the flu, which had been introduced among the Indian peoples by the white men.

Whatever the cause of the girl's tragic death, her father was grief-stricken. He ordered that she be buried upon a high hill across the river from the settlement. At her burial the old man stood at his daughter's grave, gazed out over the river, and prayed, "Oh, great Father, grant me this place for my child. Let this ground be sacred to her memory." Then he placed a curse upon that earth: "Let it never do any white man any good."

The years passed, the Indians abandoned the settlement, and Jenny and her final resting place were all but forgotten. The settlement that had grown beside the Indian camp—named Jenny Bull Falls, or Jenny for short—was renamed to honor S. S. Merrill, the manager of the Chicago, Milwaukee, St. Paul and Pacific Railroad.

But in 1884 there began a series of events so strange that the old chief's grim incantation seemed to echo down through the ages. T. B. Scott, a wealthy Merrill mill owner and lumberman, purchased "Jenny's hill" from the government and planned to build a mansion fit for a timber baron. He knew nothing of Jenny or the curse. Only two years after he bought the land in 1886, Scott died with the house only partially built. He was fifty-seven. Scott's widow, Ann, tried to complete construction on the mansion. But within a year she too was dead. It was now left to their son, Walter, to finish his parents' work. Although his mother had urged him to complete the house, Walter apparently abandoned the project. Some years later, however, Walter did visit Chicago to consult an architect about the project. During their meeting, Walter and the architect, a Mr. Sheldon, got into an argument for some reason. Young Scott was stabbed to death with a letter opener. Sheldon proved in court that he had acted in self-defense, implying that Walter Scott instigated the struggle.

The executors of the estate sold the still-incomplete mansion to a Chicago millionaire, a man named Kuechle. He wanted the house as a summer retreat and made plans to install lavish additions to it. Later he visited the World's Columbian Exposition in Chicago in 1893 and bought a number of decorations for the house, including heavy, hand-carved doors, plate glass windows, embossed mirrors, and a carved mantel. He hired workmen to install the furnishings and complete construction. Kuechle apparently spent little if any time in the mansion. Within a short time, a series of bad investments forced him to mortgage the house to a Chicago tavern owner named Barsanti. Kuechle, however, was able to avoid foreclosure on the mansion when he inherited a large sum of money. Determined to recoup his loses, Kuechle invested the fortune in a contract to build a section of the Northern Pacific Railroad, but he knew nothing of railroads or engineering, soon went bankrupt, and later died in a mental institution.

Barsanti, the tavernkeeper, took possession of the mansion, but never lived to see it. Somehow he had antagonized the notorious gang known as the Black Hand, and as he waited in Chicago's Union Station to board a train for Merrill, he was stabbed to death by one of the "Hands."

Barsanti's survivors, in turn, sold the still-vacant and only half-completed mansion to a real estate speculator, George Gibson. His intention was to build a home for elderly lawyers. An office was organized in Merrill to collect donations, and work on the mansion once again resumed.

But he vanished late one afternoon after leaving the office to go home for supper. Search parties were organized to scour the countryside. The Wisconsin River was dredged without success. Riverbanks and boom sites (sections of the river where freshly cut timber jam up) were carefully watched. There was no apparent motive for Gibson's sudden disappearance. He was never seen again after that day.

The mansion reverted once again to the Barsanti family since all payments on the house had not been made. The family retained possession for several years during which the mansion remained unoccupied. The old place now had a solid reputation for bad luck, if not evil itself. Caretakers looked after the house and grounds, mainly to protect it from vandals. One old groundsman was an Englishman known as Popcorn Dan, since he also operated a popcorn stand in Merrill. In 1911 he sailed to England for a visit to his childhood home. Returning to America in April 1912, however, he made a fatal mistake: Popcorn Dan booked his passage on the S.S. *Titanic*.

The Lloydsen family assumed the role of caretaker after Popcorn Dan's death. Mr. Lloydsen died of alcoholism.

Finally, Mrs. Mary Fehlhaber, a Merrill area midwife, bought the mansion for a small sum and took in boarders. One day, while out riding, she became ill, made her way to a nearby farm, but died before a doctor could reach her side.

In 1919 Herman Fehlhaber, Mary's husband, gave the house and adjoining property to the city of Merrill. Four years later the city offered the property to the Holy Cross Sisters, an order of Roman Catholic nuns, if they would build a hospital, which they opened a few years later and is now known as Good Samaritan Hospital. The sisters used the mansion as a residence. They also operated a small junior college and other related facilities nearby. The nuns sold the hospital some years ago and now devote their ministry to elder care.

Is it only a macabre coincidence that so many people associated with the house met with tragedy? Or did that curse pronounced so very long ago linger on through the decades to torment those who tried to build on "Jenny's hill"? Although it's impossible to parse legend from fact more than a century later, perhaps once the mansion and the grounds were used for humanitarian purposes peace was restored to that high knoll.

Should you ever see the T. B. Scott mansion at the south end of Merrill, think of Jenny and ask yourself whether the curse is over.

The Coulee Road Ghost

Hudson, Wisconsin, is a small, bustling city clinging to the bluffs of the St. Croix River, directly across the river from the sprawling Minneapolis–St. Paul metropolitan area in Minnesota. The town is a popular suburb for commuters. Its scenic beauty, river-connected recreational opportunities, lively cultural scene, and pleasant small-town living make legendary visits by the ghost of Paschal Aldrich seem quite out of place.

The story of the hauntings on what is now called Coulee Road begins nearly 140 years ago with the arrival in Hudson of one of its first residents, Dr. Philip Aldrich.

Aldrich, who was born in Ohio in 1792, could justifiably be called a pioneer entrepreneur. He became over the years a businessman, mail carrier and post-master, county commissioner, circuit judge, and landowner. No doubt the ease with which he accomplished these tasks, many of them simultaneously, was due in some measure to the small population of St. Croix County in 1845—just 1,419 inhabitants. Dr. Aldrich was also the census taker.

In those days, the county included most of northwestern Wisconsin and that part of Minnesota extending from the St. Croix River to the Mississippi, which now separates Minneapolis and St. Paul.

Shortly after Aldrich arrived in the county in 1840, the federal government awarded him a contract to carry twice-monthly mail dispatches from Point Douglas, across the St. Croix River from present-day Prescott, Wisconsin, to

83

St. Croix Falls. During the summer he piloted a bateau, or flat-bottomed river-boat, and in the winter he trod the ice-covered river by foot.

Two years after his appointment, Dr. Aldrich was elected county commissioner and continued to be closely associated with the political growth of western Wisconsin for many years. According to newspaper accounts, the first meeting of the St. Croix County Board was held September 9, 1848, at Dr. Aldrich's home, which stood at the northeast corner of Second and Elm Street in Hudson. The house was a center of many gala social events in the town's early days.

Dr. Aldrich had moved into Hudson during the previous year. He bought a large tract of land, now called the Aldrich Addition. Aldrich abandoned his mail route via the St. Croix River and took up an overland route from Hudson to St. Croix Falls. The mail was delivered on foot once a week, a round trip of some eighty miles.

In 1849 Aldrich became Hudson's first postmaster, a position he held until 1851. In that same year, he was also granted a license to operate a ferry across the St. Croix River.

A son of Dr. Aldrich, Paschal, owned a home on Buckeye Street that became the first post office. Paschal's wife, Martha, often clerked in the post office and since she could neither read nor write, the patrons picked out their own letters.

Following Dr. Philip Aldrich's death, the large holdings were passed on to Paschal. But the father's luck was not inherited by the son. Paschal Aldrich and his family moved into a small house at the head of Coulee Road, near present Interstate Highway 94. He farmed a large area for many years, but when a serious illness sunk his fortunes, he was forced to sell much of the property. There is some dispute as to the reason for the sale. One account has it that an unidentified man somehow caused the family to lose its vast holdings during Paschal's illness.

Paschal Aldrich died on October 13, 1860, in that house on Coulee Road. For years afterward, the place was known as the "haunted house." Members of his family and some neighbors said they saw Paschal's ghost wandering the premises at night, reportedly keeping watch over his family. Paschal's solicitude in death was attributed to his near financial ruin during his fatal illness.

Mrs. Paschal Aldrich also vowed to come back as a ghost. But her grand-daughter, the late Mrs. Wallace Smith, said she didn't know if there was a second ghost in the house or not. Perhaps one was enough.

A Quartet of Wisps

Will-o'-the-wisp: n.A phosphorescent light that hovers over swampy ground at night, possibly caused by rotting organic matter.

This is what a dictionary says, but Wisconsin pioneers often placed the will-o'-the-wisp in the same category as ghosts. Within the vast, dark forests, along riverbanks and lowlands, the eerie dancing lights would move and jump as if they were living, breathing creatures. No theory about "possible rotting organic matter" could shake from those hardy settlers the conviction that nothing short of Lucifer himself could be the culprit.

Mrs. Adele Cline of Eau Pleine recalls that the lights had the appearance of a man walking along in the dark, swinging a lantern, not an uncommon method of travel in the early days. Mrs. Cline's father first saw the phenomenon on a homestead near the Big Eau Pleine River in the 1880s. The first encounter took place one night on his way home from a visit to his parents' farm about a mile from his own cabin. The will-o'-the-wisp suddenly appeared beside him and shadowed him nearly to his doorstep.

Mrs. Cline's parents eventually built a barn on the land and surrounded the yard with a timber fence. The will-o'-the-wisp never entered the yard once the fence was erected.

The family homestead was quite near a widening of the Big Eau Pleine River. Between the barn and lake was a large area covered by rock the children used to call "the acre of stone." All around this section the land was cleared and under cultivation. Mrs. Cline said the light would come up from the river and cross over this stony expanse usually at twilight, although her mother once watched as two lights chased each other until the early morning hours.

The light would sometimes travel very fast, "as though it was really in a hurry," while at other times it might hover and slowly fade. A few minutes later it might reappear hundreds of feet away and continue its strange, nocturnal gyrations.

On one occasion Mrs. Cline's young aunt, twelve years old, and an uncle, who was only nine, came to visit the family. The children had been assigned the job of bringing in the livestock. Twilight descended and the youngsters had yet to complete their tasks. As they walked across a pasture, the will-o'-the-wisp appeared floating beside them. Their dog took one look at it and bolted for home. He hid for several days under the front porch. The cows wasted little time in returning to the comforts of the barn.

A few days later Mrs. Cline's grandfather was returning home at dusk when he saw the glowing will-o'-the-wisp bobbing along. At the same instant a thunderous roar bellowed from deep within the earth. The old man had been a soldier in the German Kaiser's East Prussian Army. He was familiar with the roar of cannon fire, yet the sound on that night was more frightening than anything he had ever heard.

Could there have been an underground landslide? Perhaps a minor earthquake? A neighbor boy returning along the same path heard something similar several years later. From that night on he carried a gun whenever he was out after dark.

Mrs. Cline's family eventually moved to an adjoining farm, and their original homestead was rented out. The new tenants periodically reported a man walking along with a lantern in the acre of stone.

The last sighting occurred after a bulldozer operator who was clearing stone from the farm told Mrs. Cline's father that he was surprised to see the old man out walking all alone the previous evening with only a lantern. "You could have seen the field by riding with me on the bulldozer," he offered. Mrs. Cline's father looked at him and smiled. He knew the will-o'-the-wisp had been abroad in the land once again.

The stereotypical ghost of legend may arise in the dark, brooding silences of cemeteries. But it wasn't exactly this ghost that appeared to Buffalo County pioneers but rather a fireball that hovered above a grave of an old lakeshore Indian burial ground. The size of a large orange, it swayed, like an eerie pendulum, thirty feet above the ground. As whispered word spread among the curious, residents of the area gathered nightly on the lakeshore to watch the swinging light. Occasionally, a brave man reached out to catch the light, but it always vanished before his eyes.

A will-o'-the-wisp? Old-timers had a different explanation. They said that a man named Belknap once had recurring dreams in which he saw a crock filled with immense treasures buried in the old cemetery. He was convinced that if he went there late at night and dug it up, the treasure would be his.

So vivid were these dreams that finally, one night, Belknap was impelled to action. He set forth with pick and shovels and dug until he found it. Alas, he had failed to turn around three times as he had been directed in the dream. The minute he bent down to pick up the crock he was stunned by a flash of lighting and the crock vanished.

And since that night the spot has been haunted by the glowing beacon . . . the sign of one man's folly.

The will-o'-the-wisp would often form itself into a bluish-colored fireball and then hop and skip across the fields. Some say that if a person interfered with the wisp he would become lost. Luckily that didn't happen to Alfred Ulrick Sr., who had several chilling encounters with the will-o'-the-wisp.

Ulrick was a young man a century ago when he first encountered the wisp. The mysterious ball of fire was common in his part of rural Wisconsin in those days. It would appear in an open field near his parents' farm in all manner of weather and light conditions—during rain or drought, on the darkest nights or in the brightness of a full moon. Farm animals, ironically, seemed unafraid of the object. They would continue to graze even when the wisp was close by in the pasture. But, Ulrick claimed, no one ever tried to interfere with the will-o'-the-wisp.

The closest Ulrick came to a direct encounter with the will-o'-the wisp was an incident on a late July evening. Ulrick and his father had taken the buggy and Dick, their favorite horse, into town for a supply of oats, their own grain not yet having been harvested.

Ulrick describes his father as a courageous man: "He did not seem to know the meaning of fear, regardless of what the situation was."

On their way home, the Ulricks had to travel near an area where the will-o'-the-wisp was known to frolic. Twilight descended on the pair as Dick trotted through the gathering gloom. The night air was cool; a full moon cast a glow across the nightscape. The road stretched out before them like a white ribbon laid out in the darkness.

Soon, father and son were near the wisp's playground.

They peered into the darkness. A glimpse of the fiery creature would provide ample fuel for a lively tale once they reached home.

Not far away, the will-o'-the-wisp was hovering and pulsating. It moved toward them. Ulrick's father slowed the horse to a walk for a closer look at the mysterious object. Alfred didn't appreciate his father's curiosity. The young boy didn't say anything, but his stomach was tied up in knots.

As the object continued to close the distance, Ulrick's father brought the horse to a stop. In a matter of seconds, the will-o'-the-wisp was only a few yards away. That was young Alfred's limit. "I think my body was covered with more goose pimples than a chicken has feathers. Seconds seemed like hours. I know I stopped breathing."

His father evidently felt the same dread, for he urged the horse homeward. They didn't stop until they reached their farm. Did the will-o'-the wisp follow them? They don't know; neither one ever looked back.

Sailors are familiar with a phenomenon called St. Elmo's fire, which has been likened to will-o'-the-wisps. This round flash of light often appears around ship masts during stormy weather. We know it is an electric charge, which actually does look like a flame. St. Elmo is the patron saint of sailors. It is also not unusual for St. Elmo's fire to appear on land around church steeples, airplanes, and other objects when weather is unsettled.

In early Wisconsin, St. Elmo's fire was often mistaken for the phantom-like will-o'-the-wisp by those who saw it. Such was the case of K. F. Peabody in Star Prairie.

Automobiles were still a rarity on early country roads, but travelers often ventured out after dark with the aid of strong spotlights. On one particular night Peabody was guiding a horse and rig through a light drizzle. It was late and the road was quite muddy. Suddenly a bright light surrounded the open buggy. Thinking it was someone coming up from behind, Peabody pulled to the side of the road and turned around. Nobody was there.

Where was the light coming from? Peabody lowered his umbrella. There, on the metal tip, was a bright, shimmering flame. He quickly furled the umbrella. The flame jumped to a whip in a bracket next to the seat. As he gazed at the flame, he recalled reading about St. Elmo's fire and realized that this must be the explanation. He removed the whip and looked more closely at the flame. It was brilliant, white, and similar to the flame of a candle, but it gave off no heat and, in fact, was quite cold.

Peabody finally drove on. The flame stayed with him to the top of the ridge. As he descended the other side, the flame gradually receded and eventually disappeared when he reached the bottom.

Whether it danced across a meadow, followed pioneers to their doorsteps, or hitched a ride in a buggy, the will-o'-the-wisp is a unique part of Wisconsin lore. To the superstitious pioneer, the wisp's appearance was usually a source of awe rather than fright. Today we understand that those lights pulsating over that dank swamp in the dead of night were simply the products of swamp gas.

Don't we?

No Exit

Carol, we'll be done in a few minutes so you can come down and lock the gym doors," the daycare teacher said, sticking her head through the open doorway. She was in charge of a rambunctious group of preschoolers during their playtime in the college building's old gymnasium. The daycare center was nearby. The teacher was talking to Carol Matara, the custodian in that part of the building, sitting in her small office on the first floor, directly above the gym. Carol smiled because she had no trouble whatsoever hearing the kids' happy cries echoing up through the floor beneath her feet.

"Okay, fair enough," Matara replied. She always knew when the kids were being rounded up for lunchtime—the floor seemed to reverberate with even more noise because they didn't want to stop playing. At those times Matara found it difficult to concentrate on completing the occasional paperwork required of her.

A few minutes later, when the silence below told her the kids had gone off to lunch, Matara made her way down the stairs and around the corner to the gym door. She pulled it open and looked around.

"Anybody here?" she called out. All was quiet. She locked the door and went back upstairs. She was about to sit down at her small desk when what seemed to be an old rock 'n' roll song coming up from below made her stop short.

"Wait a minute. Is that from the gym?" she asked, half to herself.

"I thought, okay, why is that [radio] on. It was loud. And on top of that I could hear someone bouncing a basketball."

"Aha," she figured, some little kid outsmarted one of the teachers and was getting some extended playtime. But the music . . . well that *was* different.

Back downstairs she went. At the gym door off the hallway she grabbed the handle and was surprised to find it unlocked. She was certain she had locked it earlier.

But that wasn't her last surprise. When she opened the door, a blast of unbearably hot air hit her in the face. And the lights were back on.

Oh my God, she thought. What's going on here?

The Ames Teacher Education Building and Lab School opened in 1962 on the campus of the University of Wisconsin–River Falls. For the first few decades of its existence, Ames housed an elementary school with kindergarten through ninth grades, which provided teacher education students with practical experience in the classroom. After the lab school closed in the early 1980s, various university offices, the College of Education faculty, and classrooms occupied the building along with a university-sponsored daycare and preschool program. The building itself was razed in 2004 to make room for the campus's new University Center.

Carol Matara liked the Ames assignment because she thought it would be interesting to be in a building where college students were learning to be teachers. Among her daily tasks was to keep the gym locked if it wasn't in use by the preschool classes or others.

Matara clearly remembered that morning in early May as anything but unusual. "(She) came to me and said she'd let me know when they were done in the gym and I could lock up. You could always tell when they were ready to wrap it up because the kids wanted to stay and play some more."

When she opened the gym door to investigate the music, however, and was almost knocked back by the heat and puzzled by the mysteries of the unlocked door and bright lights, that ordinary day would become just about the most unusual day of her life.

Her attention was quickly drawn to the far end of the gym by what seemed to be someone dribbling a basketball. Three young men wearing baggy gym shorts and dark emerald green jerseys trimmed in white scrimmaged beneath the basket. One young man — they all seemed to be about college age — wore a number eight on his jersey. Matara remembers because her daughter's birthday is on July 8.

"What are you doing in here?" she called out.

The young men glanced in her direction but continued with their pickup game. The player dribbling the ball drove toward the basket for a layup and leaped. As the ball cleared the hoop, the players suddenly vanished.

"Just like that," Matara said, amazed even now at the suddenness of it all. "It was so scary and frightening. I could feel the hair rising on my neck. I thought, wait a minute, this can't be happening to me."

Not knowing what else to do and shocked at what she'd seen, she quickly switched off the lights, ran back out the door, and slammed and locked it behind her. She scampered up the stairs and sat down at her desk. There she took a few minutes to collect her thoughts and catch her breath.

"I was scared to death. I'd never ever seen anything like that before."

Matara said the event was so remarkable, so disquieting, that she couldn't forget the details etched vividly in her mind even today. It seems, she said, like "it happened yesterday."

And then it all started up again.

Music from the gym below filtered up to where Matara sat, then she heard raucous laughter and a basketball bouncing against the floor below.

"I really didn't want to go back down there," she said, but at the same time she knew she had to, if for no other reason than to make sure some *real* students somehow hadn't gotten in.

She warily approached the gym door, listening to the faint music from inside and to what seemed to be a couple of people laughing. She was reaching out to try the door handle when it all stopped. No music, no laughter, no dribbling. "Dead silence," Matara called it. Nothing could have made her open the door. Better to leave alone whatever or whoever inside that gym seemed to be having some fun at her expense.

In a final incident a few days later, Matara accidentally dropped a sheaf of papers on the floor outside the locked gym doors. As she bent down to pick them up, a gust of frigid air swept from under the door into the hallway and across her hands. "It felt like I was going to get frostbite," she said.

Although she continued as the Ames custodian, Matara was reluctant to go back into the gym. She eventually did, and each time without problems.

Carol Matara knew she had to tell someone what had happened. It seemed reasonable that she would report the curious incidents to her supervisor. Custodial staff members were obliged to report building irregularities or issues that may raise safety or health concerns.

"I was shaking so bad when I told my supervisor [about seeing the ghostly basketball players]. I thought he'd laugh at me," Matara remembered. He neither laughed nor expressed doubt. In fact he told her he had his own odd encounter in the attic area of an even older university building. He said that early in his university career, as he reached for the pull chain on an overhead light, something icy cold swept by and touched him on the shoulder.

As word got around about Matara's extraordinary experience, she met with some skepticism but a lot of understanding. Another custodian who'd worked in Ames for two decades said nothing even remotely similar had ever happened to him. And he was to some extent jealous. A biology professor asked her if what he'd heard about her was true and begged for all the details.

The Ames building was torn down in 2004 to make way for a dramatic new University Center, which sits on the site. Some architectural pieces from the old building have been incorporated into the new center, including several stone benches and an ornamental support beam that now holds a sculpted teacup near one of the center's entrances.

Once the University Center opened in 2007, Carol Matara was assigned to its custodial crew. She wonders if two separate incidents in the new center might mean that something *else* transferred itself into the new building as well.

"When we moved in we had to clean the building after the construction guys left. It was a mess," she remembers. So she and the other custodians moved from floor to floor cleaning and making the center ready for occupancy. That included such mundane tasks as cleaning restrooms and filling dispensers with toilet paper.

"We were on the third floor to put toilet paper into the women's bathroom. Now to get the dispensers open you need a key to lower the housing onto the [toilet] seats," she said.

On this day, Matara lowered the dispensers in all seven stalls and left to get the toilet paper. As she did so, there was a rush of warm air and then a woman's giggle from inside the restroom.

"And then this *clank*. I thought, could it be possible? In every stall, the [dispenser] lid was back up in place. That was impossible! I thought, well, they've followed us into this building."

Matara didn't return to that restroom for a month.

Later, a somewhat similar episode in a second-floor women's restroom made Matara think that she had somehow become the unwitting object of another spectral practical joke.

Matara found the first stall door locked but unoccupied. She was not pleased. All she could think about was that she'd have to crawl under the door to get it open. She figured a broom handle might help so she wouldn't have to wiggle herself all the way under.

She had started out the door to find a broom when from that locked stall came the *clink* of the latch bolt sliding back. The door swung open.

"I asked my boss, 'What's going on? Why me?'" Matara added, shaking her head at the memory. She has yet to get an answer.

On a wall of University Center, a campus artist has created a mural depicting the exteriors of several venerable campus buildings. The vanished Ames Building is among them, but with one interesting addition. The mural artist included a small, ghostlike figure staring out of a window, recalling Carol Matara's singular encounter with the phantom athletes.

A ghost of a different sort may have made at least one appearance at another venue on campus, Davis Theatre, inside the Kleinpell Fine Arts Building.

It was on a late summer night that director Jim Zimmerman found himself writing notes in one of the theater's comfortable seats. Rehearsal had wrapped up for a summer theater production of *The Music Man*, and Zimmerman wanted to jot down a few observations while they were still fresh in his mind. Cast and crew had left the theater and he was alone. Or so he thought.

Zimmerman didn't know how long someone had been standing up on the stage, only that he sensed a movement. "I looked up and there he was. I didn't know where he came from," he said of the casually dressed man. He thought he might have come out from the right-hand side of the stage. He appeared to be of medium build and height, somewhere in early middle age with longish blond hair. He wore a red, short-sleeved shirt and blue jeans. Though the work lights from above the stage were on, the stranger's face was cast in shadow.

In any case, Zimmerman didn't recognize him.

"Can I help you?" he called out.

The man didn't acknowledge the question or change expression. He stood frozen still, staring out toward the puzzled director and the otherwise empty theater.

As a veteran of both professional and college theater, Jim Zimmerman was used to breathless tales of theaters haunted by tragic, suicidal actresses or murdered stagehands. So imbedded is the lore that a lamp is always kept lit on otherwise dark stages, ostensibly to keep actors and crew from tripping over cables or props. However, it *is* called a "ghost light," so its functions may be wider than assumed. At any rate, little did Zimmerman realize that on this night he would add his own bit of ghost lore to the world of theater.

The stranger's unexpected appearance didn't disturb Zimmerman at first. Though it was after ten o'clock, he could be a campus visitor who'd gotten lost trying to find his destination. It happened sometimes—the building was usually open quite late.

Zimmerman closed his notebook and was about to speak again when the stranger, who had been standing near center stage, suddenly strode to stage left, looked around for a few seconds, and then ducked behind the rear curtains. Zimmerman still wasn't too concerned. However, when he neither heard nor saw the man come back out on stage, he became uneasy. Perhaps it was someone intent on doing mischief.

The only people using the theater that summer were company members or university personnel.

"I knew them all, and I didn't know this guy," Zimmerman said. "Here he is at ten o'clock at night, walking around, not answering my question."

Zimmerman walked up on stage and looked around. The only way out was through a rear doorway that let out into a hallway. A large set of steel "barn doors" between the stage area and the scene shop were shut. A spiral staircase backstage led to a storage room for props beneath the stage. The stair light was off.

A quick look backstage proved fruitless. Then it occurred to Zimmerman that whoever this was must have left through the backstage door. But outside the door, Zimmerman found two members of the acting company sitting in the hallway feeding each other lines from a script. Both told him they hadn't seen anyone come out the door since rehearsal ended some time before. They seemed a bit puzzled at his question, especially when he described what the man was wearing.

If the man had left the stage it would have to have been out that door. Yet he hadn't. Zimmerman had no reason to doubt the actors' words.

"I didn't know where he went. It's that simple."

Simple, perhaps. Comprehensible, no.

"When I first glanced up, I thought it was an actor who'd stuck around after rehearsal and maybe wanted to talk to me. But I didn't know him and I didn't recognize that he was anyone [else from] the university."

The other oddity is that Zimmerman didn't hear any footsteps.

The wood stage flooring squeaked a bit under someone's weight, and in the quiet of the theater Zimmerman thought he would have heard the man walking around.

Zimmerman spent a few more fruitless minutes looking around for what he still thought was an intruder. Eventually he locked up, went home, and pushed the event to the back of his mind.

Zimmerman related the story a few days later in a conversation with a colleague, talking about it in terms of security. But that's not how his colleague reacted. The latter said that from the description—middle aged, slight build, blue jeans, tousled blond hair—the intruder seemed to fit the description of Sanford Syse, who had assisted in designing the theater complex back in the early 1970s, cofounded the summer theater, and taught theater courses. A straightforward explanation, it seemed. Except for one thing: Sanford Syse died years before Zimmerman's encounter. Maybe, Zimmerman's colleague said only half in jest, he'd seen Syse's ghost.

Zimmerman hadn't put the label "supernatural" on the event. He was thinking only that perhaps the theater and the building needed better security. His thoughts didn't stray any further because the man in the theater that night was, as Zimmerman emphasized, "as real as you or I."

"Here was a stranger walking around on stage and he could get hurt, or rip us off," Zimmerman said. "I told [my colleague] I didn't know where this man had gone or how he got away or who he was. The person I was talking to made the connection to Sanford Syse."

Syse taught theater at UW–River Falls for ten years until his death from cancer in 1974, shortly after the fine arts building opened. Today, a smaller experimental, "black box" theater adjacent to Davis Theatre is named after him, as is a drama scholarship awarded each year.

Zimmerman had never crossed paths with Sanford Syse. "I wish I would have known [that night] what he looked like because I might have recognized him," he said. It wasn't until later that Zimmerman saw a picture of Syse. He thought the man he had seen looked like Syse, but because the stranger's face was shadowed he wasn't entirely certain.

But even with that it took him a long time to reconcile with the idea that perhaps what he had seen was a ghost.

"I never thought it was a ghost at the time," he mused. "He looked absolutely real. I wasn't looking for the theater ghost, and to this day I don't know if it *was* a ghost. I do know it was a bunch of anomalies that I can't answer."

Zimmerman believed his predecessor did a good job in designing the theater complex. "For a space built in the 1970s, it's still functioning pretty well today."

Perhaps that's why Sanford Syse checked in that night. He wanted nothing more than to take a look at the theater, his legacy, and to make a brief, albeit unforgettable, acquaintance with one of his successors.

The young drama major relaxed in a theater seat, idly passing the time until her next class. Suddenly she had the eerie sense that someone stood nearby watching her. She glanced back, toward the main door. An "iridescent glow" stood in the doorframe. Within seconds it silently vanished. She had met Raphael, a ghost that dwells in the Ripon College theater.

This particular theater ghost's origins are murky, but apparently he made his first appearance when the school's Red Barn Theater burned down in 1964. No cause for the fire was ever found, leading theater folks to put the blame on "the ghost."

After the fire, the theater department used an old church on the edge of campus where Raphael was held responsible for leaving lights on, locking students out of the building, and ringing the former church's bells, still in the belfry.

Perhaps the most famous tale involving Raphael originated during a production of Mary Chase's classic comedy *Harvey*. The play centers on Elwood P. Dowd and his giant, albeit unseen, rabbit friend Harvey. But during the play's run in the converted church, Raphael was "cast" in that role. Whether he actually made an appearance or initiated any shenanigans isn't clear.

No one seems to know why the ghost is named Raphael. Instead, people prefer to recount doors opening and closing of their own accord, mysterious footfalls in different parts of the old church, and other eerie sounds, especially late at night.

When at last the old church was demolished and the theater moved to Rodman Center, the question became whether or not Raphael moved with it.

According to researcher Bev Christ, he did.

Students say electric plugs left in wall sockets are found lying on the floor, as if to conserve energy, yet locked doors are found ajar, with lights on in the rooms beyond.

As theater ghosts go, Raphael is a benign, prankish, hard-to-spot fellow, but that doesn't matter to theater folks at Ripon College. Alumni, students, and faculty are quite possessive of him. Bev Christ called Raphael "our" theater ghost.

The Pendant

Her name was Jan. She was a pretty girl. Gold-tinged hair framed a cameo face. Her large, gray-green eyes held the sunlight of today and the dreams of tomorrow. She fell in love; she fell out of love. She knew joy and despair. She studied art in college. During the summers of her young woman-hood she loved to swim, boat, and picnic at her parents' lakeside home near Spooner. Although shy and sensitive, she had the restless, searching mind that longs to know the world, to hold it close. Those who knew her hoped that all good things would come to her.

At age twenty-eight she was dead, the loser in a three-year battle against mental illness. Her life had ended at the moment when doctors said that complete recovery was within sight, when bright tomorrows were again within her grasp. For her parents, Marion and Dick Stresau, and their other children, the tomorrows were filled with the particular sadness that attends the death of one who has been taken too soon.

But that sadness was overshadowed by a series of puzzling incidents that began to occur in the Stresau home—events that, in time, changed the lives of every member of the family.

It was Marion who had the first experience. Less than two weeks after her daughter's death, she had been sound asleep when she was suddenly awakened. She glanced at the clock. It was just after three in the morning. Then she felt it—a soft touch upon her arm. She was certain that she hadn't been dreaming.

Her husband, deep in slumber, lay beside her. Drifting into sleep again, she felt once more the light touch upon her arm. A spider perhaps. Although by now fully awake, Marion was surprisingly unconcerned. She felt only a strange sense of peace and relaxation. She drifted back toward sleep, but her husband had awakened and wanted to know what was troubling her. After she muttered something about a spider, Dick got up and turned on the light. Marion got up also, and both searched the bed, but found nothing.

Many months later, on a trip east, Marion was to learn that her mother had also been awakened on that same night at about the same time to see an oval blue mist float slowly across the end of her bed. The older woman, who had been close to her granddaughter, was convinced that the mist was Jan.

Later on that morning of Marion's experience, Dick was not able to go back to sleep. He awoke his wife with his restless squirming. "Hey!" he shouted. "There's something moving under my arm!"

Both leaped out of bed, pulled the bedding, pillows, and mattress off the bed, and examined everything thoroughly. Dick had been sleeping on his side. Had he had a muscle cramp? Had his arm gone numb? No. He was positive that something had been crawling under his arm. Unable to find a logical explanation, they put the matter out of mind and never discussed it again. Marion kept to herself the strange feelings she had that both episodes might have something to do with Jan. Was that possible?

That likelihood strengthened a short time later when a friend sent Marion a pamphlet with her sympathy note. Although Marion was not one to be consoled by what she calls "commercialized words of comfort," she was intrigued by the author's statement that sometimes the personality of a deceased loved one seems to make contact with the living in the form of a touch. Was Jan really trying to communicate with her parents? Or was Marion merely the victim of "fantasies of a mind recovering from grief," as she wrote in her personal diary? Neither she nor her husband gave credence to psychic phenomena or superstitions of any kind. Yet there was that persistent feeling that someone was trying to communicate with them, a sensation that Marion thought had some-thing to do with the circumstances of Jan's death. She vividly remembered the details of that day two weeks earlier: that dreadful phone call from the mental institution saying that Jan had escaped, that she'd attempted to cross a busy highway and had been hit by a truck. It might have been suicide, as she had made previous attempts. Or was it a tragic accident? These were questions Marion could never answer.

A few weeks later, only days before Christmas, Marion started to unpack the boxes of tree ornaments. Discovering the treetop angel that Jan had made many years earlier, Marion hesitated. Should she put it on the tree this year or would the memories be too painful? She noticed that the angel's dress was soiled and rumpled and would have to be replaced if it were to adorn the tree. Instinctively she thought Jan would have made a new dress. But just as quickly, Marion, suddenly overwhelmed by a sense of love and joy, understood that it was now up to her to make the dress. Family Christmas traditions are for tender keeping.

In the morning Marion drove to town and bought the white tulle with silver sparkles that would reflect the tree lights. Back home, she worked all morning, carefully cutting, fitting, and sewing the dress. Just before noon, she stopped to prepare lunch. Suddenly a flash of blinding light filled the room. Marion dismissed it as eyestrain. On her way to the kitchen, the light flared again.

On the Saturday afternoon before Christmas, the Stresaus' thirteen-year-old son Steve set out to search the woods for a Christmas tree. Although he had always gone with his father, Marion decided that this year he was old enough to go by himself. At dusk he returned, dragging a blue spruce with thick clusters of cones. Marion remembers that it was the most beautiful spruce she had ever seen. Steve told his mother an uncanny story. He said he had hiked a long way and couldn't find any suitable tree. Then, when he was ready to give up, the spruce suddenly appeared before him "almost like in a dream."

He took the tree into the kitchen to cut off the lower branches. Marion was working at the sink, her back to her son.

Suddenly Steve shouted, "What was that flash of light?"

Marion wheeled around. She had said nothing to anyone about the flashes she had seen a few days earlier, but after Steve described a "very bright, white light," she knew that they had both witnessed the same phenomenon.

On Christmas Eve, the Stresaus' third child, their daughter Pat, arrived home from college for the holidays. After a long, cold drive, she welcomed the cheerful warmth of the blazing fire on the hearth. She settled into the orange leather swivel chair that her mother usually occupied, and Marion sat on a hassock in front of her. The family was engaged in animated conversation, catching up on Pat's news, laughing and talking, when all of a sudden Pat's chair tipped over backward, coming to rest against a window ledge. Pat was thrown backward, her legs straight up in the air. Her parents helped set the chair up, but it tipped backward again almost immediately. Bewildered, Pat stammered, "I . . . I didn't do a thing!"

Marion, who had been facing her daughter, knew she had made no movement that could have upset the chair. The two women exchanged places and the chair did not move again. If other family members forgot about the incident, Marion did not. The episode was inexplicable. The chair had been the center of roughhousing for years by boisterous teens and never before had it tipped over.

The next morning, Marion conducted an experiment. She found that the only way she could tip the chair back was by bracing her feet against the hassock and pushing. Yet Pat hadn't had her feet on the hassock because her mother had been sitting on it. Again, Marion thought of Jan. Could she somehow have resented the fact that her sister occupied the chair usually reserved for their mother and indicated her displeasure in a physical way?

Future events were more puzzling. Several nights after the chair incident, Steve spent the night with a friend. After everyone had gone to sleep, loud banging on the wall awakened Marion. There was a pause, and then the blows began again. The family's dog began barking, but the blows continued intermittently for fifteen or twenty minutes. Marion reasoned that Pat must be doing exercises in her room, and was annoyed by her daughter's lack of consideration. Dick, a sound sleeper, was not awakened by the disturbance.

In the morning Marion spoke to Pat about her exercising at unorthodox hours.

"It wasn't me," Pat insisted. "I haven't done exercises for years. I was sitting up in bed scared to death! I didn't move out of the bed the whole time the banging was going on."

The family searched outside the house. Their home did not have any shutters or loose siding or doors that might have banged in the wind, nor could they recall any neighboring homes from which the sounds might have come. Besides, Marion remembered it as a deeply cold, silent night outside. There were no footprints or animal tracks in the freshly fallen snow. Could the two women have imagined the noises? Perhaps. And the dog? Not likely.

The strange events of a Christmas season. Marion pondered them often, and then one day she confided in Steve that she too had seen flashes of light. In turn, he told his mother that for some strange reason he had felt a warmth and goodness during the holiday season that wasn't connected to anything materialistic. Both shared the tenuous thought that the mysterious happenings were somehow related to Jan, that she was trying to reach them, to share once again in the happiness of a special time. The closeness of Jan seemed a reality. Marion wished she could be sure.

According to Marion's diary, the next strange occurrence was on a date when Pat was home on her spring break from college. She, her little brother Steve, and their dad were outdoors on a Sunday afternoon when Marion decided to tidy up the living room. As she reached for the clutter of newspapers on the coffee table, she noticed a clipping—a picture of three young women skating at an indoor ice rink in Duluth. It had been so carefully torn from the paper that the sides were nearly scissor-straight. She read the girls' names in the caption below the picture but knew none of them. Nor did she know why anyone in her family would be interested in such a picture. Puzzled, she put the clipping aside.

When the rest of the family came inside, Marion asked them about the picture. Pat and her father recalled having seen it when flipping through the paper that morning, but that was all.

The next morning, Marion threw the clipping away but later, on impulse, retrieved it. A few days later, she showed it to a friend who claimed to have some talent in the extrasensory perception field. The friend thought that the meaning of the picture was quite clear. She explained that the three smiling women holding hands were symbolic figures representing Marion, Pat, and Jan. The joining of hands symbolized the closeness and happiness they had always shared. Marion thought the symbolism made sense, but still it didn't explain how the picture had been physically removed from the newspaper.

On the following Sunday, just before noon, Marion and Dick arrived home from a short trip to find their son studying boat-building catalogs, excited about a particular small boat that he hoped to build that summer. Marion was immediately aware of the odor of glycerin and rosewater. As she moved closer to Steve the scent became stronger. The only thing in the house with that scent was a bottle of hand lotion that Jan had left. Then, as if reading his mother's mind, the boy looked up and said, "What is that awful perfume smell? It's been driving me nuts all morning. Must be some of Pat's stuff."

Steve went off to check, and about that time a pajama-clad Pat came into the room. She hadn't seen the bottle of lotion since her mother had given it to her several days previously, and no one had been in her room. Steve opened a number of bottles on Pat's bureau, and when he found the lotion bottle that had belonged to Jan, he identified the smell immediately. But how could the odor have filled the room when no one had opened the bottle? Marion wondered if Jan was trying to make her presence known. Jan was the only one in the family who had ever used that particular lotion.

About a year later, in the summer, Marion, Dick, and Steve had been talking about a book they had all read and enjoyed, and Jan's name came into the conversation. Marion recalled, "There was a happy feeling of closeness among the three of us that evening." When darkness closed in, Steve and his father left Marion reading a book. Their cat was curled up on the hassock. Soon Marion noticed that she seemed to be staring at something across the room in the partly closed door of the studio/writing room. The cat's pupils were large and black but she didn't act frightened. Marion followed her gaze, but she couldn't see anything unusual, not even shadows as the room beyond was well lit.

The family's dog Tuffy, which had been asleep at Marion's feet, suddenly jumped up and stared at the glass-paneled door that opened onto the porch. The terrier's tail wagged as she trotted to the door. Marion was startled by the dog's behavior because, like many small dogs, she was an excellent watchdog, accepting only the family and barking furiously at the approach of any stranger or animal. Yet her husband and son were still in Steve's room. Marion could hear their voices.

Perplexed, she got up, opened the sliding door, and let the dog out. Tuffy circled the area beyond the porch but evidently picked up no scent and bounded back inside. Several minutes later, Marion realized that the studio door was directly in line with the glass door. Whatever the cat had seen in the studio door might have been reflected in the glass door across the room. Could that be? It has been suggested that animals often have the ability to see discarnate entities invisible to humans. Marion concluded that Jan's presence must be in the room and that the animals, recognizing it, were not afraid.

The dog and cat eventually lost interest in whatever had attracted their attention, and wandered off. Marion resumed her reading. Suddenly, a clattering noise shattered the silence. It was as if something metallic had crashed to the floor, and the noise seemed to have come from the studio doorway. Marion got up and checked the room and both sides of the door. The cat, alarmed by the noise, ran into the studio and sniffed and pawed around. Marion found nothing that could have explained the commotion.

The touch in the night . . . the brilliant light . . . the tipping chair . . . the banging on the wall . . . the newspaper clipping . . . the aroma of glycerin and rosemary . . . a presence felt only by the animals—were these only a series of unconnected events? The imaginings of a sensitive, bereaved family? Or had the ghost of Jan returned to brighten the lives of those she had loved? One classic theory is that the ghost of a person who has died an unexpected death often returns to familiar places. Another theory holds that ghosts of those who do not know how to proceed to further spiritual development after death come back to stay with loved ones. It's all speculation, of course.

But the Stresaus were not content to speculate. They wanted proof of Jan's continuing presence. The long search was encouraging at times, disheartening at other times. It culminated in the family's participation in a prayer group near Chicago. It was in this prayer circle that the Stresaus believe they received irrefutable evidence of Jan's existence after death.

One of the psychics, in a semi-trance, spoke of a pendant—teardrop shaped and edged with small seed pearls and filigree work. The pendant's stone was described as being mottled in color. This information was not significant at first. Marion was certain that there was no pendant of that type in the family.

Then, one day about three weeks after the family had returned home, Marion decided that she could no longer postpone sorting through the boxes of Jan's personal effects that had been sent on from the girl's city apartment after she became ill. Although she had gone through everything earlier in order to send to the hospital the things Jan had wanted, Marion dreaded facing the sad task—making the difficult decisions about the final disposition of her daughter's clothing, letters, jewelry, and other precious items that Jan had accumulated over the years. But it had to be done and one Friday morning Marion began the task.

In the bottom of a large packing box, she found her daughter's green leather jewel case. The top tray held an undistinguished jumble of jewelry pins, loose beads including a collection of baby pearls, and a pair of filigreed gold earrings. Marion picked up a round glass bead and was about to toss it into her giveaway pile when she saw something moving inside the bead. She held it up for a closer look and, in doing so, nearly dropped it. The bead was not round at all; it was a teardrop-shaped globe. And something inside was moving indeed. Tiny, iridescent white chips floated in a liquid and, as Marion moved it, the particles changed position, flashing darts of red, aquamarine, and purple-blue. The pointed end of the globe was inserted into a four-pronged silver shaft to which was attached a ring for a chain. A pendant! Yet it wasn't the one the psychic had described; it had no mottled stone.

Marion laid it aside and resumed her sorting. But, drawn irresistibly back to the pendant, she kept glancing over at it. Then she realized that, in looking at it from that particular angle of vision, it did appear to be a mottled stone, the chips motionless in the liquid. But there were no small seed pearls or filigree work that the psychic had "seen." Of course! Pearls had surrounded the pendant as it lay in the case; the filigree must have referred to the gold earrings close by. Now deeply moved, Marion sat staring at the jewel in her palm.

The next day at the jeweler's she bought a silver chain for the pendant. She learned that the iridescent chips inside the globe were cuttings from a flame opal suspended in glycerin. The jeweler added that she had never seen a floating opal so large and so beautiful.

The pendant on the silver chain became the family's most cherished possession.

The Lady in Brown

*S*cores of ghost stories detail visitations to houses by the spirits of former occupants. Stories of people somehow "left behind" after death to watch over a home to which they had a strong emotional attachment weren't unfamiliar to one young woman who lived near Durand. She knew all about such things.

Brenda Weidner lived for five years in a haunted house southwest of Durand. She, her husband, Robert, and the couple's two-year-old son moved into the rented, rural, two-story frame home without the slightest indication the house was anything but what it appeared to be—a rather rundown farmhouse in a grove of elm and oak trees on a county highway, not unlike thousands of other homes across the Wisconsin countryside.

Everything seemed normal the first year. Robert Weidner drove each day to a factory where he worked the night shift. Brenda stayed home with young Derek. But the idyllic country life was shattered late one spring evening as Brenda waited for her husband.

It was that night when she first heard insistent pounding in the walls, gently at first, almost too faint to detect. Then the sound grew in intensity. The walls vibrated so much that the curtains shook. She thought at first it was someone outside with a baseball bat. It happened first on one living room wall and then on another wall, and then back and forth. It would go on for five or ten minutes, just like someone was trying to get out. When the hammering ceased, Brenda sat frozen on the couch, afraid to move and reluctant to search outside on a cold, starless night. Her husband fruitlessly searched the house and grounds when he returned home from work. The pounding continued periodically, but only for a few minutes shortly after ten o'clock at night. Brenda didn't think it had anything to do with mice or squirrels trying to find a way out. The sounds were absent during the day and at other times of the night. Robert never heard the sounds, as he was most often still at work.

A few months later, however, Brenda learned she was not the only person to have heard the strange noises. A local teenager had been employed by the Weidners to watch over Derek when the couple went out for an evening, but the young woman became "unavailable" after only a short while. Brenda and her husband were perplexed.

The girl said it was nothing the family had done; it was the house that upset her. She said she couldn't stand the pounding inside the walls, first behind a wood stove and then from across the room. That's where Brenda had heard it as well. They had never mentioned it to the babysitter.

The pounding in the walls was not the only frightening experience the young girl had in the home. Brenda explained:

> Every time she shut off the basement lights they would go on again and the basement door would swing open. She could shut off the lights and close the door and go back in there in five minutes and the lights would be on again and the door open. She couldn't take it any more. Every time I called she would have excuses. I finally found out why. It was the house.

Young Derek provided the first hint as to an identity for what they came to believe was their unseen tenant. The boy's bedroom was adjacent to the living room and only a few feet from the small kitchen. Brenda was preparing lunch one afternoon when she heard her son's voice coming from behind the closed door of his room. The young mother walked over and stood outside the bedroom. She heard only her son's muffled voice. He would say a few words, stop, and then continue. Brenda thought at the time the child was carrying on a conversation with someone. But only *his* voice was audible. For several minutes Brenda listened. At length the boy came out with a confused expression.

"Mommy," he said, "I just talked to an old, old lady in my room." Brenda glanced past her son into the small bedroom and saw no one. She asked him if he was positive. Yes, the child replied, vigorously nodding his head.

His mother said he wasn't so much scared as bewildered by the experience. She would have dismissed the child's report but for the earlier experience. Derek had never before made up imaginary people or playmates. Brenda began to wonder if there was a connection between this mysterious "old woman" and the knockings.

Other events reinforced Brenda's belief that some unseen entity was at work in the house. She might hear moaning, or groans, in the kitchen area. It would come from behind, but no one else was in the house.

"It was like someone was in pain," she said.

Brenda had never taken seriously the stories of haunted houses or ghostly apparitions. But now she began to wonder if there wasn't some truth to those tales.

Determined to learn more about the house and its history, Brenda began questioning neighbors and the present owner of the house, the elderly son of the original family. Gradually she pieced together the story of Mrs. Gerda Biermann, the late wife of the house's builder. Her entire life had been spent in the house; she died there in the 1950s. But what startled Brenda were two peculiar facts relating to the woman's last days on earth: Gerda Biermann had died in the room now occupied by young Derek Weidner, and she reportedly had told a housekeeper that she would never leave that house.

A few months later, it seemed that Gerda's vow was more than the idle ramblings of an elderly woman.

Brenda was sitting on the couch in the comfortably furnished living room shortly after midnight, watching a television program and waiting for her husband to arrive home. She expected him within a few minutes.

Suddenly Brenda heard the kitchen door swing open and then slam shut moments later.

"Robert, is that you?" she called out.

There was no answer. Surprised, she rose quickly and walked into the kitchen. The nearly transparent image of a woman wearing a brown dress hovered near the outside door. The specter hung motionless in the air, its vacant eyes staring past the frightened young woman. Brenda saw that although her body was perfectly outlined, a vaporous mist formed an aura around the figure. Several inches of space separated the specter's feet from the kitchen floor.

Suddenly the ghost floated slowly across the room. Within seconds it disappeared into the pantry. Brenda walked over cautiously and peered in. The small room was empty.

Brenda was dazed. It was the first time a "physical" presence had presented itself to her. As she turned to walk into the living room, her thoughts raced back to all she had learned of the late Gerda Biermann. Yes, she realized, the specter in the kitchen did fit her description. The dress was plain and old-fashioned, her face haggard and old. Yet Brenda couldn't grasp the possibilities of having just seen a ghost.

She certainly hadn't dreamed the entire episode, and returned to the kitchen for a glass of water to calm her frayed nerves. But what she beheld didn't help assuage her nerves: the pantry light was now on, the basement door stood wide open, and the basement lights were ablaze. She had just checked the pantry minutes before. And yet her eyes didn't lie. She gazed down the rough, wooden basement steps, silently listening. She switched off the lights and closed the basement door. Now she understood the babysitter's concern about the basement and its perplexing lights. What hand had turned them on? What fingers had encircled the basement doorknob and softly pulled it open?

Until the Weidner family moved out of the house, Brenda often found the basement door open and the downstairs lights switched on without reason. Brenda wondered if there was some significance to these odd happenings and searched the old, musty, and rather forbidding earthen cellar several times, but it contained nothing out of the ordinary as far as she could tell.

Other events were equally puzzling. A vase Brenda often filled with flowers would be moved from in front of a kitchen radio to beside it. She never saw it move, but would find it shifted even when she was home alone. Perhaps Gerda preferred the vase in a different position.

The Weidner's dog, a German shepherd, also sensed a ghostly presence in the house. Brenda said that on numerous occasions the dog crouched down on her stomach. Brenda thinks at those times Gerda was around.

Shortly before the Weidners moved from the house, Brenda had her final, and in many ways most chilling, encounter with the ghost of Gerda Biermann. The late woman's son had recently built a new porch onto the rear of the house. On a February afternoon a few days after the job was finished Brenda was in the kitchen fixing a meal; the dog lay at her feet while her son napped in his bedroom. From the new porch off the kitchen she heard a woman's voice: "Look what my son has done to the house. He built this porch."

The dog's ears perked up and her fur stood on end. She started to growl. With a sort of low, articulated mumble, the voice from the porch then spoke in what sounded to Brenda like German, though she did not know the language. Brenda threw open the door. The voice stopped. Her dog ran out and sniffed at the corners, on the steps, even down on the ground. She knew someone had been out there. Snow was on the ground but there were no footprints or tire tracks. Yet there had been that voice. That was the last time Brenda Weidner ever heard from her elderly, live-in ghost. And for that she was grateful.

Psychic Sisters

Rachel Harper* and Diane Bonner* are sisters who shared a curious talent: the ability to act as a magnet for ghosts.

The first time a ghost visited Rachel she was laying next to her slumbering husband in the bedroom of their small frame home near Neillsville. Her husband and their two young children had been asleep for hours. But Rachel was still alert, gazing at the darkened ceiling, somewhere between wakefulness and sleep.

Suddenly she felt a presence in the room. A third person was watching her. Rachel looked across the room and saw a man's form pulsating in a fog-like haze.

Rachel recognized him—his name was Billy . . . Billy Fulham*—and he had been dead for nearly ten years. They had been high school sweethearts. But, as with many teenage romances, love withered and the couple went their separate ways—Rachel to marriage and homemaking and Billy to the army shortly after graduation.

No one knew precisely what happened, but Billy left his army camp one night without permission and was killed in an automobile accident. The young man who had died too soon was buried in the small town where he had grown to manhood.

Rachel couldn't attend the funeral, but she often thought of Billy during the ensuing years. He had an intense love for the outdoors, and whenever Rachel

gazed at a particularly spectacular sunset, or walked across a low hill after a
gentle rain, or trod softly in a misty morning fog, she remembered Billy and
how he would have reveled in these simple pleasures.

All these memories flooded back to her as he floated toward her in that
night-shrouded room. Rachel could sense a deep sorrow, almost as if he wanted
to be consoled over a great loss. And then Billy vanished as suddenly as he had
materialized.

The next morning Rachel told her husband about the strange visit during
the night. "It wasn't a dream," Rachel told him. "Billy was *in* that room."

She had remembered her dreams before, as many of us do. But Billy was
most definitely not the product of the fragmented experiences released in the
eerie world of dreams.

Her husband scoffed at the incident. Rachel, too, was outwardly jocular
over the "ghost." Yet she was secretly distressed and puzzled by the visit. Rachel
wanted to dismiss it as a hallucination or imagination . . . or something. On the
following night, however, Billy came again. Just as on the previous evening, she
though he was trying to communicate with her. Yet there was still some barrier
between him and Rachel.

"There was this sadness, though, this deep depression. I couldn't understand
what he was saying." Rachel also felt that Billy was trying to draw her away; he
wanted her to join him.

For three consecutive nights Billy appeared and tried to make Rachel
understand his sense of sorrow.

On the fourth night, Billy came as before. But this time Rachel left with
him. There was no conscious movement, Rachel said, no action. She felt
herself being lifted by the shoulders and suddenly accelerated to "a different
dimension."

Rachel found herself in a place of whiteness and such brilliant light that it
seemed as if the entire world's light grid had been turned on at once.

"It was cold. The beings I saw weren't human and they weren't three-
dimensional. But, they had faces, and you recognized them as people but could
only see faces."

Rachel again sensed a suffering, an emptiness in the beings around her as
though they needed to be released from some indefinable shackles.

The couple passed through this world of silence and moved into a void
occupied by a single stone bench with intricate, etched scrollwork on the
backrest. There was no talk. In fact, there was no sound at all.

As suddenly as she had entered this realm, Rachel was back next to her
husband. She still wasn't sure if it hadn't all been a dream.

By the following day Rachel was afraid for darkness to fall. What was Billy trying to say? Why was he coming to her? Were these all dreams or something else entirely?

On Friday night, Rachel lay awake wondering if the pattern of the previous evenings would be repeated. She was not to be disappointed. Rachel saw him in the doorway, shimmering and beckoning toward her. He wore the same sorrowful countenance about him. But something was wrong. Rachel knew then that he was saying good-bye. Billy had been unable to reach her. He seemed to want to make her understand that something was wrong and that she had to look into it.

When Rachel awoke the next morning she was frightened.

She decided to telephone Billy's mother. It had been years since they'd last spoken to each other, and perhaps his mother could understand the reason for his visits.

Mrs. Fulham answered after several rings and seemed delighted to hear from Rachel. Casual conversation followed. Rachel asked the woman how she had been.

"Well, all right, under the circumstances." Mrs. Fulham replied.

"What do you mean?"

"Rachel, my husband died last Sunday night."

She froze at the words. So, that was it.

Billy first appeared the night after his father died. That was the sorrow he felt. Somehow, Billy knew that Rachel could tell his mother how sad he was and how much he wanted to be there to comfort her.

Rachel tried to tell Mrs. Fulham about Billy but the woman refused to listen. "I don't want to hear about or talk about such things," the older woman said.

But the puzzle had been solved. The final missing piece had been put into place. The visits of the ghost had not been a product of Rachel's imagination.

As the months passed, Rachel gradually eased Billy Fulham from her mind. But she was not able to escape the ghost of Billy Fulham.

It was just past nine thirty in the evening nearly a year later. Rachel was propped up in bed reading a novel. Suddenly she felt Billy coming down the hallway. Rachel didn't know how she knew, only that she looked up and fully expected to see him standing in her doorway once again.

But he was not there.

"You could just feel him though," Rachel explained. "It was like electricity charging through the air."

She spoke out loud and told him that she couldn't go through the same experience again.

Rachel reached over to a bedside telephone and dialed Mrs. Fulham. She was in clear distress. "What has happened?" Rachel asked. Earlier in the day, Mrs. Fulham said, her bank mortgage had been canceled. She had been unable to make the monthly payments and would have to move within thirty days!

Two visits from a dead soldier, and two tragic events in the life of his mother. Perhaps it was a hand reaching out from the grave to console a grief-stricken parent. Rachel never again saw the ghost of Billy Fulham.

Diane Bonner is Rachel's younger sister by several years. She has encountered three ghosts and seen a vivid dream turn inexplicably into reality.

Diane moved with Rachel and their mother to Chippewa Falls when she was a junior in high school. On a particular Sunday night in August she looked forward to her new school starting the next morning. She and her sister were staying with their grandmother until a house could be found to rent.

Diane had gone to bed at about ten o'clock. How long she had been asleep she didn't know. But she was suddenly awake and alert, sitting up in bed. Through an open window she saw stars shining in the hot, clear night.

Then she saw the upper half of an old man wrapped in a vaporous mist at the foot of her bed. He wore work trousers and a blue short-sleeved shirt. A bushy white moustache curled over his upper lip, and a full white beard reached down to his chest. His white hair was receded to nearly the middle of his head. His deep-set, extraordinarily blue eyes bore into Diane as she sat transfixed on the bed. A kind of light seemed to emanate from them.

Nothing was said and the old man did not move. As quickly as he had come, he was gone.

The next day after school Diane found her grandmother chatting with a neighbor woman. The young girl told the women about her visitor. Her grandmother scoffed at the tale, but the neighbor did not.

"Why, that sounds like old Mr. Banks*," she said. "He died in that house about twenty years ago!"

A few years later Diane had an encounter with a ghost strikingly similar to her sister Rachel's. It was shortly after Diane had graduated from high school. A good friend of hers, Tom Kearsley*, had been told that his headaches were the result of an inoperable brain tumor. He apparently had been born with it.

Kearsley was one of the most popular boys in Diane's high school class. He was the type of boy nearly everyone respected and liked, always ready to help his friends. Selfless was the word used often to describe his outlook on life.

As the youngest child in his family, Tom was particularly close to his parents and especially his father, whom he idolized.

Diane and her boyfriend, whom she would later marry, were the only close friends to whom Tom confided the tragic news. Six months after the tumor was first diagnosed, Tom, Diane, her boyfriend, and a group of friends attended a party. The next morning Diane learned that Tom had been rushed to a hospital and doctors were preparing to perform brain surgery. Before the operation could begin, Tom Kearsley passed away.

Diane recalled, "About eleven in the morning I suddenly felt my skin tingle and I immediately thought of Tom. A friend called later and said Tom had died about ten thirty that morning."

He was buried a few days later. The next night Diane awoke with a start at 11:30 p.m. She looked across the room and Tom was standing only a few feet from her bed. He looked as he did in life, as if he had never died.

Diane described what happened next: "There was no verbal communication between us, but it was almost as if I could read his thoughts. And he said, 'Diane, I know everyone feels bad about my death, but please tell them not to worry. I'm happy here.' And then he was gone."

It was very difficult for his friends to accept Tom's death.

Whenever they would gather, the conversation inevitably turned to Tom and how he was missed so very much. Diane accepted his death better than most of his grieving friends and relatives.

"He was only nineteen but he had a very good life. People adored him. What more could anyone want?" she would remind them.

Perhaps that's why the ghost of Tom Kearsley came once again to Diane. It was about a week after his burial. Just as before she awoke in the middle of the night to see a vague form of a man standing before her.

"Please tell everyone to leave me alone," the ghost told Diane. "I know everyone is still upset. But, please, have them remember the good times and leave me alone."

Even after life Tom was concerned and moved by friends in distress. Diane carried out his commands, and the ghost was released from his earthly wanderings.

Two years later Diane had her third session with a ghost. By then married, she and her husband were in a century-old house on Elm Street in Chippewa Falls.

Shortly after the couple moved in, Diane was busying herself with makeup in front of a large mirror in the upstairs bathroom. She reached down for a brush, and when she glanced back into the mirror she saw two reflections! The disembodied head of an old woman was staring at her from over her shoulder. Her emaciated face looked like old leather, weathered and deeply etched with wrinkles, cheeks sunken, thin lips hardly distinguishable. Her long, gray hair was pulled tightly back into a bun and parted straight down the middle. Diane swung around but saw no one behind her. The old lady's image had vanished from the mirror as well.

She never again encountered the old woman in the mirror, and she never discovered who the ghost might have been.

Diane Bonner's last encounter with the unknown happened upon her father's death. Her parents had been divorced, and Diane and Rachel lived with their mother. They rarely saw their father.

Diane clearly remembered the "dream" she had the night before she learned of her father's death.

"The dream wasn't about my father, but he kept appearing in it," Diane recalled. "I don't believe I'd dreamed about him since he left us."

At the end of the dream, Diane saw herself at a table with a stack of large-denomination bills in front of her. A stranger was beside her. The money was hers, he said.

The next evening Diane's mother called. She had somber news. "Well," Diane replied, "if it has anything to do with money it has to be good news."

Her mother was strangely silent. Then she told her daughter that Diane's father had died. Further, her mother said, Diane would receive an inheritance from her father's estate. Depending upon the settlement, she could receive as much as ten thousand dollars.

How had her mother known about the inheritance so shortly after her former husband's death? Diane learned that her father had discussed his will with his former wife only a few weeks before, but he had made her promise to keep the terms of the estate confidential from his daughters until after he died.

In this instance, a dream turned out to be amazingly exact.

The Phantom Congregation

$\mathbf{A}$ few miles from Amery, down a winding country lane, past trim farmhouses and grazing cattle, perched atop a windswept knoll, there stands an old Lutheran church. Its profile juts out sentinel-like over the rolling fields, casting its shadow over the old church cemetery. The building, painted a brilliant white, is a plain structure, a large cross affixed to an outside wall near the main entrance the only decorative touch. A bell tower rises dramatically from the roofline, its spire visible for several miles in any direction. A modern, single-story addition housing offices and classrooms angles away from the main building.

Like hundreds of other country Protestant churches across the Midwest, pioneer Norwegian immigrants erected the building. Sunday worshippers first assembled there nearly 150 years ago. The old ways died hard: services weren't offered in English until the 1940s.

But this church is very different from most other rural houses of worship.

For nearly fifty years, there have been reports that within its walls are trapped phantom worshippers speaking in muted tones.

And once, in that majestic steeple, the heavy iron bell tolled *all by itself*.

The people who have witnessed the peculiar incidents—including a former pastor—were all hardworking, practical people not prone to belief in ghosts, phantoms, or bells that ring without a human touch. Yet at least some of them would never venture into the church alone . . . *at night*.

The phantom congregants were first heard over forty years ago when Barbara Anderson* was the church organist. She had always been reluctant to enter the church at night, but never out of fear of anything unseen. Even in rural areas, women sometimes hesitate to travel alone after sunset, or to enter isolated buildings. She therefore decided upon daylight hours as those in which to practice at the organ.

Anderson didn't think anything peculiar could happen during the day. But then she heard the voices.

"It sounded like people talking, so loud I could almost hear what they were saying. The first time, it was just kind of a mumbling though. I didn't bother to go downstairs where the voices were coming from. I thought it was somebody in the church [basement]."

The voices continued as she tried to concentrate on her music. Her curiosity got the better of her. She decided to go downstairs to see who was there. The room was empty.

"I even went to the outside door to look into the churchyard because the voices had been so loud," she explained. Except for the quiet old parishioners buried in the church cemetery, she was quite alone.

On two separate occasions Anderson heard clear, distinct conversations in the church. But at other times, on other days, the voices seemed distant, muffled.

And each time, Anderson packed up her sheet music and left for home.

She told no one of her experiences. Nearly fifteen years passed before she found out that another church parishioner also heard phantom voices there.

Sheila Larsen* was a volunteer who spent countless hours helping to operate the small country parish on a tight budget. One of her jobs had been to assist with the annual financial report.

On the first Friday of a December some years ago, Larsen and another woman sat in the small church office poring over ledgers and balance sheets. A small electric space heater warmed the room, while an electric mimeograph machine hummed in a corner, churning out pages of figures that would be discussed later that week by the congregation at its annual budget meeting. It was past ten o'clock at night and the two women were anxious to finish the job and return home to their families.

Ever so slowly, almost without a conscious realization of *when* it started, the women became aware of a low murmuring of voices coming from somewhere deep within the darkened church. They thought they had been alone; no one else had been scheduled to use the church that night. The voices grew more distinct as the pair anxiously stared through the open office door and down the dimly lit hallway. The murmuring voices seemed to be coming from the direction of the basement, where Barbara Anderson had noticed them, though Larsen and her companion had never heard the story. "You couldn't hear what they said, but it was loud enough so that we thought a meeting was going on," Larsen explained.

The mysterious conversation seemed to get louder, as if someone turned up the volume on some unseen radio. But there was no radio, nor any other possible cause for the voices.

Bravely, the women looked through the main part of the church. They even ducked down the basement steps and poked around the dark basement.

"Of course, there was nobody there. We came back up and went back to work. But the voices began again, just as before. We hurried up, got our work done, and left!"

The voices still drifted through the church as the women scurried out the door.

Sheila Larsen never could explain what happened to her that night. She tried to rationalize the experience. Was it the wind? No, the evening air was quiet and cold. Was it someone yelling out the window of a passing vehicle? Highly doubtful since the church office in which Larsen was working is some distance from the county highway and all the doors and windows were tightly closed. The nearest house was several hundred yards away, save for the parsonage across the road; and no one was at home there that night.

When Anderson and Larsen later happened to compare notes, they were struck by the similarity of their experiences: the voices always faded as the women neared the apparent source, the church basement; the voices seemed to be part of a rather large gathering; and both discerned men's and women's voices within the murmurings. However, neither could distinguish specific words or phrases, nor could they even be certain it was English they were hearing.

Then there is the church bell. It once rang—by itself.

The ponderous, cast iron object hangs in the church steeple, of course. A long, heavy cord twists downward from the bell to the bottom of a narrow stairway adjacent to the choir loft. The door to the staircase is usually kept locked to keep curious youngsters out of the musty, dimly lit tower.

The bell's strange behavior took place on a day in June. Three people were in the yard of the parsonage across the street—Rachel Halvorsen*, Barbara Anderson, and the church pastor, the Rev. Elizabeth Robinson*, a young woman not long out of the seminary who was serving her first congregation in the Amery church. She and her husband lived in the church-owned house.

The trio had been talking only a short while when the clear, reverberating ring of the church bell echoed from across the quiet road. Anderson and the

Rev. Robinson stared at each other, and then glanced over toward the bell tower. Though neither could believe what they had heard, they agreed that it had been the bell. The church was empty, or so they had thought. In a bizarre twist, the third woman, Rachel Halvorsen, heard nothing.

"I don't know if it rang once or twice," Anderson said. "Although the other woman with us didn't hear it, we all decided to go over and see who was in [the church]."

They considered several scenarios, including the possibility that a youngster had been accidentally locked inside the church and was using the bell to summon help.

They unlocked the main door and checked through the basement, kitchen, bathrooms, every hiding place they could think of. They climbed up onto the balcony to see if someone was there.

"The door to the steeple was closed, and the rope was not moving," Anderson recalled.

There was nothing that could move that bell save for a solid tug on the rope. Yet Anderson and her pastor heard the bell ring, a soft pealing, they said, as if someone had gently pulled the rope.

Could they have been mistaken? Might it perhaps have been a cowbell off in the distance?

Not likely. "Women in rural areas know the difference between a cowbell and a church bell!" the Rev. Robinson said emphatically.

And what she heard on that June day was most definitely a church bell . . . her church's bell . . . rung by unseen hands.

The history of the church is for the most part unexceptional. To the best of anyone's knowledge, there have been no spectacular or peculiar deaths there to account for a possible haunting. The only noteworthy element of the church's history concerns the graveyard touched by the building's long shadow. In a previous era, people who committed suicide were denied burial in consecrated ground and instead were interred outside a white picket fence surrounding the cemetery. Over the years, the wood rotted and the fence collapsed. Eventually it was taken down; so one might imagine that the spirits of those who died natural and unnatural deaths now mingle freely in their musty graves.

Hauntings do seem to center on people who may be especially sensitive to paranormal events. Perhaps Sheila Larsen, Barbara Anderson, and the Rev. Elizabeth Robinson were three of those rare individuals.

For her part, however, Rev. Robinson rejected the idea of ghosts at the church. "I don't think that when people die their spirits float around."

But she trusted the witnesses who heard the voices in the church and what she heard for herself—the tolling of the church bell.

Although she remained skeptical, the Rev. Robinson was open to the possibility that the voices in the church might have been of a paranormal nature even if they did not belong to ghosts per se. That is some consolation to Sheila Larsen and Barbara Anderson. They believe *something* not of this world was congregating in their church.

In the years since, Elizabeth Robinson took a position at another parish, and other ministers have taken her place at the Amery church. Stories continue to circulate about other odd events at the church—a ladder that mysteriously ended up back in a storeroom after a custodian had set it up when he wanted to change a light bulb in the ceiling, several parishioners watching as a soft drink can glided toward the edge of a cafeteria table in the basement . . . and then back to the middle again. Many others continue to avoid the church at night altogether. Who could blame them?

Summerwind

The young Wauwatosa woman and her family were doing what thousands of American families do every summer: spending their treasured vacation days at a beautiful lake resort in Wisconsin's North Woods. In this case the family was about as far north in the state as you can travel, near Boulder Junction, in Vilas County, only a handful of miles from Michigan's Upper Peninsula. One evening as the family dined at a nearby supper club, the family struck up a conversation with their waitress. Among the stories she told them was an intriguing one about a strange, crumbling mansion on West Bay Lake, near the Wisconsin–Michigan border and only a few miles from where they were staying. Not long before, it had been listed as one of the nine most haunted places in the nation by *Life* magazine.

The story was captivating, especially to Mary Beth, the family's teenage daughter, who listened intently.

She decided to do more than listen to the tale — she wanted to pay a visit to the place. A few days later, she and several friends found the rambling, abandoned house, after some searching, on the wide lake's pine shores. From a distance, the wood and stone exterior looked like a set from a horror movie, albeit not nearly as terrifying with the sun shining. The girls found that someone had tried to nail shut the doors and windows, but to the curious, drawn by the house's growing celebrity, getting inside was not that difficult. Poking through the rooms in the hulking mass did give pause if for no other reason than its dangerous physical condition. However, Mary Beth and the others, excited to have found a "real" haunted mansion, carefully made their way through the debris of shattered glass, past sagging walls with moldering wallpaper, and tiptoed their way across barely navigable, rotting floorboards. They discovered the two bullet holes in a door leading to the basement, allegedly made by someone shooting at a "ghost" in the house's early years. A big old sprawling lake house slowly succumbing to the elements, yes, but certainly nothing outwardly unnerving or supernatural.

But that brief, daytime visit wasn't enough for Mary Beth and her friends. Soon after, they decided to return—at midnight, with a Ouija board.

Immediately they were struck by a sense of foreboding.

"As we passed through the kitchen, we all noticed that it was about ten degrees colder than any other room," Mary Beth remembered about that night.

The group settled into a back room. Mary Beth and a friend sat across from one another, the Ouija board balanced on their knees, their fingers lightly holding the planchette. First they "asked" the board a series of simple questions, waiting for the heart-shaped marker to spell out its answers.

At length, the pair was curious about the house's reputation for being especially malevolent to women who lived or visited there.

"Do you want us to leave?" came their question. They waited anxiously for the Ouija to respond.

Slowly the planchette began moving, first to the "N" and then to the "O." After a brief pause, it raced to the "W."

N–O–W.

"We were all pretty terrified," Mary Beth said. They hastily made their way out of that dark, dank backroom toward the wide door at the rear of the mansion through which they had come.

The small group hustled out the door and into the pitch-blackness, but once outside, Mary Beth paused long enough to swing around and take a photograph of a second-floor window above the portico. Earlier, a friend had told her she had seen what looked like someone peering out. She snapped a photograph using her small 35mm camera and a flash.

The night might have been deemed a fun, if somewhat creepy, midnight caper if not for what Mary Beth discovered when she got home.

"I had the pictures developed and that's when I noticed there was a face peering out of the window," she said. "There was absolutely no one in the house at the time. Everybody was outside."

The grainy photograph clearly showed a wide, fieldstone arch entryway to the rear door, out of which Mary Beth and her friends had just fled. Tall weeds on either side of the small, sheltered porch threatened to overtake the pathway. The flash illuminated portions of the house's grimy, wood shingle exterior. Above the door was a triple-paned window. And through the left pane of that window, in the lower left-hand corner, there appeared the rather clear image of *someone* gazing out. It was a murky face to be sure, but a hairline, a pair of dark, hollow eyes, and the bridge of . . . its? nose stood in stark contrast to the surrounding darkness.

That mysterious "face in the window" photograph was Mary Beth's permanent reminder of one strange nighttime visit to one of Wisconsin's most notorious haunted houses, though most traces of it have now vanished.

It was Summerwind.

The name itself evokes a picture of a stately home, light and airy, expansive windows open to the breeze. So it once was. But now the famous North Woods mansion is no more. What Mary Beth and her friends saw that night— a dilapidated hulk, broken windows and rotted roof, dormers filled with bats, fieldstone foundations and broad walkways to the lake—all of that has virtually vanished. But that doesn't mean the house or its many legends have been forgotten. It continues to fascinate and confound all those irresistibly drawn to a place that evokes the classic "haunted house." Books and television shows feature its story, Internet sites and cable television "ghost hunters" debate its history, and even the occasional car disgorges inquisitive visitors at the isolated location. Perhaps its appeal has as much to do with its convoluted history and colorful owners as with anything else.

President Herbert Hoover's one-time Secretary of Commerce, Robert P. Lamont, erected the mansion in 1916. It was reputedly built on the site of an earlier fishing camp. For years, Summerwind was the Lamont family's quiet summer escape, a twenty-room "cabin" of high ceilings, multiple staircases, grand entrances, and several outbuildings (including servants' quarters, a laundry building, and a boathouse) all nestled on several acres along several hundred feet of prime lakeshore property. Lamont and his family used it for many years as their summer getaway, far from the oppressive heat of Washington, D.C. When Lamont died, Summerwind was sold . . . and sold . . . and sold again but always remained the "Lamont place" to locals. The Keefer family eventually bought the property in 1940. They tried to sell it several times over the years but without success. New owners seemed inevitably to default after having insurmountable difficulties in realizing their plans for the property. And so it remained associated with the family until the late 1980s when the land and its remaining structures were at last sold for the final time.

Skeptics maintain that nothing supernatural *really* happened there, that any ghostly manifestations or unexplained incidents took place purely in the imagination of the tenants. Or did they?

The paranormal "history" that became indelibly attached to Summerwind seems to have begun in the early 1970s when Arnold Hinshaw, his wife, Ginger, and their six children lived at the mansion. Hinshaw's father-in-law, Raymond Bober, had actually rented the house but let his daughter and her family live there. Within six months, according to the family, "ghosts" drove Arnold "mad" and his wife attempted suicide.

From the day the Hinshaw family moved in they say they saw vague shapes flitting down the hallways and heard voices mumbling in dark corners; in the evening, as they dined, a ghost they named Mathilda would float just beyond the French doors leading into the living room.

For a time Ginger wondered if they were imagining all this. But then it became too odd, too frequent, to ignore. The litany of mysterious events never seemed to end: a hot-water heater stopped functioning but started up again before the repairman arrived; a water pump performed the same self-recovery. Appliances died and were resurrected with astonishing regularity. Skeptics say it was because of the irregular electrical service.

Windows and doors closed tightly at night were open by morning. The lower sash of a window in the master bedroom, heavy and without weights, was nearly impossible to lift. One morning Arnold closed the window and started downstairs. Remembering that he had left his wallet on the dresser, he returned to the bedroom. The window was standing open.

The couple said they hired subcontractors to undertake restoration projects in the house, but invariably the workers failed to show up, pleading illness or non-delivery of materials. A few confided in Ginger that they just didn't want to work on *this* house.

Perhaps the most bizarre episode reported by the family took place after they decided to finish all of the remodeling themselves. One day they began painting a hallway closet. A large shoe drawer ran along its back wall. The Hinshaws removed it to paint around it. Behind the drawer they found a hole in the wall and a deep, dark recess. Ginger got a flashlight and Arnold wedged himself into the opening. He shone the light back and forth, then suddenly backed out. He said what looked like a corpse was jammed into the back of the cubicle. Plumbing pipes and old building material prevented him from going in any further, he said.

The family's children were in school, but when they got home Arnold and Ginger told them about the weird discovery. Their daughter Mary volunteered to take the flashlight and crawl into the space. Moments later she yelled out. She said she saw a head of dirty black hair, a dried-up brown arm, and part of a leg.

The other children looked too and somberly backed out. Their mother made them promise never to tell anyone what they had found.

The Hinshaws said they didn't call the police because nothing could have been done about the crime so many years after it had taken place. Their claims of a decayed corpse wedged in the crawlspace were never substantiated by independent sources.

About this time Arnold began to stay up late and play the Hammond organ the couple brought with them to Summerwind. He enjoyed playing in the evenings, as he found it relaxing. But now Arnold's playing became a frenetic jumble of melodies and chords, growing louder as the night hours passed. Ginger pleaded with him to stop, but he said the "demons" in his head demanded that he keep playing. Night after night, the cacophony kept the family awake until dawn. The frightened children huddled together in one bedroom.

Arnold's breakdown came quickly, followed by his wife's attempted suicide. While Arnold was in treatment, Ginger and the children moved in with her parents in another northern Wisconsin community. The couple eventually divorced. In time Ginger regained her health and remarried. Her new life was happy and tranquil, and the days at Summerwind seemed only a distant nightmare.

But the past came rushing back far too soon.

Ginger's father, Raymond Bober, announced that he would purchase Summerwind and there, with his wife, open a restaurant and perhaps an inn. He thought the beautiful North Woods location on a tranquil lake would attract a steady stream of customers.

Ginger was horrified. Although she had never given her parents all the details of the frightening experiences in the house, she begged them *not* to move in. But Bober's mind was made up. Further, he knew the place was haunted and he said he knew who the ghost was—the eighteenth-century English explorer Jonathan Carver! Bober claimed that Carver was searching for an old deed to the land granted to him by the Sioux Indians in return for negotiating peace between two warring nations. The grant supposedly took in most of the northern third of Wisconsin. The deed itself was locked in a black box and sealed in the foundation of Summerwind. Carver's ghost was seeking Bober's help in locating it.

And how did Bober know all this? He communicated with Carver through dreams, hypnotic trances, and a Ouija board. At least that's what he claimed in his book, *The Carver Effect*, published under the pseudonym Wolfgang von Bober.

Shortly after Bober moved into Summerwind, he, his son, Ginger, and her new husband spent a full day inspecting the mansion. The group was just leaving the second floor when Ginger's husband George spotted the closet at the end of the hall. He began pulling out drawers and looking behind it. Ginger begged him to stop. He didn't know what she was talking about, but later around the kitchen table she told the small group the entire story.

The men were undaunted at the prospect of finding a corpse. With flashlights in hand, they returned to the closet, moved the shoe chest away from the wall, and found the crawl space. Ginger's brother was first in, but backed out in a few minutes. What did he find? Pipes, beams, insulation, and debris but that was all—nothing even remotely like a corpse.

One by one the other men poked around the tight space. Where had the body gone? Had someone removed it? Or had there never been a body there in the first place?

Over the following Labor Day weekend, Karl Bober, Ginger's brother, traveled alone to Summerwind. He had gone to get a repair estimate on the outside water well and also to look for an exterminator who could rid the house of its profuse bat population. He thought he might even trim some trees and tidy up the lawn if the good weather prevailed and he had some extra time.

The story he later told claimed that when it started to rain on the first day, he ran upstairs to make sure the windows were closed. In the long, dark hallway, a deep voice suddenly called out his name. The young man spun around just as the disembodied voice repeated the greeting. In the quiet that followed, no one showed his face.

Bober closed the windows and went back downstairs. But when he reached the living room, he was again shocked when two pistol shots rang out from somewhere close by. He couldn't tell if they'd come from within or outside the house.

He found the kitchen filled with the acrid smoke of gunpowder. It seemed that someone had fired from *inside* the house. How could an intruder have entered or left without Karl knowing? The back door always stuck and had to be noisily pushed open or slammed shut, and the other doors all had inside security bars across them.

A quick look around the room led to the discovery of two bullet holes in the basement door. But those holes looked as if they'd been there for some time, worn smooth around the edges. Karl Bober left the house that afternoon.

In his book, Raymond Bober wrote that the original owner of the house, Robert Lamont, whom he called Patterson, had fired twice at a ghost, though there was nothing to substantiate the claim. And that had been many decades earlier.

Raymond Bober's attempts to renovate the house were as futile as those of his daughter. Workmen refused to stay on the job, complaining about being watched by "evil eyes." Bober's wife understood that complaint. She was always uneasy around the house. Every time she sat in the sunny courtyard it seemed that someone watched her from the windows of the master bedroom.

Most disturbing to Bober, he reported, was his discovery that the mansion apparently shrank and expanded at will. Bober said he measured rooms one day only to find their dimensions different the next. Usually his measurements were larger than those given on the house blueprints. Through measuring rooms, Bober estimated he could seat one hundred fifty people if he created a restaurant on the main floor, but after he laid out the plans on the blueprints, he realized the place would seat no more than seventy-five.

He said photographs he took from the same position with the same camera and only a few seconds apart likewise displayed amazing distortions of space. The living room in particular seemed to expand and contract.

On one occasion Bober compared his pictures of the living room with those Ginger had taken before she and her family had moved in. Ginger's pictures showed curtains at the living room windows, which she took down after she moved in. Bober said the curtains "reappeared" in the photograph he took.

If indeed the ghost of Jonathan Carver wanted help in finding his "deed," why did he manifest himself in such diabolical ways? Bober explained this by saying Carver did not want any improvements made in the property and that he resented anyone living in the house or renovating it in any manner whatsoever.

The Bobers never attempted to stay in Summerwind. Instead they cooked and slept in a camper on the property. And what of Jonathan Carver's hidden deed? Bober spent many days unsuccessfully searching the basement and chipping away at the foundation in a futile effort to find it.

Wisconsin writer Will Pooley was among the first to visit Summerwind with the aim of discovering the truths hidden behind the old mansion's many tales. He found, for instance, that even if Bober had come across Carver's deed, it would have been worthless. Not only had the British government ruled against an individual's purchase of lands from the Indians, but it was also later determined that the Sioux had never owned land east of the Mississippi River.

In addition, although the original deed was apparently found during the 1930s in an old land office in Wausau, Wisconsin, historians argue that it is very unlikely Carver ever traveled as far north as Vilas County. Thus, how could the deed have been sealed up in the foundation of a house built 136 years after the explorer died?

Neighbors, too, were skeptical of the supernatural claims.

Herb Dickman of Land O'Lakes helped pour the foundation for the Lamont mansion. He recalled that the only thing they put in there was stone. There was no black box. Dickman also lived in the house for three months after it was finished. He said nothing unusual ever occurred there during that time.

Another sixty-year neighbor said the mansion didn't get a reputation for being haunted until after it had been abandoned and dilapidated. It never had that reputation while it was occupied, save for the short-lived Hinshaw and Bober occupancy.

Carolyn Ashby, also of Land O'Lakes, spent a number of summers in the mansion as a child. She didn't remember any ghosts about the premises, but she did admit that the place seemed "spooky" at night, especially with the large number of drafty old rooms.

Other neighbors told Pooley that the Bobers spent less than two full summers on the estate. Bober abandoned plans for his restaurant, but then tried to get a government permit to operate a concession stand near the house; a local ordinance prohibited it. At one time Bober toured the country with a nineteenth-century popcorn wagon.

Also, there is some uncertainty as to whether Bober ever actually owned Summerwind; instead, he may have been trying unsuccessfully to buy it on a contract for deed basis.

Is the mystique of this Wisconsin haunted house based on publicity and the gradual disintegration of a once-magnificent home? Summerwind's neighbors thought so. And they resented strangers tramping over lawns and driveways to get there, or knocking on their doors at all hours of the day. At one time there were even chartered buses that disgorged amateur "ghost hunters" onto the grounds.

And what did the visitors see? Only the gray, bat-and-guano-filled skeleton of a turn-of-the-century relic decaying in a grove of scrub oak and gaunt northern pines. Yet for even the most skeptical of visitors, when the winds blew through the shattered windows and the doors creaked on rusted hinges, it was easy to believe that something lurked behind those weathered, crumbling walls.

Even today, long after a lightning-generated late night fire left Summerwind a smoldering relic, the mansion's isolation and lingering questions about all that went on there keep television producers and Internet sites speculating on its haunted history. Even its few remaining traces—part of a massive wall, sections of stone steps descending to the lake, a portion of a fieldstone fireplace and chimney—add to the unnerving feeling that the place might well have once harbored spirits.

Perhaps its allure, and its thrill, come from imagining what a young Wauwatosa woman experienced on that late-night visit: a stern warning from one of Summerwind's undying occupants to go away, and possibly even a glimpse of its pallid face. One long-time area resident may have put it best when he said, "I don't believe in ghosts, but I've been afraid of them all my life."

Part II
Southern Frights

The Music Box

It was a hot, muggy late July evening in Madison. The young University of Wisconsin–Madison student hadn't lived in the city very long. A recent transfer from another University of Wisconsin campus, she was subletting a second-floor apartment with her best friend and two other girls in a plain, old, American foursquare house on the city's near west side. It was a spacious apartment with separate bedrooms for each girl. They shared a living room and kitchen. On this evening, she was studying, her roommates at work or out of town.

Even with the windows open there wasn't much of a breeze, and her bedroom at the rear of the house was especially stifling. She got up to stretch her legs, and wandered into the kitchen and on into the living room hoping to find some relief from the heat.

Instead, she found a whodunit.

From her friend's bedroom off the living room she heard a music box playing "My Funny Valentine."

"I thought it really was odd that the music box would just start . . . on its own. I hoped that a breeze might be the cause."

But that was not the case.

Her friend kept the inner mechanism of a music box sitting on a shelf. She walked over to the open bedroom door and glanced in. The mechanism was indeed tinkling away, playing the old standard. Across the room the window was open, but there was no breeze coming through it.

"Okay, I thought. I'll just stop freaking myself out. I'll shut the window so the wind can't blow against it," she said to herself at the time, while knowing full well the open window could not explain the curious event.

And then her evening got really strange.

She was taking a step into the bedroom when suddenly her right arm shot straight out in front of her, parallel to the floor and stiff, but her hand remained relaxed. It was, she said, like someone had lifted her arm and didn't want to let go. She felt no pressure being applied, nothing had grabbed it, yet she could not move her arm.

"I just stood there. I thought, well, this is weird. Then I took a step and sat down on the bed."

Her arm was still thrust outward, immobile.

That's when she started talking . . . to whatever might be with her in that room—something unseen, something letting her know it was there. She couldn't think of anything else to do.

"I said 'Okay, I don't know what's happening here but I don't mean you any harm.' I tried to see if I could put my arm down. And I could. I let it drop to my side."

Part of her, quite naturally, felt very foolish "talking to the air," but, on the other hand, "I *thought* I *had* been by myself."

She went on to introduce herself and say that she was living in the house only for the summer and didn't want to disturb anyone and that she was now going back to her bedroom to study, which she proceeded to do.

This may seem an improbable episode to many, yet for Krista Clumpner it was an enigma so very real that it mystifies her even now. Today a university librarian in Marquette, Michigan, Clumpner spent just one summer in that Madison apartment. By the end of August, she and her roommates had moved out, but that was because their subletting lease was up and not because of the music box incident.

Clumpner did tell her best friend and the other two roommates about the incident, but they were skeptical. Her friend said the music box only played when she wound it up, so perhaps it had been wound too tight and the wind somehow released it.

"Okaaay," Clumpner replied, clearly not believing that rationalization.

"I think it was a ghost or spirit, whatever you want to call it. It obviously wasn't something that was too angry or threatening. I talked to it, I acknowledged it, and I never had another incident. I wasn't afraid to live there even though that had happened. I simply thought it was odd, but that it was okay."

She didn't have time to look into the history of the house because of the brevity of her residence there, but wishes now that she had. The young men who lived in the apartment during the school year couldn't provide any answers, though Clumpner and her roommates told them about the incident. They didn't seem terribly surprised. The men did tell her the bedroom most recently had been occupied by a biology major who kept the remains of dead animals, including a bird skeleton dangling from a light cord. She thought that strange, but didn't see any connection between dead birds and her experience.

Krista Clumpner went on to receive her undergraduate degree in art history and a master's in library science. From there she worked at various historical libraries in Wisconsin, Iowa, and Michigan before settling in Marquette, where she is the head of technical services and systems at the local university library.

Various professional advancements, her marriage, and the arrival of children have not diminished Clumpner's occasional interactions with the otherworldly. She believes she is more open to the paranormal than the average person, and not just because of the music box incident. Several incidents at her home in Marquette seem to bear her out.

After a year of renting following their move to Marquette, Clumpner and her artist-husband bought a large, old, early-twentieth-century house, with some Victorian flourishes. Designed primarily in the American Foursquare tradition, it has spacious rooms and a walk-up attic. Yet it's been a very "odd" home from the very beginning, she said.

Before moving in their furniture, Clumpner insisted that the living and dining rooms be painted. She picked an off-white color with a peach tinge. After they moved in, her husband went to work trying to dislodge a pair of pocket doors that slid back into the walls between the two rooms. After tugging and pushing and prying, he at last pried one loose. The couple discovered the door had been painted the same color his wife had chosen for the two rooms.

"We kept having things like that happen," she remarked. "We decided to put in a white picket fence. While the workmen were digging the holes to put in the fence, they came across the top part of an old white picket fence. We were meant to have this house because we're taking it back to the way it was, to what it was."

Coincidental color schemes and duplicate picket fences were one thing, but her discovery soon thereafter that her family may have been sharing the home with a ghost was quite another.

"Every now and then I'd see something out of the corner of my eye, but when I turned directly toward it, it wouldn't be there." She attributed it to "seeing things" or simply being tired—the "regular notions" one resorts to when something like that happens.

One night her three-year-old daughter wandered downstairs in her pajamas, rubbing her eyes.

"Mommy, can you tell that little boy to get off the landing?"

She made the request quite matter-of-factly. The family had never talked about the earlier "coincidences," nor had Clumpner spoken to anyone about the "shadows" she'd been seeing—coincidentally on the same landing her young daughter was now referring to.

"It was a 'he's keeping me up' kind of statement she made," she explained. "I said, 'Okay, don't worry about it. He won't hurt you. Maybe you should just tell him to go away?' That calmed her down."

Krista Clumpner and her husband had been sitting together when their daughter came downstairs. After she'd gone back to bed, they looked at each other and began comparing notes. She told him she'd seen a shadow on that landing too. Her husband admitted he'd glimpsed what looked like a person's shadow passing by in the attic. But neither had seen anything definite or found anything intimidating.

Some time later, when Clumpner's son was a preschooler, on what otherwise seemed a typical evening, she tucked him into bed and then walked over to shut the closet door.

"No! He doesn't want that door shut," the child insisted.

"He who?" his mom wanted to know. "Your dad?"

"No, the little boy who lives here, he doesn't want it shut."

Again Clumpner complied with the unusual request of one of her children. She left it open. Perhaps the boy was an imaginary playmate—or perhaps something else.

But once she got back downstairs and told her husband, they decided to ask a friend who was also a psychic to help them out. They wanted to know what was going on and who might be making these periodic visits. Neither one wanted to send away the child spirit—if indeed that's what it was—but rather simply sought to understand the nature of the haunting.

The psychic told them there was indeed a "presence" in their home, a child whose name was Jeremy, and that he had been confined to a lonely life in the bedroom that now belonged to Clumpner's son because of a debilitating illness, perhaps tuberculosis. He could only watch through his windows as other children played outside. The psychic said at some point the house caught fire, trapping the boy in his bedroom. He died while hiding in his closet to escape the smoke and flames.

The psychic worked to "release" the boy's spirit and told him he didn't have to stay there. Though Clumpner and her husband made it clear they were willing to share the house with the boy's spirit, she says that after that evening everything seemed to quiet down. Her children didn't have any further encounters with the boy and neither Clumpner nor her husband again caught sight of shadows flitting by.

Clumpner took the psychic's findings for what they were, a heartbreaking story that couldn't be proven one way or the other. She did some research into the house's history and found that its original owner had been a doctor, but learned little else.

That's when the couple's penchant for remodeling may have helped solve the mystery. As in many older homes, some of the rooms had been paneled over. Their son's room was one of them. When they stripped the paneling away from the walls and ceiling near the bedroom closet, they found scorched wood. Similar remnants of scorched wood were located in the attic over that same bedroom.

Krista Clumpner and her family still live in and continue to be fond of their big old home, despite the occasional hints of dark secrets. She holds out enough hope that this may not be the end of her brushes with the supernatural.

"I'm not sure [the little boy] will come back. We haven't seen anything more but maybe someday we'll move somewhere and I'll have another experience."

Someone to Watch over Me

Tales of early American wayside inns or century-old hotels inevitably stir visions of romance, danger, . . . and ghosts. Today, many have succumbed to the ravages of time, while others manage to survive in one form or another as restaurants, hotels, or a combination of the two. But in any case, it is inevitable that where there was so much transient, sometimes tumultuous life there would be some *afterlife*—guests who refuse to bring down the curtain on their final act. Sometimes the word "guest" is a misnomer when applied to what might haunt a few of Wisconsin's old hostelries.

The Walker House is generally considered Wisconsin's oldest inn, having opened in 1836 at Mineral Point, then the "metropolis" of the lead-mining region in the state's southwestern corner. The handsome, three-story stone building, with its later two-story addition at one end, exuded a decidedly continental atmosphere. In its heyday, tucked into a hillside and set off by a row of sentinel-like trees, the Walker House could have been a European baron's hunting lodge with heavy, rough-hewn ceiling beams, the bark still on them, throughout the ground-floor rooms. An upstairs tavern featured a polished, room-length bar and walls adorned with hunting trophies.

From the beginning, the Walker House did a brisk business. Wisconsin's territorial officers were sworn in at Mineral Point the same year the inn was built, and the little village teemed with politicians traveling back and forth between the temporary state capital at nearby Belmont and their home communities. The inn welcomed all the Cornish miners, frontiersmen, immigrants, and speculators pouring into the region, eager for the riches that the lead and zinc deposits promised. At night, the inn burst with life as the rough men jostled with one another for drink, food, and perhaps a bed on the uppermost floor.

But one customer was different from all the rest. He hadn't come there willingly, for his brief stay preceded his hanging directly in front of the Walker House. He was an outlaw by the name of William Caffee . . . and it's his ghost that may haunt this very oldest of Wisconsin inns.

The date was November 1, 1842, six years before Wisconsin obtained statehood. Caffee had been convicted of shooting Samuel Southwick to death during an argument. A throng of over four thousand men and women—many with children in tow—turned out for the hanging, most of them with picnic baskets and camped on the hills ringing the town. The execution rite itself was macabre. Caffee was put astride his casket, where he beat out the rhythm of a funeral march with two empty beer bottles. He marched up to the scaffold erected in front of the inn with such a nonchalant and contemptuous attitude toward his own death that it brought him a sort of posthumous notoriety. No one who witnessed the spectacle would ever forget it or him.

Yet if this by itself weren't enough to secure his place in posterity, Caffee, if we are to believe the numerous stories about him, made one final gesture to ensure his memory would remain alive forever: his ghost returned and settled in the Walker House.

The earliest reports of Caffee's ghost arose in the mid-twentieth century when new owners took over the inn. It had sat vacant for a number of years, ruined by neglect and vandalism. Soon, the owners and a crew of young people had dug out dead trees, replaced eight hundred windowpanes, and built a native stone fireplace in the pub. Oak planking from an abandoned barn was used to cover over the pub's walls. One dining room was refurbished and opened, serving Cornish-style luncheons and dinners. Another dining room soon followed, and then a second-floor tavern with a massive bar was made ready for guests.

Unfortunately, the business did not succeed and the Walker House was sold to a local physician. It was at about this time that a student from Madison was temporarily living in a second-floor apartment, above the inn's office. He wasn't happy about what he said went on when the place closed for the night: someone turned his doorknob from the outside, and he heard strange noises that he couldn't locate or even identify. After many sleepless nights, he moved out.

Walker Calvert could understand the young man's fear. The new owners had just hired him as a chef-manager when he discovered that sometimes things just *happened* in that old inn. On three different occasions, Calvert found himself talking to *someone* in the main dining room, but no one was ever there . . . nor could he recall the conversations or describe the person he was talking to. He said it was almost as if he had been hypnotized.

"I didn't know I *wasn't* talking to a real person," he said. Waitresses who heard two voices before going into the dining room found Calvert alone. They said the other voice they'd heard through the door was definitely male.

In the kitchen, the banging and clanking of pots and pans created a din each morning . . . except no one was using any of the pans at the time. One older kitchen worker refused to work alone. Calvert understood: "When I was in there, I always felt that someone was following me around."

The other waitresses felt the same way. Several of them told Calvert they would fix drinks and then feel themselves bump into something as they carried the loaded tray to tables. Only nothing was ever in their way to bump into. At other times it was a white shape that might quickly flit by.

One waitress who scoffed at the ghost tales got her comeuppance in the kitchen when her ponytail shot straight up in the air. The girl hollered, "Get away!" Her ponytail slowly dropped. But then just as suddenly it shot upright again. She became a believer. Several women customers also reported their hair being tousled or played with.

"The ghost was always doing something," Calvert said. "It was as if he tried to prove to everyone . . . that he was there."

For example, one might hear the sudden heavy breathing from close by, or the hurried footsteps, which scared a number of employees. On one occasion, a bartender was stooped over to check his supply of clean glasses beneath the bar when what he thought was a man's heavy breathing made him freeze.

"Leave me alone!" he yelled.

As he straightened up, gripping the edge of the counter, the breaths grew shallower, while the slow footfalls across the aged floorboards receded across the room.

On a December morning shortly before the Walker House closed for the winter, Walker Calvert was working alone in the office. He heard someone walk up to the open door behind him and stop.

He had just turned in his chair to look when a deep groan and then a howl split the quiet, cold air. He ran from the building: "It scared me to death."

Still no one had actually *seen* a ghost at the inn, nor did they have any solid proof that it was William Caffee. Everyone seemed to think it was him hanging about the property, so to speak, because his was the best-documented death in or near the inn.

Walker Calvert noted, for instance, that it seemed the ghost wanted to keep customers and employees out of the building, as if he resented crowds of people, which was certainly understandable if it was the unfortunate Caffee. Several times, either in the early morning hours or late at night, there would be the jangle of keys in the front door lock, yet no one entered. Or a door that was unlocked would be found locked tight.

Sometimes at night, Calvert and the waitresses discovered the main entrance locked even before they left. "The door we used has a deadbolt lock opened with a key. We'd have to get that key and unlock the door to get out of the building. There was no way that door could have gotten locked. I didn't lock it, and I had the only key."

At last, the reluctant ghost made its first visible appearance just before sunset on a crisp October evening. Appropriately, Walker Calvert was the first to see him. He had gone upstairs to check the door that opens from the far end of the barroom onto a porch, containing, at that time, an L-shaped wooden bench. An exterior, wooden staircase led down to the ground level.

As Calvert reached to lock the door to the porch, he noticed what *appeared* to be an older man slumped on the outside bench barely two feet away from him. It was difficult to tell from the rough clothing alone, though—the figure had no head! A black felt hat rested flat on his shoulders where his head should have been. He wore a gray miner's jacket and dusty denims.

Calvert quickly locked the door and glanced back out the window, but whatever had been there was no more.

Oddly enough, during that same week a waitress saw the ghost of a young man, head still attached, in the second-floor bar. He stood alongside the bar rail for a few moments and then vanished.

The ghost of William Caffee—if indeed it was he who haunted the Walker House—never seemed to harm anyone, nor did it seem that he posed any threat. He didn't smash dishes or try to set fire to the place, though he did throw a beer bottle or two when no one was looking. However, large crowds did irritate the ghost of the man whose last earthly sight was the raucous mob pushing against the scaffold, eager to see him dance in the air.

Caffee's ghost was certainly prankish, and, at times, downright frightening. Yet perhaps he was only trying to be "helpful," rattling the pans in the kitchen, checking out the bar, and locking up at night. It's not always possible to understand a ghost.

And what did Walker Calvert make of his experiences?

Before he went to work at the Walker House, he scoffed at the supernatural. "Absolutely no way," he said, shaking his head.

And after?

"Now, I'm sure it's all possible."

The Walker House has changed hands several times in recent years. In early 2011 it appeared that at least part of it was again on the market.

The historic Chances Restaurant in Rochester had just gone through some extensive remodeling, including the installation of a new roof, when co-owner Debbie Schuerman got one of those telephone calls every business owner dreads—an alert that an electronic alarm had gone off and a motion detector had identified movement in the dining room. Even worse, the call came in the middle of a rainy night and the last thing she wanted to do was to accompany the sheriff's deputies as they checked the premises.

But to the restaurant she went, not knowing what to expect. A systematic search failed to turn up any plausible reason for the motion detector to have activated. The possibility of a false alarm seemed especially unlikely given that the system could not be triggered by pets or other small animals. Spiders, mice, squirrels, or even most household pets would not have set it off.

Debbie and the sheriff's deputies made sure everything was secure inside before they reset the alarm and started down the back hallway to the rear door. At that point she discovered what she thinks was the *real* reason she had been "summoned" to the restaurant. She felt drops of water hitting her face as the small group walked down a hallway. The water seemed to be coming through the ceiling near a doorway in a section recently remodeled.

Apparently the roofers hadn't completely covered the seam between the old section of the restaurant and the newer addition. She decided to call the roofing company the next morning and have them fix the problem. But as she was locking up she saw the real danger—the leak was only a few inches from a light fixture. She got some rags to plug the small crack through which the water was dripping and then shut off the power to the light fixture.

No doubt the deputies were startled when Debbie turned toward the empty restaurant and called out, "Thank you! I'll catch you in the morning. Keep an eye on the place!"

With that she also thanked the puzzled deputies, turned the key in the lock for the last time, and went home.

And to whom was she speaking?

It might have been Sadie, the African American cook, or the Civil War soldier, or perhaps his lover, the lady in green. They are just three of the seven ghosts that Debbie and her family believe stand watch over their 150-year-old establishment.

Debbie has learned to be sensitive to what is not obvious. She thinks the ghosts warn her of potential danger. If there's a late-night alarm, police look for prowlers but she'll check for electrical problems or perhaps sniff the air for a natural gas leak or smoke.

But over the years, none of the alarms has meant a living intruder. The Schuermans have never had a break-in or a burglary while other businesses in the small, western Racine County community have not been so fortunate.

The owners think they know why.

Early Racine County settlers Levi Godfrey and John Wade staked a claim on the Fox River near the present site of Chances in the early 1830s and soon built a double log house that was opened as the first tavern in the western portion of the county. Although the quarters were primitive, that didn't impede travelers from stopping there to share meals and spend the night sleeping on the packed dirt floor.

According to legend, disgruntled Indians burned the log cabin in the early 1840s. Peter Campbell bought the property and built the existing brick building in 1843. The Union House, as he named it, continued to serve travelers on the old Plank Road from Racine to Janesville. Rochester was the -largest city in Wisconsin at the time and Campbell's hostelry was one of the most popular stops along what could be considered the interstate highway of its day.

A large stone addition with eighteen-inch-thick walls was added to the Union House before the Civil War. An expanded dining room was situated downstairs while a two-thousand-square-foot dance hall took up most of the second floor. The original springboard dance floor is still intact and is thought to be among the last of its type anywhere in Wisconsin.

Unfortunately, the 1850s also brought the decline of business along the Plank Road as railroads bypassed Rochester in favor of nearby Burlington. The Union House closed as a hotel, but it has continued in business as a tavern and restaurant almost uninterrupted to this day.

Perhaps the Union House's most fascinating period came during the years just prior to the Civil War when it and the Willard House across the Fox River were purportedly stops along the Underground Railroad. Local legend has it that escaping African Americans were clandestinely taken up the Fox River to tunnels on the riverbank that led either to the basements of the Union House or the Willard House. The escaped slaves hid in the cellars until they could be sent on their way to their next stop and on to eventual freedom in Canada. What looks to be a patched circular hole in an exterior basement wall at Chances is routinely pointed out as a possible entrance to the old passageway.

Over the past 150 years, the inn has gone through countless owners and several name changes. Until Tom and Debbie Schuerman bought the business, it had been known in the modern era as Big John's or simply the Rochester Inn.

"We fell in love with the place because of its history," Debbie said of their decision to buy the then-closed restaurant. Neither Debbie nor her husband had previously owned or managed a business, but both had familiarity with the food and liquor trade.

"We jumped in with both feet, thus the name. We took 'chances.'"

The couple set about cleaning the well-maintained building, adding a few room dividers and shortening the bar, which once extended into the dining room. Today, the front portion of the inn holds an entrance hallway, the cozy bar, and restrooms, while the rear section accommodates two separate dining rooms. In one of these, Debbie displays her collection of antique dishes and teapots. She wanted it to look like "her grandmother's dining room," she said. The second floor is no longer in public use, but it continued to be a dance hall until shortly before the Schuermans bought the business; additionally there was a small apartment at one end.

The two-story brick and stone edifice on County Road D in downtown Rochester occupies a prominent place in the local business district. Since the building was in "pretty decent shape," in Debbie's words, it didn't take long to get Chances open for business. From the original pressed-tin ceiling in the dining room to the brick and stone walls and period furnishings, the old wayside looks today much as it did a century ago, as is clear when a visitor studies the old photographs that adorn the walls.

What the Schuermans didn't anticipate was that along with the period furnishings and historic architecture would come a few otherworldly residents almost as old as the building itself.

"We didn't have any idea that the place had any so-called spirits or ghosts," Debbie said matter-of-factly. One of their new employees—whose husband's family once owned the place—told her ghost stories about the place. Debbie didn't pay all that much attention to them.

Perhaps she should have.

It all began with small annoyances shortly after the restaurant opened. Chairs in the dining room were pulled away from the tables each morning when Debbie came in to clean. She had to push the chairs back in just to walk through.

Then her shoes started to go missing. "It drove me nuts. I wore high heels to work. I'd bring in a pair of flats so that through the night as my feet got tired I'd slip into my flats and put my heels back in the liquor [storage] room. The next day I'd come in and they'd be gone. I think I lost half a dozen pairs of heels before I finally decided I wasn't going to wear high heels any more."

At first, Debbie thought someone was trying to tell her something by playing these peculiar practical jokes. But her high heels continued to vanish even after she started hiding them.

"I decided I couldn't afford it anymore so I just kept wearing my flats. My feet were more comfortable and I didn't have shoes disappearing."

It took a long time and a lot of convincing before she thought something, well, odd was going on. Unbeknownst to her, Chances had a ghostly reputation not spelled out in the Schuermans' purchase agreement.

"I thought there was always some logical explanation to it. That's how I felt about it. But within the first year, we would get small groups of people who claimed to be psychics coming to dinner. Some of them would say, '*They* like you.' The spirits were going to watch over us, protect us, and make sure we're happy." Debbie usually nodded politely and smiled when visitors told her that, not quite knowing how to take these compliments, if that's how they were intended.

She wasn't won over until a night a couple of years after Chances opened, a night on which the Schuermans came perilously close to losing all they had worked so hard to build. Debbie was bartending on a Wednesday around eight o'clock when she discovered that she had run out of carbon dioxide gas for pressurizing the tavern's soft drink and beer hoses. The problem was that the gas tanks that fed the bar's spigots were located in the basement, a room in which Debbie is decidedly uncomfortable at night. She isn't necessarily afraid or uneasy, but she usually had another person accompany her down there.

So with the help of a regular customer who volunteered to help her, Debbie went to the basement room where the gas tanks are located to supervise while he exchanged the empty tank for a full one.

"Then I heard this hissing sound above my head," Debbie said, shivering at the memory. "I have a phobia about snakes and I thought that's what it was."

She stayed crouched and backed away but couldn't resist trying to see the source of the sound.

She looked up and noticed water leaking through the ceiling. It appeared to be coming from the sinks in the kitchen. It was trickling down on top of a light fixture and had blown the glass off the light bulb. But the filaments were still glowing. The hissing was coming from the water hitting the live electrical wires.

Once they had quickly changed the tank, Debbie and the customer, also a volunteer firefighter, disconnected the power to the light fixture and capped the wires on what they both knew posed a very real and potentially catastrophic fire hazard.

The porcelain on the fixture was black and the floorboards above it were the same. The heat was very intense. If they hadn't noticed it that night the business may very well have gone up in flames.

Early the next day, the company that maintained the carbon dioxide tanks came out to replace the one Debbie thought was empty. But after checking the tank, the serviceman came back upstairs looking perplexed. He asked why the tank had been replaced the night before. It was half full, had pressure, and had nothing wrong with it. It didn't need to be replaced.

Then Debbie remembered the visiting psychics who had told her the ghosts at Chances liked her and her husband and that they would be around to see that no harm befell them.

"I was being protected. Because I had to go downstairs, we found that hazard." Since she had been drawn to the basement she was able to discover the problem with the light socket and perhaps avoid a catastrophe.

It was a few years later that the episode with the leaky roof offered more corroboration that the Chances ghosts have been able to warn the owners when something is amiss or there is danger. Often this has come in the form of the burglar alarm being activated, such as the night of the roof leak.

Debbie described the times she's been called after hours when the alarm goes off as "attention-getters."

She's found something wrong most of the time. It makes her nervous when she can't find any problem. Even on the night three squad cars showed up, she looked over every square inch of the restaurant, including the garbage cans, in case a burning cigarette had been tossed inside one. When the alarm company again tested the system, everything checked out just fine.

"After a while, I figure that if I missed something, the ghosts will set the alarm off again. That's the confidence I have. But I want them to make it more obvious."

The identity of the seven ghosts who may haunt Chances is as shrouded in legend as befits such a historic place. A fire that destroyed the Rochester town hall took with it city records dealing with the history of many Rochester businesses, including Chances.

Only one ghost has a name, Sadie, a black woman and supposed runaway slave who cooked at the Union House. The others are known by their physical descriptions, including two women, one wearing a green gown, the other a blue dress.

Sadie was the first ghost Debbie became aware of.

"This is where she ended up settling and for some reason she lived in the basement. She would only come up to cook," Debbie said, adding that what she has learned of the resident spirits has come from previous owners. The ghost had no name so it was Debbie who first called her Sadie.

She is the "kitchen spirit" because she usually doesn't go beyond that area. If there are odd things going on back there, it's Sadie who is thought to be responsible.

"Our chefs change their clothes in a bathroom back there. I've been here when they've come running out white as can be and with their clothes in hand because as they're bending over they were touched. They're just terrified."

Other problems associated with Sadie involve stove burners being shut off while food is cooking, a basement door off the kitchen that will not stay closed, and food that vanishes. In fact she doesn't like the kitchen staff much at all for invading what she may still consider "her" kitchen.

Although no one has actually *seen* Sadie, the same cannot be said for the mysterious entity known as the Civil War soldier, whose haunt is confined to the first floor of Chances.

Stacy Kopchinski is Debbie and Tom's married daughter. She works at Chances and helps manage the facility and is one of only a few people who say they've seen the soldier.

For Stacy, the sighting came on a bright, early weekday morning as she vacuumed the carpet under tables in the dining room. "I don't know why but I turned around, and I saw him sitting there at the bar as if he were waiting for someone to come and serve him a cocktail. He had on a hat with a brim and a long coat. He was dark and looked very much like a real person."

So real, in fact, that Stacy grabbed a fork off the table, fearful that an intruder had somehow gotten in, although the doors were still locked. Then he was gone.

"I thought, what the heck? I looked in the bathrooms and then called my dad and asked him to come right down. It was scarier thinking a real person had gotten in." A cleaning woman is also said to have seen him and promptly quit.

The soldier displays another irksome bit of behavior—he pinches female customers and waitstaff.

"He's a ladies' man," Debbie said with a laugh. "We've always thought he's the one who pinches ladies' butts, or pats your butt all the time. Then you'll get this chill like something is [back] there and you're swiping it away all the time."

The sense of being touched is annoying, but Debbie hardly pays attention to it anymore since "he's doing it all the time."

Stacy said once she was seating a couple at a table when the woman quickly turned around and glared. "She thought I'd pinched her!"

The old soldier may long for female companionship because, by legend, his girlfriend in life is the lady in the green dress who haunts the second floor. She is said to have been a prostitute trading her charms for cash at the Union House.

"The story we've been told is that the Civil War soldier and the prostitute were a couple. She fell in love with him but decided she was unworthy of his love because of what she did and killed herself upstairs. But the soldier was so distraught over what she did that he committed suicide downstairs. The two can never get together because they're on different [spectral] planes."

Although Debbie has not seen the spectral woman in green, her daughter Stacy has driven by the restaurant late at night and seen, at least twice, the face of a blonde-haired woman staring out the upstairs windows. Electric Christmas candles in the windows and outside lights have illuminated her face. On other occasions, customers have asked if someone lives upstairs because they "see" someone in one of the windows.

Debbie told the story of a former bartender who lived in the small apartment at one end of the otherwise unused second floor. He once heard faint harp music. When he looked around for its source, he saw the woman in the green dress standing in a far corner of the old dance floor. It happened more than once. He scurried downstairs each time he heard the music, but eventually decided to stand his ground to see what she would do. Apparently, she floated right to him and passed through his body, leaving him with a cold, clammy sensation. A decidedly unpleasant odor lingered in the air.

Music played a role in another incident as well.

Debbie explained, "I'd gone upstairs to do inventory on a Sunday morning. All of a sudden I hear this music, beautiful music that sounds like it's from an old piano. I wondered where it was coming from, but no matter where I walked around the ballroom, it was always the same volume. I thought someone was playing a joke, so I quickly opened the door, thinking someone was there. I went downstairs where a cook and his assistant were getting ready for Sunday brunch and a bartender was setting up. Everybody's doing their job, there's no music, no nothing."

She went back upstairs to continue with the inventory, and after a few minutes the music started up again. It was calming, she said, but unnerving at the same time because she couldn't figure out the source. Debbie was tired from working long hours and taking care of the myriad details necessary to operate a successful business.

"I kicked a box across the room, and just as it hit the floor the music stopped. Then I thought [the ghosts] were only trying to be good, to be nice. I apologized. I said I was sorry and that they could play music for me any time they wanted. But I've never heard it again. I really insulted them."

In the quiet early morning hours or late at night there's often other activity in the old ballroom. "You have the feeling someone else is here. Either you hear movement or some muffled talking. Footsteps, too, a *click, click, click* across the floor, like someone [wearing] heels—very well defined. It makes you wonder if someone is up there. You do get used to it . . . because you hear it all the time."

Another female ghost, in a dark blue polka-dot dress, inhabits the first floor along with the soldier.

One day a waitress watched as she walked calmly through the dining room and into the kitchen. The woman looked so real that the waitress followed her back to the kitchen to find her.

Debbie recalled, "When you're sitting at the bar late at night and the lights are off in the dining room . . . the doors to the kitchen will open up. We've run back to see if somebody had walked into the kitchen but nobody would be there. The doors swing open so the lights in the kitchen filter in and draw our attention to them. There was a period of time when she was around a lot. It was always after the dining room closed and she was always going into the kitchen."

A fourth presence dwells with the lady in green on the second floor. He is a bearded man glimpsed once by Tom Schuerman.

Tom had turned off several spotlights that had been used to illuminate some carved gargoyles on the facade. He was going through the old kitchen upstairs when he glanced into a mirror above the sink and saw an older, bearded, dark-haired man's face staring back at him. The outside lights have remained on since then.

The last two ghosts at Chances have only been seen in a painting of the restaurant that hangs on a dining room wall. They are twin children, a boy and a girl, portrayed playing around a kid's wagon in the foreground of the picture. The artist lives in the area. She is also a psychic.

"When she gave me the painting, I asked her where she got the idea for the kids in the painting and she said that they're playing here, this is their play area. Someone had told me about the [ghost] kids before but I didn't want to believe it."

Debbie said the children are the ones "doing their playful things."

In fact, all the ghosts at Chances are illustrated in the picture. The psychic painted everyone she felt was at the restaurant. But she didn't know their names, nor very much about them.

"What I've come to terms with over the years is that the ghosts are souls that are lost, that they're in this in-between stage with unfinished business. I don't know what that unfinished business is, but I've always thought that if the Civil War soldier could be reunited with his love upstairs then their business would be finished and they'd move on."

Does Debbie ever want to help them "move on"? Absolutely not.

"This is their home and we're the guests more or less. I get very protective of them. We have a comfortable coexistence. We're comfortable with them. They help us and we entertain them, I guess. I do have this sense when it comes to them of calm and peace."

That does not mean, however, that she would want to live with their steady presence. "I don't know if I'd feel this way if they were in my house. I can walk away from it here every day."

She does have the habit, however, of locking the doors, turning around, and calling "good night" to the lingerers.

Stacy Kopchinski seems almost as comfortable with her unseen helpmates as does her mother. "It's just nice to know they're here, especially when I'm alone closing up the bar. Sometimes you can feel them everywhere, then you know they're all out, but then there are other long periods when they're not around."

Except for a short paragraph on their menu, the Schuermans have not exploited their unique guests. That would be taking advantage of them. And besides, if changes have been made in the building that the ghosts haven't liked, or if there are visitors to whom they've taken a disliking, "we'll know," Debbie added.

Owners and staff keep a wary eye around the place. Stacy avoids the upstairs rooms whenever possible and Debbie does not go alone into the basement.

"Sometimes it's the fear of actually confronting something face to face. What would you do if one of [the ghosts] was actually standing there?" asked Debbie.

What would you do indeed?

Kurt Muellner was pleased that his plans to celebrate his mother's ninetieth birthday were proceeding without a hitch. His son and daughter-in-law were going to attend, as were his cousin and her husband; his godson came up from Chicago. They were all staying overnight at the historic Kewaunee Inn, formerly the Karsten Inn, in the Lake Michigan shoreline community of Kewaunee. His mother's celebration would be held in the inn's dining room. The party was a great success. At the end of the evening, Muellner bid his guests a good night and arranged to meet them the next day for breakfast at the inn. But he wasn't prepared for what they told him when they all came downstairs the next morning.

Muellner's daughter-in-law wanted to know what kind of hotel he'd booked his family into.

At about two o'clock in the morning she awoke to a loud commotion outside her door: laughing, screaming, and hollering suddenly followed by dead silence. Then shortly afterward she heard what sounded like toilets in nearby rooms being flushed all night long.

Muellner's cousin and godson echoed the young woman's complaints when they arrived for breakfast. Loud noises in the middle of the night had kept them awake.

But Muellner, a local businessman and history buff, knew that none of that was possible—his relatives had been the only overnight guests. They could not have heard a commotion from anyone living.

That late night revelry may well have been a "welcome" by the three mischievous ghosts that call the Karsten Inn home. They include old William "Big Bill" Karsten, the inn's 300-pound namesake who bought the property in 1911; a maid named Agatha*, who worked at the inn in the 1920s and '30s and who according to local lore had been Big Bill's mistress; and a five-year-old boy named Billy, Big Bill's grandson who died during a meningitis outbreak in 1940, a few weeks after his grandfather's death.

A front desk clerk says she's heard many stories from departing guests, especially those who stay along the second-floor corridor.

"They tell me they've heard kids running up and down the hall around three in the morning. They get up to look out the door but nobody is there. Some have even heard a kid playing with a ball because the bouncing is what woke them up."

The Kewaunee Inn is actually the second hotel on the corner of Ellis and Lake Streets, within sight of Lake Michigan. The Steamboat House opened there in 1858 and, following numerous owners and name changes, "Big Bill" Karsten bought it in 1911. Less than a year later it burned to the ground. Karsten soon rebuilt a grand, fifty-two room, three-story brick hotel. Included in the new inn were a ninety-seat dining room, a long, elegant tavern with a separate street entrance, and a wide, attractive summer porch.

Remodeling undertaken in the 1960s and '80s seems to have triggered at least part of the ghostly activity. Carpenters working on the third floor felt sudden, bone-numbing drafts but attributed them to typical conditions in an old, poorly insulated hotel. But they weren't entirely convinced.

Nothing evil or dangerous has ever been attributed to the ghosts of the Kewaunee Inn, but they do seem intent on reminding staff and guests in particular of their continued presence.

Sometimes the ghost of a little boy shows up wanting to play, but only if there's a child staying in a room. A typical example is the experience of a family who once stayed for the weekend. After they checked in and had gone to their room to unpack, the couple let their three-year-old daughter explore the hallways. A few minutes later they heard doors slamming from the hallway, looked out, and found their girl looking into the various unoccupied and unlocked rooms.

Her mother asked what she was doing. The child replied, "Looking for that little boy." She wanted to play with him. Her parents quietly explained that there were no little children around.

Inexplicably, the family packed up and left in the middle of the night. As they were checking out with the surprised night clerk, the child ran up to a photo on a lobby wall.

"Mommy, that's the boy I was playing with," she cried out.

The picture was actually that of Bill Karsten Jr., Big Bill's son, taken when he was a little boy. Though he died as an adult in 1964, there was a resemblance between him and his own son, Billy, who died so young.

Another couple had a scarier moment with their own young son. Several times he ran out of the room because he wanted to "play" with the other child he'd seen earlier. Though his parents tried to dissuade him, he kept insisting that the "other boy" wanted him to come out and play. Sometime that night both parents awoke to the sound of the boy's sharp cry. They found a teddy bear on his bed that earlier had been sitting on a shelf. More disturbing was that an old hat pin was stuck in the bear. Apparently the pin had also stuck the boy in the foot. Neither parent had put the teddy in the bed, and the shelf on which it had rested was too tall for the boy to reach.

In Agatha's old room, the former maid seems to be playful or helpful, depending on the guest. A female guest once jotted down a comment in her room's diary and placed the fountain pen alongside it on the desk. Minutes later, when she finished with her shower, the pen was lying several feet away on the floor.

Two overnight guests from Arizona found items in their room rearranged. A straw hat had been moved to the bedpost and the water pitcher moved closer to the sink.

Two men staying in Agatha's room were perplexed that the toilet kept flushing all night, even though one or the other got up several times to adjust it. There seemed to be nothing to account for it.

Agatha insists on having the doors and windows open in her old room.

They are found open "all the time," claims a former owner, even though no one has been in the room. The overhead light might be shut off, windows and door locked, but within a short time hotel workers discover them on and open.

Though he loved to be in the lobby sitting in his favorite club chair, "Big Bill" Karsten spent most of his final days in his private suite, now room numbers 205–210, battling obesity, arthritis, and heart trouble before his eventual death in 1940 at the age of seventy-eight.

It is his ghost that may appear as a dark shadow in those rooms or, as one guest in his old suite found, be the source of the mysterious heavy breathing and wheezing that greeted him when he checked into the room. At other times he'll give out a sharp, unpleasant odor that drifts through the building. Cold spots and mysteriously rearranged furniture in his old room may surprise guests. Another guest suggests Big Bill may wander the hotel—he swears he saw the old man's ghost sitting at the bar, quaffing a beer.

The Kewaunee Inn, through many owners and name changes, seems to survive, arising Lazarus-like from the commercial grave. The mischief-making ghosts seem to thrive as well, leaving guests with special memories they may not have anticipated.

It took Samuel Bradley six years to build the landmark Cobblestone Waystation Inn at East Troy. Beginning in 1843—five years before Wisconsin's statehood— Bradley dutifully hauled thousands of selected cobblestones he'd gathered from the glacial drift fields in southeastern Wisconsin and from along the shores of area lakes. Once he had enough stones he began constructing his "monument," as he termed it, on a corner lot on what is now South Church Street. When it was finished in 1849, Bradley's three-and-a-half-story Buena Vista House was the community's landmark hostelry, noted especially for the unusual third-floor springboard dance floor.

During its first three years, well-known personages stayed there, including, according to legend, Abraham Lincoln during one of his infrequent forays into the state.

But then something caused it all to change. Shortly after the Bradleys paid off the mortgage—years ahead of schedule—Samuel and his English-born wife said they were returning to Britain to visit her family. They never returned, nor is there any evidence to indicate what became of them.

However, some claim that Samuel never really left the old inn and that his ghost is still there.

During the building's late-twentieth-century renovation, workmen and employees reported enough oddities to think *someone* made their home there, someone who made his presence known in most peculiar ways.

A carpenter claimed that someone always seemed to be watching him as he worked. He'd find his tape measure a yard or more away from where he'd put it down. And somehow a clock radio's volume would be cranked up *only* when music came on the air. A remodeling on the third floor included new curtains for the windows. Someone, however, didn't like them; one day employees found them all on the floor. No one admitted being up there.

New pictures were hung throughout the second floor. A manager checking through the rooms is said to have found them all turned against the wall. She straightened them all around, but within half an hour she again found them facing backward. The workmen were working on the exterior that day, and the other three employees were all accounted for.

Then there was the rocking chair. Employees heard it from the third floor—a distinct *creak-creak-creak* on the ancient flooring, especially as managers were closing up around ten o'clock at night. The problem? There was no rocking chair on the third floor.

Though many remain skeptical of the inn's haunting, there is some evidence that as far back as the 1940s, restaurant menus included some brief anecdotes about their "Cobblestone ghost."

Perhaps a former manager got it right when she said that in such an old building "there can't *not* be anything here. Something's got to be around."

The waitress at the Hotel Boscobel had just finished making salads for a private dinner-party when a sudden draught of cold air swept over her. From around the corner in the kitchen came the quick steps of someone walking away. But when she peered through the doorway no one was there. She reported the incident to the manager, who then realized that he had forgotten to turn on the deep fryers. He went in but was astonished to see that they were already switched on. He checked with his son, at work in a different section of the restaurant, but the latter denied having anything to do with it.

Was this another in a line of visits from the ghost of Adam Bobel?

Best known today as the home of the Gideon Bible, the old Boscobel inn dates to a few years after its founder, Adam Bobel, a Prussian emigrant, arrived in town in 1861. Bobel and a partner built the three-story stone structure as a saloon and small hotel. When the Civil War broke out, he served in the Union Army as a sutler, or government approved vendor, selling supplies to soldiers at often-inflated prices. Back in Boscobel, Bobel eventually became the sole proprietor of the hotel, but fire leveled it in 1881. He rebuilt and opened it as the Central House in May 1881. He continued to operate it until he died in 1885.

In later years, it was the chance to greet old Adam Bobel himself and his mysterious girlfriend that attracted visitors to the establishment.

A former bartender said Bobel's girlfriend sometimes joined Bobel on late night, spectral visits. A chef once saw a woman sporting a Victorian, "Gay '90s" bonnet stroll by the bar on her way to the dining room. He quickly followed to take her order, but the dining room was empty.

Bobel sometimes opened and closed doors—and even left tips on occasion for long-suffering waitresses. "I never worried when I was there," one former waitress said. "He never played malicious tricks."

Overnight guests would ask about the elderly man and woman they'd seen strolling down the hall. They were surprised at the couple, as they'd been told they were the only guests that night. When a picture of Adam Bobel was pointed out to them, they readily identified it as the man they had seen.

Sometimes there were only voices. Once, half a dozen of them floated down a hallway where two employees there overheard them. They thought it odd that a group of people might be walking through the place, but soon discovered that no one else was about that night.

The Gideons International had its beginnings in 1898 when two salesmen—John Nicholson and Samuel Hill—stayed at the hotel and fell into a discussion about the lack of an organization for "mutual help and recognition for Christian travelers." They met a year later and decided to act upon their earlier discussion. A subsequent organization meeting in Janesville led to the founding of the organization, best known today for placing Bibles in the nation's hotel rooms.

Adam Bobel may have approved of the project, as he was a helpful sort of person, both in life and after. A waitress was once asked to retrieve a bottle of wine from the wine cellar. When she got downstairs she found the very bottle she wanted propped on top of the wine rack. Someone was trying to make her life easier, she thought.

Though much of the original 1881 exterior remains, the hotel has been closed in recent years. With less overnight traffic through the building, Adam and his lady may now have decided to take up residence elsewhere.

What was known to old-timers as the Harris House Hotel in the town of Brodhead has been around for a century and a half. Through name changes, neglect, closings, disasters, and rebirths, this landmark has been through it all—including the visits of a certain gentle lady ghost.

A vaporous woman drops in infrequently and instigates unusual activities, according to reports of former owners and managers. She seems to be a protective spirit, interested mostly in seeing that the business continues in operation. The building is no longer used as a hotel, but has housed a popular restaurant and bar in more recent years.

A former owner claims to have had two encounters with the ghost: on the first occasion she felt someone's hand touch her shoulder; on the second she followed someone who walked past her down the hallway and into the dining room. But once she got there, there was no sign of anyone present.

Some believe the ghost might be the daughter of the hotel's builder, John Young. The young woman was killed in a 1905 fire there. However, other records indicate that while Young's daughter did indeed die in a fire, it was at her home and not in the hotel.

Perhaps because it may be the first owner's daughter, the ghost seems especially attentive to money matters. Once after tallying up the day's receipts, a manager had taken them to an upstairs office. But as she reached to turn on the lights she saw a woman in a starched, high-collar dress with her hair tied back. She dropped the money and ran. A few minutes later she was returning cautiously to retrieve the cash when she came upon a stranger passed out on the hall floor. She later learned he had broken in sometime earlier with the intention of stealing the day's earnings but had collapsed unconscious from the effects of a drug overdose. The manager thought the ghostly woman might have been trying to warn her about the robber's approach.

Who among us would not welcome a little help with our personal safety— even if offered by a ghost?

Undoubtedly the largest commercial lodging in Wisconsin with resident ghost stories is the Pfister Hotel, in Milwaukee, known for decades as the eternal tramping ground of its founder, Charles Pfister. By his nightly strolls he means no more than to wish his many guests a pleasant stay.

This Victorian "Grand Hotel of the West," as the hotel was termed when it opened in 1893, was built at a cost of over one million dollars. It was described as one of the finest hotels between New York and San Francisco. Electricity, fireproofing, and thermostatic controls for every room were innovations at the time. An extensive remodeling in 1962 saw the addition of a twenty-three-story tower and refurbishment of its rooms.

Charles Pfister, according to those who have spotted him standing on the hotel's grand staircase, is an older, portly gentleman whose ethereal poses seem to mirror his posture in his formal lobby portrait. Pfister has also been seen in the "minstrel's gallery" of the hotel ballroom and checking out hotel cleaning supplies in a ninth-floor storage room.

Wayfaring Strangers

At early Wisconsin inns, the very transience of nameless lodgers invited speculation about their purposes. The weary traveler might have emerged on horseback from the woodland trail to see the welcoming glow of oil lamps through curtained windows. Or perhaps he peered through the stagecoach window as the brace of winded horses pulled up under a weathered signboard rocking in the wind on a gusty night. Just through the heavy oaken door, the tired, dusty stranger would find welcome respite, even if the bed were made of straw and thrown upon the cold floor, and the food a nearly inedible gruel made palatable by liberal shots of cheap liquor.

Even worse for the unwary visitor who seemed to have money or possessions or both was the threat of sudden, deadly violence by those without a conscience, whose thirst for quick riches meant a swift stiletto between the ribs, a razor-sharp blade across the neck, or a quick bullet in the back of the skull. Those wayside inns provide the stuff of which ghostly legends are made.

Ethel Van Patten was a child of eight when her parents bought the Evansville House in 1894 and converted it into a boardinghouse. The sixty-year-old former hotel had innumerable rooms, halls, and musty corners where the curious girl reveled in exploring. An old barn, once used as a livery stable, offered a glimpse of pioneer life with its hand-hewn log rafters and windowsills. On the veranda, which stretched halfway around the house, little Ethel would sit for hours listening to the legends and mysteries connected with the aged structure. One particular story came startlingly to life.

One eccentric boarder, Patrick McGlinn, told Ethel that the Evansville House once served as a stagecoach stop on the road between Madison and Janesville, Beloit, and other points southward. A number of servants were employed to look after the guests, cook their meals, clean their rooms, and generally attend to the numerous chores connected with the bustling hostelry.

A certain young and willing chambermaid had the misfortune of falling in love with a married salesman who made the Evansville House a frequent stop on his travels. The liaison continued for several months until the salesman, despairing of his inability to marry his lover and not wanting her to marry another, strangled her. The salesman fled the inn in the middle of the night with the intention to jump aboard a passing freight train. Instead, he slipped and was crushed under the train wheels.

Little Ethel Van Patten was thrilled by the tale. Less enthralled were her parents, who, as good, skeptical Yankees, placed little credence in McGlinn's narrative and were upset at the man's earthy language and rough ways. He was not, they thought, the best influence on their daughter. But Ethel didn't care. Mr. McGlinn told terribly exciting stories filled with history and romance and danger.

Even Patrick McGlinn may not have known the full impact of his story, for on one cold winter's night the long-dead salesman seemed to be on the prowl once again.

Mr. and Mrs. Van Patten heard footfalls descend a staircase near their bedroom. It sounded like a man wearing heavy boots walking down the steps. Night after wintry night the scenario repeated itself—footsteps echoing through the quiet halls at about three o'clock in the morning.

At first the family suspected McGlinn, figuring he was adding a bit of mischief to his morbid tale. Further, he claimed to be a former sea captain and habitually wore heavy brogans.

Van Patten confronted McGlinn, but, as might be expected, the merry Scotsman in his rich burr and heady vocabulary steadfastly denied being the culprit.

On one particular winter's night, the couple settled down in bed and listened for their mysterious intruder, determined that on this occasion they would catch McGlinn in the act and put an end to this nonsense once and for all. Right on schedule they heard the footfalls . . . down the staircase . . . into an office on the first floor . . . and finally the front door opened and slammed shut.

Mr. Van Patten raced down the stairs. The outer door was bolted from the inside! He unhitched the latch and looked out. A fresh snowfall revealed no footprints. It was undeniable: no one had passed through the front door, at least physically, despite what the Van Pattens seemed to have heard.

Undeterred, Mr. Van Patten scurried back upstairs and threw open the door to McGlinn's room. In the bed near the wall he lay, sleeping quite soundly in his nightshirt and snoring away.

And what's more, the mysterious intruder was never heard from again. Future owners of the place were reportedly never troubled by the phantom . . . or at least never admitted that they were. Was it only Patrick McGlinn adding a bit of playful sound effects to his tale? Perhaps.

The Evansville House was operated as the East Side Inn for many years before being torn down. Today in its place on East Main Street is a gas and convenience store.

Much to the chagrin of one Simon Brechler*, a badly weathered, rundown inn was the only available lodging in the small Wisconsin frontier village he rode into that night. He had spent weeks scouting for a farmstead, and now that he had found the site, he decided to spend the night in a nearby settlement. Simon's family awaited word from him in New York State. All that could be said in favor of the old inn is that it provided a roof over his head, a cheap meal, and a dry room. Perhaps tomorrow he would find something better.

He went directly to his room. The furnishings were sparse—a bed and washstand—but there was one object that seemed terribly out of place in the rundown hostel: against a wall stood an immense, ancient bookcase, its shelves sagging under the weight of scores of volumes covered in dust.

Yet Brechler hardly noticed; he fell asleep before the sun had slipped below the horizon. The night was not half gone when he awoke with a start, sensing movement in the corner of the dark room. He lay perfectly still, unsure if his inner alarm had not been triggered by a dream. He rolled over in bed and looked around the room. The moonlight filtering in through the dusty, uncurtained window fell upon a cloaked figure huddled near the bookcase. Silently and methodically she—for the slight figure made him quite sure it was female— lifted books from the case and placed them in piles on the floor. When the last shelf had been emptied, she reversed the process until once again the bookcase was full. With that, the figure faded away.

To say Simon Brechler was astonished, puzzled, and distressed by his night caller would be quite an understatement. He did not have a clue as to the figure's identity, nor what she may have been searching for. He was too tired to think much more about it. Perhaps in the morning a few discreet questions asked of the locals might solve the mystery.

After breakfast, he found an old man willing to talk about the specter. Yes, there was such a thing in the hotel, the codger admitted.

"But don't you never speak to it!" he warned. "I say that in earnest, sir. It's plain awful what's happened to them who did."

Really not wanting to chance another night in the hotel, Brechler looked for other lodgings but could find none. At sundown he reluctantly retreated to his room. Sleep came in fits and starts. Then, as on the previous night, he heard a faint rustling near the bookcase. She was back—hunched over the bookcase, performing the same bizarre ritual as the night before.

"What in heaven's name do you want?" Brechler cried out. "Who are you? Why do you so disturb my sleep?"

The dark-robed figure stopped what she was doing and turned slowly toward the bed. She glided silently across the room toward him. Brechler drew back in horror. He was looking not into the face of a woman but rather the hollow eyes and gaping mouth of a skull. The form bent slowly over the cowering homesteader and raised its bony hands. The wraith's thumbs came down upon his forehead and pushed him deep into the mattress and into unconsciousness.

How long he remained senseless he did not know. When at last he was able to look around, it was daylight and the apparition was gone. His head burned and ached as if a flaming log had been dropped on his skull.

He struggled out of bed and looked into the mirror above the washstand. Two black thumbprints were burned into his forehead. Simon Brechler carried those scars until the day he died.

The Wisconsin Dells is the most popular vacation destination in Wisconsin. Tens of thousands of tourists flock each year to this spectacular terrain of towering bluffs and deep ravines sculpted over the millennia by the Wisconsin River. The twenty-first-century visitor enjoys water parks and ski shows, boat rides and musical performances, dozens of campgrounds, novelty shops by the score, faux Indian pageants, and other man-made attractions too numerous to mention.

Little does the modern visitor imagine, however, the eerie entertainment once provided at the Dell House, a riverside inn built in 1837 alongside a sandy beach and near a fresh water spring not far from the Narrows.

A man named Allen built the inn with an eye toward providing the river men with a bit of entertainment, 1800s style. The temptations were those of the flesh—bad whiskey, crooked gambling, bawdy songs, and frontier ladies more than willing to exchange what was left of their virtue for a few dollars. More often than not, violence capped the evening's "festivities." The churning, muddy waters of the Wisconsin River claimed the earthly remains of not a few luckless revelers.

The days when river traffic was king soon passed and the Dell House lost its reason for being. By the turn of the twentieth century, the hostelry was abandoned, its empty hulk mute testimony to an earlier, vanished—but not mourned—way of life. Only a few adventurous tourists and locals camped in the shaded glen where the hotel once stood.

By daylight the old place had what an early resident of the Dells described as "an indescribable charm of romantic interest."

But nightfall brought stories of unquiet happenings within the decaying hulk. Some campers swore that cursing and drunken laughter and crashing crockery joined the sighting of vague, fleeting figures in the moonlight. The violent and bloody history of the inn replayed in startling, supernatural fashion.

The legacy of the Dell House ended for good late one night in 1910 when what was left of the place burned to the ground. A towering brick chimney above a fireplace as tall as a man remained for many years. In time the unforgiving forest claimed it as well.

Peace officers were few and far between on the early Wisconsin frontier. The only law was that which pioneers established among themselves. Justice was usually meted out swiftly to those transgressors unfortunate enough to be captured.

So it was that the old Ferry House Inn at Merrimac came to be associated with a "galloping ghost" during the nineteenth century. The grim visage raced along the road near the inn astride a coal-black stallion.

Those who claimed to have seen the mounted, spectral horseman believe he was in some way connected to a bloody murder at the inn, though official records fail to show such an event. Victim or perpetrator—we will never know which.

Mrs. Courtney's Return

Mr. and Mrs. William Courtney had never gotten along. Mrs. Courtney had left her moody Irish-Canadian husband at least once, but she always returned to him and their small farm in Brooks' Corners, a section of Vinland about seven miles north of Oshkosh.

The uneasy truce between the bickering pair ended on November 4, 1873, when Mrs. Courtney died of natural causes. Not long after William Courtney discovered his wife's body in her bedroom, he moved out of the house and into the home of his mother-in-law about a mile away. He returned only to plant and harvest crops and do the farm chores.

William continued to employ a girl they had hired to keep up with the housework, but she soon decided a new job elsewhere would be better for her health. That's because several days after Mrs. Courtney's funeral, the girl heard sharp raps on the windowpanes in a room adjoining the bedroom where her mistress had died. The girl lifted a corner of the window curtain and peered out. Although she could see no one, the girl was badly shaken and fled to a neighbor's house. She quit that same day.

Hiram Mericle and his family lived on an adjoining farm only a few hundred feet from the Courtney's. Shortly after the hired girl quit, Hiram noticed a light burning in the Courtney house. He knew the place was empty, so with two of his older children he walked over to investigate. From the front yard, they could see that the light was in Mrs. Courtney's old bedroom. As they got closer, the

160

light dimmed and finally went out. Mericle and his children went home quite puzzled. But then before dawn the next morning as Mericle prepared for his morning farm chores, he saw the light again shining from next door as brightly as before.

Other neighbors soon noticed lights in the Courtney house. When several of the neighbors investigated, they claimed to have seen a shadowy form pass in front of the light. "Look, it's Mrs. Courtney!" one of them screamed.

From then on everyone in Brooks' Corners said Mrs. Courtney haunted her old house. Lights of varying shapes and forms continued to appear regularly. Sometimes they were circles about six or seven inches in diameter, with smaller lights circling the larger ones. At other times, the lights were ovular in shape. Unnervingly, the light most frequently seen was a flame with clearly defined edges, surrounded by inky darkness.

The light came from all parts of the main house as well as the one-story rear addition that housed the kitchen.

On November 20, 1873, the *Oshkosh Weekly Times* dispatched a reporter to check out the rapidly spreading ghost story.

The reporter reached the house of one Jacob Whitacre by nightfall, about half a mile from Courtney's. The newspaperman dined with the Whitacres and listened to their stories; each family member had seen the lights at one time or another. The Whitacres seemed to him to be intelligent, straightforward people who had seen something for which they had no explanation.

After supper, Jacob Whitacre led his guest down the road to the mysterious house. There a group of about a hundred men and boys had already gathered in the late-autumn snow, stamping their feet to keep warm and comparing notes on what each claimed to have seen. A bright light suddenly blazed in one of the windows and just as quickly vanished, again plunging the house into darkness. Gusts of wind churned the loose snow and finally the reporter grew cold and disappointed at not witnessing further manifestations. He and Whitacre walked over to the Mericles' farm to warm up. They returned a few hours later, arriving in time to see a series of bright lights in the house exploding like, as the reporter termed it, flashes of lightning.

On November 21 and 22, large crowds again converged on the haunted house but no lights appeared. The Oshkosh newsman speculated that since a family was planning to move into the house no more lights of a ghostly nature would be seen. He didn't explain how he had arrived at this conclusion.

The reporter continued to try to solve the mystery lights puzzle. He interviewed William Courtney, who claimed the lights were the work of a prankster who had gained access to the house through an unlocked cellar door.

Courtney also said he had found the kitchen door kicked in. He thought the culprit was someone who wanted to rent the place and was trying to scare off the man to whom Courtney had promised it.

The hundreds of nightly witnesses did not agree. Many told the reporter that no one in their right mind would brave the wild winds and deep snows to break into a vacant house night after night. Observers noted that the lights did not reflect off anything around them, often flashed like lightning, and sometimes changed shape or created halos. It seemed unlikely that kerosene or oil lamps could have produced such effects.

The puzzle was never really solved. The Oshkosh newsman did not think the witnesses were fantasizing, although the possibility of pranksters at work could never be ruled out completely. Apparently no one in the crowd was brave enough or foolhardy enough to break into the Courtney home at the moment when the lights made an appearance.

Voice on the Bridge

The village of Omro, Wisconsin, was a center of Spiritualist activity in the nineteenth century. In this little settlement near Oshkosh, the First Spiritualist Society hosted eminent Spiritualists and mediums from all over the United States—the Davenport brothers, Moses Hull of Boston, Benjamin Todd of Michigan, Susan Johnson of California, and many others. Séances were performed, spirits materialized, but the combined efforts of local and visiting mediums failed to solve the murder of a local man.

Sometime between nine and ten o'clock one night, farmer John Sullivan left Omro, where he had spent the day trading. His thoughts must have been on home and a good night's sleep after a long day in town.

His movements were later reconstructed, as there were no eyewitnesses to what happened. Several people who lived near the Fox River said they heard a sharp cry followed by a gunshot. A short time later, Sullivan's body, with a single, fatal gunshot wound, was found next to a footbridge across the river. Law enforcement officials were baffled because Sullivan had no known enemies nor was he carrying a large amount of money after having spent most of it on supplies.

Séances buzzed with questions directed toward the nether world asking for the identity of the killer; there was never an answer.

Then some weeks later, a Mr. Wilson happened to be crossing the same bridge at the same time of night when out of the darkness he noticed what appeared to be a man just ahead of him shouldering a rifle. A voice from out of nowhere whispered, "That is the gun that killed John Sullivan!" Wilson heard a terrified scream, a loud gunshot, and then the man and rifle vanished.

Wilson ran back to the village to relate his experience. He swore that he would recognize the murder weapon—and the murderer—if he ever saw them again. He later claimed that he had indeed seen both but then refused to identify them. The spirits remained silent as well. Sullivan's murder remained unsolved.

He Comes by Night

The winter nights were long and lonely for the families of nineteenth-century Wisconsin lumberjacks. While husbands and fathers lived in lumber camps as they cleared the great northern pine forests, wives and children stayed behind in scores of small settlements, sometimes hardly more than clusters of log shanties, scattered across the state. From Brule in the northwest through Minocqua, Hazelhurst, Conover, and Split Rock toward the east, the villages, especially during the harsh winter months, were as isolated as any place on earth.

One such village was West Algoma, near Lake Winnebago and since incorporated into the city of Oshkosh.

The legend has persisted that in one particular year over a century ago, West Algoma's isolation was disrupted each winter night by the terrifying appearance of a towering figure swathed in a black cape.

The stranger's routine never varied. At the stroke of midnight he would emerge from the shadows at the edge of town, walk slowly with the aid of a crooked cane down the wooden sidewalk, and then vanish into the night. He never spoke aloud to anyone nor did he alter his gait. Villagers claimed the timing of his arrival varied by less than a minute.

Townsfolk hid behind barred doors and curtained windows, afraid to interfere with or question the mysterious visitor. Few could sleep until he was gone.

On one particular night, however, a teenage boy approached the stranger. He claimed that beneath the figure's dark cap he had seen a pallid, expressionless face devoid of life. Terrified, the boy fled.

Night after night, week after week, and month after month of that long winter this *thing* walked the streets of West Algoma. But on the day in spring when the men returned from the woods the visitor vanished, never to return.

Some claimed he was a ghostly town crier keeping watch over the lonely families until their menfolk returned from the forest. Then again, the night walker may just have been one villager's imaginative and ultimately successful effort to keep wives and children close to home on those cold and desolate nights.

The Phantom Rider
of Pumpkin Hollow

As dusk settles on quiet autumn nights over the south line road near the crossroads settlement of Oak Hill, a few miles south of Sullivan, in Jefferson County, old-timers say an Indian brave still gallops through the gathering darkness, a garland of sliced pumpkin around his neck. High above his head he holds his ancient rifle, a pumpkin speared around its barrel. His fast pony is festooned with even more pumpkin chunks. The legend of the phantom rider begins in Wisconsin's early pioneer days and bears more than a casual resemblance to Washington Irving's "Legend of Sleepy Hollow."

Harry Osgood operated a tavern on that road frequented by ox drivers and travelers on their way to Milwaukee. The structure was little more than a log shelter along the rutted trail. Nevertheless, it was a favorite stop.

Early one fall evening, an Indian arrived at the tavern astride a lively pinto pony. He was already tipsy when he stumbled into the establishment but demanded more whiskey. Osgood refused. Instead, he gave the brave a number of ripe, bright orange pumpkins. The Indian was delighted, impaling the largest one on the barrel of his rifle. He cut the others into chunks and with some twine draped them around the pony's neck. Pleased with his work, he set off down the trail.

A short way off, pioneer physician Doc Powers was riding toward the tavern after making calls at several homesteads. As he gazed down the trail, he saw the pumpkin-bedecked Indian galloping toward him. The trail was narrow near the spot where the two met. Powers demanded to pass first but the Indian refused. Instead, he bashed Doc over the head with his rifle.

Powers fell from his horse, but what happened next is unclear. One rendering of the legend holds that the physician recovered his senses and grabbed the rifle from the Indian, smashing the weapon against a tree trunk. The young Indian fled across the marsh, and both horses bolted into the forest. Powers knew that men from the tavern would help find his horse.

Another version of the story claims the doctor lay unconscious for some time. When he awoke, pieces of the pumpkin littered the road, but the Indian was nowhere to be seen. The doctor's horse was found a short way off.

Whichever version is correct, Doc Powers swore vengeance on the Indian who attacked him. The doctor made his way to the tavern, where Osgood agreed to help him search for his horse. When the pair reached the spot where the attack had occurred, Powers shook his head over the chunks of pumpkin scattered about. He declared that the name of the area really ought to be changed from Pleasant Valley to Pumpkin Hollow. And so it was.

The Indian was never again seen at the tavern or anywhere else in the region. Wayfarers, however, frequently reported the ghost of an Indian bedecked with pumpkins galloping up and down the south line road for many years. And, some say, when the chill autumn wind scatters brittle leaves down Pumpkin Hollow, the Indian brave is still seen in his garish costume.

The Possession of Carl Seige

Can an evil spirit take over an individual's mind, body, and soul? People have always thought so. In every culture, in every period of history, demonic possession has been recognized. Loud, obscene curses and bile issue from the victim's mouth, body contorting and eyes gleaming with hatred. Often, it's all accompanied by paranormal manifestations—pounding in the walls, the levitation of furniture, and the presence of fireballs.

The causes of demonic possession are little understood. Since possession closely resembles some forms of mental illness, medical treatment is usually tried first. For intractable cases that do not respond to medication, the religious rite of exorcism may be performed to cast out the "demons." No one knows how many exorcisms are performed in this country in any given year because the possessed usually insist upon anonymity and church records are closely held by church authorities.

But the possession of Watertown's Carl Seige became something of a cause célèbre. He was harassed by demons for twenty years and the whole town knew it. His exorcism and the other lurid details of his sensational case were reported breathlessly by Wisconsin newspapers and reprinted by periodicals nationwide. The case remains one of the most often cited reports of "demonic possession."

According to the contemporary accounts, the diabolical manifestations first began when Carl was five years old and living with his family in their native Germany. One day one of Carl's sisters found a duck egg under a tree just

169

outside the door of their small cabin. With typical childlike curiosity, she picked it up and took it to her mother. Mrs. Seige noticed that the egg had a small pinhole in one end. She cautioned her daughter to put the egg back where she had found it. The girl did so. At that moment, the family dog appeared, seized the egg, and ate it. Immediately, he was struck blind and, raging with fright, ran in wide circles through the yard. The child fled, screaming. The dog was promptly shot.

A short time later, the little girl was seized with blindness and spasms and soon was bedridden. She lingered in agony for a year before she died. Carl was attacked with blindness and severe pains that continued for a number of months, leaving him with a limp and a withered, twisted hand. His sight was partially restored, and he survived.

But when Carl turned twelve years old, he endured more physical anguish. Uncontrollable seizures set in, his head was jerked like a puppet by unseen forces, his shoulders twisted, and he was often thrown violently to the ground where he struck out at all who tried to approach him. He frothed at the mouth, his eyes filled with malevolence. If a "fit" overtook him while he was eating, his hands struck his dinner plate, scattering food all over the floor. Sometimes one of these spells would last an entire day. Between attacks, he prayed for deliverance and made the sign of the cross. His prayers went unanswered. So did those of his pious Lutheran family. German doctors, using roots and herbs and all the medicines available at that time, were unable to cure, or even alleviate, the dreadful symptoms of Carl's strange malady.

Finally, in the spring of 1867, when Carl was twenty-four years old, the despairing family—father, mother, three sons, and five daughters—immigrated to Watertown, Wisconsin, a community with a sizeable German population. But their troubles followed them. The sixteen-year-old Seige daughter, a beautiful young woman, was sent to live in the home of the local Lutheran minister to help with the housework and to care for the family's several children. Before long, she became pregnant by the minister and bore a son. In sorrow and shame, she returned to her own family.

But her return precipitated a series of terrifying events. Her brother's demonic symptoms greatly increased. Now the violence was focused upon the baby. Screaming that he intended to kill the infant, Carl would spring toward the child with eyes wild in his pale face, froth glistening on his lips. His terror-stricken sister sheltered the infant as best she could during these tantrums. She slept only fitfully at night, keeping the infant close by; during the day she never let him out of her sight. As fears and tensions mounted, the whole family suffered strange, recurring illnesses marked by dizziness and severe headaches.

In the evenings, unearthly noises shook the house. Open doors slammed shut with no one near them, the windowpanes rattled loudly, even on windless nights, and weird, hollow-sounding noises emanated from one of the rooms.

Late one evening, to the family's horror, an enormous ball of fire appeared on the top of the cooking stove. As they watched, frozen with fear, Carl dashed forward and struck the fireball with his fist. It broke apart, scattering small, glowing globules into all corners of the room. Yet nothing burned, and the fire gradually went out.

Shortly after this incident, the family cow, tied in the backyard, started behaving strangely. She began to rear on her hind legs, and lash out with her tail. Carl, watching her from the kitchen window, gave great shouts of joy. His father could not get near the beast to milk her, and he and his wife were convinced that somehow the demons had gotten into the cow.

The simple family, who had sought sanctuary in the New World from the evil, supernatural forces that seemed to beleaguer them, were engulfed once again by fear and despair. At first they had tried to keep Carl's illness a secret. But as his attacks increased with awesome intensity, Seige knew he needed outside help. In the winter of 1868, he called in a Dr. Quinney, son of a prominent Stockbridge Indian chief. His medical "specialty," if any, isn't known.

Quinney listened to the young man's history, and then administered an herbal remedy. He also applied poultices to Carl's shoulders in an attempt to "draw out" the evil spirits. When the compresses were removed the next day, they were covered with bristles! Those bristles were of different colors and ranged in length from half an inch to three inches. The Indian doctor could not account for them. But the spirit of a long-deceased Mohawk Indian, speaking through a Milwaukee medium, later offered an explanation. This spirit claimed that the bristles were actually "long, hairy worms generated by microscopic animals" found in a spring in Germany, whose waters Carl had drunk as a child. The spirit said these worms were feeding upon Carl's muscles and would eventually kill him. This was an extraordinary diagnosis, to be sure.

Sometime after the bristles appeared, Carl had a violent seizure during which he gave the names of the devils possessing him. One was named Wilhelm Bührer. Seige recalled that Bührer was a desperate man who many years before had murdered a hog drover in Germany for his money. Was the soul of this murderer tormenting Carl? Some people thought so.

When Dr. Quinney could offer no further help, the family turned to a Spiritualist medium. He arrived at the house to find Carl black in the face and gasping for breath. The medium claimed that a snake was inside the young man, pushing its head up into his throat. Some pointed to Carl's chest, where they said they could feel the lashings of its tail. The medium pushed a goose quill down Carl's throat then waved the quill over his head. Finally, Carl became quiet and was helped into bed. Relief, however, was short lived.

When the demons returned, the Seiges decided to appeal to the local Catholic priest. He declined to intervene, however, because Carl was not Catholic. However, when the Milwaukee bishop visited Watertown and heard the story, he agreed to arrange for an exorcism.

On an early November day, Carl was brought to the Catholic church in Watertown for the rites. The church pews were crammed with Catholics, Protestants, and others of no particular religious persuasion. A sudden hush spread over the congregation as Carl Seige was laid upon the altar. His face was wan, his slender, wasted body corpselike. Seven priests, in cassocks, white surplices, and purple stoles, took their places beside the stricken man. Their faces divulged no fear, yet each, in his heart, recognized the dangers inherent in the ritual—of conversing with the demons, of being attacked psychologically in such ways that they themselves might be overcome by the evil spirits they sought to cast out.

"Almighty Father, Everlasting God . . ."

They recited in unison, each priest tracing the sign of the cross over the young man's head.

"We beseech thee, this day, to help us cast out from thy beloved servant, Carl Seige . . ."

Each priest sprinkled holy water upon the victim.

"Those demons that torment and seek to destroy . . . and by thy infinite mercy . . ."

Each priest laid hands upon the prostrate form before him.

"In the name of the Father, and of the Son, and of the Holy Ghost."

Then came the words of ancient prayers, powerful incantations used for centuries to drive evil from the earth. The clerics knelt in a circle around Carl. At the back of the altar a picture of the Holy Virgin glowed in the candlelight, and flanking her was burning incense giving off a heavy, pungent fragrance.

The prayers, the sprinklings of holy water, the sign of the cross were repeated—over and over with soft yet urgent insistence.

Suddenly Carl's head jerked, and from his gaping mouth the evil spirit spewed invectives. It shouted obscenities in German, mocking the holy water, threatening to surround the church with its own water, which it would purify. The forces of God and Satan had met. The priests' faces, shadowed by the flickering candlelight, were fixed as if carved of stone. The demon laughed raucously at the prayers, telling the priests they had not found the right one. Then it began speaking in tongues—snatches of Gaelic and Latin mingled with a strange vocalizing that resembled no spoken language. Undeterred, the priests continued their prayers, beads of sweat sparkling their brows. Yet they spoke with confidence, with a discipline born of long training. And the congregation watched, some moved to tears by the rite, others stoic and calm.

When the last cold rays of the setting sun vanished below the windowsills of the church, the exorcism was halted. The exhausted priests were cautiously optimistic—they told the assembled congregants that four demons had been cast out. But there were more.

On the next day, Carl was again placed upon the altar before the picture of the Holy Virgin, and the priests resumed the long ritual. Three more demons were cast out.

And on the third, and final, day, the last demon agreed to leave if all the persons assembled would leave with him. All but three acquiesced, and, to the great joy and relief of Carl, the churchmen, and the congregation, the devil departed. The miracle was complete.

A subdued and grateful Carl, along with his family, joined the Catholic Church. They hung a crucifix on the wall and bought prayer books and rosaries. And Carl attended Mass each morning.

One month later, however, another devil appeared. This one was successfully cast out, but not before shouting, with glee, that four more demons remained.

Here the story of Carl Seige fades from the newspapers. Perhaps the demon was wrong and its four brethren decided to leave on their own. It was 1870 and the press had more important stories to write about. Wisconsin communities were astir with the issuance of railway bonds, and with the outbreak of the Franco-Prussian War in Europe.

No one will ever know the true nature and dimensions of Carl's illness. Was he mentally ill? Or was he really possessed by supernatural, earthbound entities that invaded his body to torment him with their evil thoughts and fears? Today's physician may have diagnosed Carl as an epileptic. The many films, books, and television programs about the rite of exorcism, however, illustrate the continuing fascination we have with this ancient evil. The Catholic Church revised its Rite of Exorcism as recently as 1999. Today, doctors must examine a candidate to determine if the person has a mental or physical ailment before an exorcism will be considered.

There is one postscript to the story of the Seige family. The minister who fathered Carl's nephew was arrested on a charge of seduction and committed to the county jail. After being confined for a month, he tore his blankets into strips and hanged himself in his cell. It is said that the child and his young mother continued to live happily in her parents' home.

Murder on the Boardwalk

Back when Oshkosh was a bustling frontier town that spilled across the plain, sawmills on both banks of the Fox River hummed incessantly, turning out pine lumber and shingles, while factories produced finished wood products. Lumberjacks roared into town on payday and their heavy drinking in Main Street saloons often ended in brawls.

One night, a rural man who had been shopping in town started homeward carrying a rocking chair. His young son accompanied him. The sidewalks at that time were high boardwalks, and as the pair passed a large grove of gnarled oak trees, the father decided to rest for a moment. He put down the chair and, elated over the splendid bargain he had struck with the shopkeeper, sat down to rock.

Suddenly from out of the darkness beyond the trees two drunks appeared. Resentful of the man's obvious delight in his new chair, and spoiling for a fight, they taunted the stranger. The quarrel soon got out of hand and the drunks killed the man and ran off.

The boy, meanwhile, had dived under the boardwalk. When the assailants left, the child raced across the street for help. By the time help arrived, his father was dead in his chair.

For years afterward, travelers claimed that they heard the creaks of the rocker and the groans of the dying man in the grove where he had been slain. And those who are keen of ear say that the eerie sounds can still be heard, carried by the wild wind of a stormy night.

Footsteps in the Dark

The house at the crest of High Street in Pewaukee projects the solidity of a medieval fortress. Built in the nineteenth century when the octagon craze swept the Midwest, the three-story, eight-sided cement home, with walls eighteen inches thick, has permanence about it that modern houses lack. Yet the dark hardwood trim, the lofty windows, the carpenter's lace that embellishes a second floor porch, and the towering ash and maple trees that surround it soften the severity of its lines. To the casual observer, the house appears an intriguing architectural folly; to those familiar with its history, it is remembered as the house of haunting footsteps—the abode of some unseen, unknown, ghostly nightwalker.

The site originally held a log house. But after this structure burned to the ground, Deacon West, a blacksmith, bought the property and had a house put up in the late 1850s. Several years later, West too lost his home in a devastating fire. Only the massive walls remained.

The next owner, Ira Rowe, sold the place to Col. N. P. Iglehart from Kentucky. Iglehart, who spent his summers in Pewaukee, rebuilt the house into its present form in about 1873. He also discovered springs on the expansive property and soon established a small home business, bottling the water and selling it under the label Oakton Springs Water.

In the early 1900s, Audrey D. Hyle, a Milwaukee attorney, owned the house. And it was during his proprietorship that the unearthly footsteps were first heard. Someone or something seemed to wander through the vast rooms

175

and corridors at precisely ten forty-five each evening. Whatever "it" was never bothered anyone nor showed itself. Sleeping residents were sometimes half awakened by the footfalls but drifted back to sleep as they faded.

In the 1930s, Mr. and Mrs. Joseph Zupet lived in the haunted house, and by this time the nocturnal visitor had varied its wanderings slightly. It now ascended the staircase from the front hall to the second floor five minutes later, at precisely 10:50 p.m., and descended by another staircase into the garden at 1:20 a.m. Sometimes it paused outside a closed bedroom door, then moved on down the wide hallway. Whatever it was searching for could never be determined. Nothing was ever disturbed or taken.

Nevertheless, the Zupets became apprehensive about what they believed to be their resident ghost and invited a mystic by the name of Koran to visit their home. He was performing at the Milwaukee Theater at the time and welcomed the opportunity to make the twenty-mile trip to Pewaukee. Koran made a thorough investigation and, although he did not identify the phantom, he did assure the homeowners that it was a friendly one. The Zupets put the house up for sale about three years later, but tales of their "haunted house" had already spread; consequently no one wanted to live there.

The octagon house remained vacant for a number of years, but then the housing shortage following World War II brought a succession of renters. Finally, in 1948, Mr. and Mrs. John T. Oswald of Milwaukee bought the house and lived in it until 1966. Today the home remains in private hands.

A possible explanation of sorts for the "mysterious" footsteps came to light when it was discovered that old speaking tubes had been installed throughout the house when it was built so that family members could communicate with each other and with household staff. Over the years the wall openings were covered over, but the tubes were still in place and could transmit sound from one part of the house to another. Yet that doesn't explain the ghost's "punctuality" or the fact that the footfalls seemed to be loud enough to wake sleeping family members.

There have been no reports of ghosts in the Pewaukee octagon house for many decades.

The Hille Curse

Mrs. Dorothy Ransome had a very clear idea of who the phantom was that approached her farmhouse near Waukesha and then vanished at the kitchen door. The ghost was John Hille, the man who built the house over a century ago.

What the ghost of John Hille may not have known is that those appearances were just another chapter in a saga of bizarre, and often tragic, events, including the untimely deaths of a half dozen or more people associated with the farm, that led many to believe the farm known as Ravensholme was cursed.

Dorothy Ransome and her husband, Ralph, purchased the property in 1948. The ghost of John Hille made regular trips to their back door starting in the early 1970s. It was after the ghost's first appearance that Mrs. Ransome began delving into the history of the farm. What she found was chilling.

The history of the farmstead began in 1848, the year Wisconsin was admitted to the Union. John Hille, thirty-seven years old at the time, brought his young wife, Magdelena, and their several children to settle the 146 acres of virgin wilderness bordering the Fox River, six miles southwest of Waukesha. Hille had been born in Hanover, Germany, and immigrated to America in 1837 following the death of both of his parents. He had been apprenticed to a cabinet-maker in Hanover and utilized his skill in New York, where he worked until his move to the Wisconsin frontier. Magdelena Jaquiltard Hille was also an immigrant. She married John in 1837, five years after her own family reached the East Coast from France.

177

The Hilles began their new life in a log cabin near Waukesha. Gradually they built their holdings into a prosperous 215-acre farm with several granaries, barns, sheds, and a spacious stone farmhouse erected from the granite boulders Hille had cleared from nearby fields.

The curse claimed its first victim in 1898 when the Hille family numbered eight. Magdelena Hille became ill and a doctor was summoned. No one knows precisely what happened, but somehow the family physician mistakenly gave Mrs. Hille a fatal dose of poison. A short time later John Hille, the immigrant who had turned a Wisconsin forest into thriving farmland, died at nearly ninety years of age. His death was attributed to natural causes. Shortly thereafter a son, who had been an invalid for some time, followed his parents in death. Two of his brothers had died many years before.

The family, which had been eight, was now five.

Two Hille sons, Oscar and William, and their sister Hulda inherited the large estate. Several other children had moved away and showed no interest in farming. By all accounts, the trio that remained on the farm was well respected by their neighbors and thrifty in their financial affairs, making the farm one of the most profitable in the county.

Nearly a decade passed before tragedy again struck the Hille family.

Oscar Hille died unexpectedly in 1916. He had taken a bull to a water trough early one morning. The animal had been led back to its stall and tethered to a post when it suddenly bolted and crushed Oscar against a wall. He died of internal injuries two days later.

The strangest of all deaths attributed to the "curse" was the macabre scenario played out at the Hille farm two years after Oscar's death.

The war in Europe had reached into America's heartland as young men marched off to battle the armies of Germany's Kaiser Wilhelm. At home, sewing circles formed to make warm woolen clothing for the forces overseas, the Red Cross and YMCA asked for donations, and the purchase of Liberty Bonds and War Stamps were seen as marks of patriotism.

William and Hulda were particularly touched by the war. Both their parents had been born in the land now being torn asunder by battle. They still had many Old World customs; as with other German-heritage families, their hearts must have ached at the suffering and loss on both sides. William didn't like to discuss the war. "It's useless to argue," he often said. That hesitancy to engage his neighbors in talk about the war because of his Germanic background may have led some of his neighbors to suspect him of disloyalty, although members of his family later convincingly rebutted such speculation. The suspicions stalked William and Hulda with tragic consequences.

The morning of July 11, 1918, broke gently over the lazily moving Fox River a hundred yards behind the Hille house. The couple went about their chores as they did each day, but there was tension about them, almost as if their world was about to crumble.

Several weeks earlier, a man named Elder Krause had ingratiated himself with the Hilles and persuaded them to take him on as a hired man. Krause told his new employers that he was from South Milwaukee. But after several days his behavior changed abruptly. Apparently Krause said he was actually an "agent" of the U.S. Secret Service and was there because of reports that the couple were disloyal. It soon became clear that the story was false and Krause's actual purpose was to extort money from William and Hulda, perhaps preying upon the couple's uneasiness. He enlisted the aid of a neighbor boy, Ernest Fentz, who performed odd jobs for William Hille. Newspaper accounts of the day say Krause and Fentz threatened the Hilles with "exposure" as disloyal Americans unless they acquiesced to their demands.

There is little, if any, evidence that either William or Hulda were disloyal; on the contrary, they gave generously to the war effort. But a packet of letters found later in the Hille farmhouse indicated something mysterious and sinister in Krause's ways. One note from Hulda alluded to some past misdeed that was so bad that she had torn up the letter Krause sent threatening her with its exposure. There is no proof that either brother or sister gave in immediately to Krause's extortion attempt.

Fentz's role in the blackmail is unclear. William Hille had always liked the boy, buying him gifts and often allowing him to ride in a car the Hilles had recently purchased. But he turned against the boy when he teamed up with Krause in the blackmail scheme. Fentz was fired from his job at the Hille farm in late June and told never to return.

The climax to this peculiar chain of events took place shortly before noon on July 11. Krause stopped by young Fentz's home, saying he wanted him to come along to the Hille farm because he "had a good position for him." The lad's stepfather tried to persuade him not to go, but Fentz wouldn't listen and left with Krause.

At the farm, William apparently relented and gave Krause and Fentz thirty dollars for "protection against exposure." Fentz handed Hille a crudely written receipt for the money. It is not known what information would be "exposed" or from whom the Hilles would be safe. The money may have been given to them as much to get them off the property as to buy their silence. Krause, Fentz, and William then fell to arguing. Hulda Hille, who was deeply fearful that the pair were "after them," telephoned a neighbor, Mrs. William Dingeldine, and asked her to hurry over. She had just stepped through the kitchen door when a sharp gunshot blast came from the direction of the living room. Seconds later William walked into the kitchen holding a shotgun. When he saw Mrs. Dingeldine he offered to shake hands, but instead she tried to grab the gun. Hulda stopped her neighbor. "Let him go," she said. "It is for the best. They're after us anyway, and you cannot prevent this. We will be dead before anyone can get here."

In the living room, Ernest Fentz was dead, his body slumped in a rocking chair, the left side of his face torn away by William's shotgun.

William hurriedly pushed past Mrs. Dingeldine and started for the barn. She tried to reason with him, but he brushed her aside, echoing his sister's grim prediction: "They are after me," he said.

Hulda then handed a small wooden box to her neighbor and told her to leave. Hulda said there were valuable papers in the container and she feared that Krause, who was still somewhere on the farm, might find them if he searched the house. Mrs. Dingeldine ran toward home to telephone other neighbors for help. But when she reached the gate, more shotgun blasts came from the direction of a barn. At about the same time Mrs. Dingeldine heard Hulda yelling at Krause to "stay away from here." Krause had apparently heard Hille shoot Fentz and came out to investigate. After Hulda's unexpected warning he fled across a nearby field.

At the Hille farm a slaughter was underway. William methodically killed five horses with shots fired into their heads. Back in the kitchen, he shot and killed a pet dog. Hulda had retreated to her upstairs bedroom, where she lay in bed, an empty bottle of arsenic and a razor blade next to her on a table. The poison acted swiftly, as life drained from her body. The last sound she may have heard was her brother climbing the stairs and going into his bedroom. He sat down in his favorite chair and balanced the shotgun against his legs, its barrel pointing directly at his midsection. Against the trigger was the end of a long, thin strip of wood. He looked for one last time out the window to his beloved farm and remembered that it was the land his father and mother had wrestled from the wilderness and made prosperous. Now he was an old man, and "they" were after him. The crashing roar of his shotgun shattered the stillness. The buckshot tore a gaping wound in his chest. Down the hall, his sister lay dying.

One person murdered, two others dead by their own hands, six farm animals slaughtered. Why? What motivated this orgy of violence? A coroner's inquest and the recollections of the three surviving Hille sisters shed some light on the tragedy.

The sisters claimed that their late brother and sister had been "loyal American citizens." They said Krause's only object in coming to work for William and Hulda had been to get money from them on one pretext or another, and when he could not persuade them in any way he made threats by posing as a secret serviceman. William gave Krause the money, hoping to be rid of him. When Krause and Fentz didn't seem satisfied and William threatened to call the authorities, an argument took place that led to the deaths.

The coroner's inquest left many questions unanswered. Krause was finally located in St. Paul, Minnesota, trying to enlist in the army. The Waukesha authorities were said to have attempted to bring Krause back for the inquest, but his testimony was not included in the coroner's report, according to contemporary newspaper accounts.

The most mysterious aspect of the investigation dealt with a letter found in the box given to Mrs. Dingeldine by Hulda, in which the latter predicted her own death.

It read: "Say girls, the other night there was a slapping noise on the wall. I knew what that meant, so good-bye. All be good with Eliza. There are only these three left. We will try our best to get our rights. Don't take it hard because Bill would have to be in prison for life; he [Krause] was telling Bill about the Japs [*sic*] coming over and how they will come. And then Bill—we would go in the house and shoot them. Give the machine to H. and A. That is W's wish."

Hulda then listed the pallbearers she wanted at her funeral.

What crime had William committed that would be punishable by life imprisonment? How did Hulda know in advance that their deaths were imminent? Was the slapping noise an omen? The questions cannot satisfactorily be answered. We can only surmise that the harassment of the elderly couple by Krause and Fentz had caused some initial anxiety that soon became fear and paranoia. William and Hulda were convinced that some unspoken past deed or utterance would cause their arrest and imprisonment. Sadly, there is little evidence to support their fears. They seemed to be trapped by the malevolent accusations of Krause and Fentz . . . and the Hille curse.

The farm reverted to Mrs. Jacob Hahn of Delafield, Wisconsin, one of the three surviving sisters. Over the next decades a cloud of disaster hung over those who lived in the great old stone farmhouse.

Mrs. Hahn sold the farm in late 1918 to H. S. Kuhtz. The Kuhtz family built a milk house and enlarged the barn. But Kuhtz went bankrupt in 1927 and Mrs. Hahn took the farm back.

From 1927 until 1929, a young couple whose names have been lost to history rented the house. They too suffered the Hille curse. Two of their children died of crib death.

After 1929 no one lived on the farm for nearly twenty years, but that didn't prevent the curse from working its evil. In 1932 a man named Pratt was killed while dynamiting stone in a farm pasture.

On a clear, bright, beautiful morning in September of 1948, Mr. and Mrs. Ralph Ransome first saw the bittersweet sight of the stone house standing abandoned amid weeds as they drove slowly down River Road. The Ransomes owned several health spas in the Chicago area and were looking for property on which they might retire someday. As Dorothy Ransome gazed at the house sitting in a grove of thirteen massive oak trees, she knew it was the house for her family. The couple walked around the yard and peered into the dimly lit rooms through dust-encrusted windows. Mrs. Ransome was determined to find the owner. Incredibly, the house was still in the possession of Mrs. Jacob Hahn, the last surviving Hille sister. The octogenarian agreed to sell the house only after the Ransomes promised to return the home to its original splendor.

Various architects said it would be extraordinarily expensive to restore the house, but Dorothy Ransome insisted that it be saved since she had promised Mrs. Hahn to do so.

The roof was removed and the interior of the house gutted and rebuilt. The only part of the house to remain intact was the eighteen-inch-thick fieldstone walls. The Ransomes lavished vast sums on the house's rebirth. Stained glass from an old funeral home was fitted into several windows; a marble fireplace, which has been the centerpiece of a New Orleans mansion, went into the living room. Crystal chandeliers from the old McCormick mansion in Chicago were wired into the dining room and parlor. At last, the house stood proud and beautiful, surrounded by spacious lawns and clipped hedges. Work on the restoration had taken four years.

In 1953 Anita Ransome, the Ransomes' only daughter, met and married young Andrew Kennedy while they were both students at Northwestern University. The couple moved to the farm that same year, while the Ransomes continued their business obligations in Chicago.

Meanwhile, they began to hear about the tragedies connected with the old farm. Neighbors warned them that terrible things happened to anyone who lived at the old Hille house. Tear it down, the neighbors told them, or dynamite it, but don't live on that farm! The Ransomes were to learn they were not immune to the curse.

The first calamity in the Ransome family was not, however, directly connected with the farm. During a family outing, their grandson, seven-year-old Philip Kennedy, drowned while swimming in Lake Mendota. Nine years later the farm would claim its next victim.

Ralph and Dorothy Ransome retired and moved to the farm they called Ravensholme, adapted from the original English spelling of Ralph Ransome's last name. By then, their daughter and son-in-law had separated. Their son, five-year-old Ransome Kennedy, was living with his grandparents on the farm, enjoying the delights and distractions a young boy can find in the country. But on a March day while the young lad was playing in the barn he fell into an auger and was crushed to death. The curse had struck again.

Dorothy Ransome first saw the ghost of the man on her driveway when on several occasions she would be sitting at the kitchen table stringing beans or reading. A furtive, fleeting shadow slipped across the backyard and approached the kitchen door. Yet when she reached the door to meet the visitor no one was ever there.

At first she thought it simply a shadow cast by a passing cloud on a sunny day. But it persisted. She saw it cross the backyard and later move quickly up the driveway toward the house. She came to believe it was John Hille wearing an old black coat and a crouched hat. The coat rode high on his back but hung down in the front. On each occasion he came to the kitchen door, the entrance the Ransomes believed he used most often in life. Dorothy said he arrived at different times of the day but never at night, always moving briskly with his arms swinging at his sides as if he were in a hurry. Often her cat sat up and stared at the back door at about the same time she saw the figure crossing toward the house.

Dorothy Ransome didn't fear the ghost. She only wanted John Hille—if indeed that's who it was—to be happy and pleased that his old farm has been well cared for.

Why would John Hille haunt his old farm? Because, Dorothy Ransome reasoned, he put his whole being into the farm. "He built this house with his own hands, cleared all the land, too. His family was raised here. I think he loved it so deeply and it meant so much to him that his spirit is still around. The neighbors are scared to death of this place. But I have nothing but love for it."

Mrs. Ransome did not, however, understand the tragedies that afflicted her home. "The neighbors still say there is a curse on this farm. We laughed at it at first. But there has been a constant stream of tragedies. . . . It's always been the same."

Perhaps it always will be.

Marie

The old two-story, brick house in the sixteen-hundred block of Milwaukee's National Avenue looks out of place in a neighborhood of undistinguished apartment buildings, light industrial firms, and small businesses. The place is easy to miss—lofty buildings on either side seem to cast it in perpetual shadow. Sitting rather forlornly as it does atop a raised yard, the house looks every bit its age of a century and a half. But even so there are indications of its once grand appearance—little touches of filigreed wood trim and some decorative patterns in the brick facade around the narrow windows.

Thousands of Milwaukeeans pass along that block every day, ignoring this house just as they would most any other inner city dwelling long past its prime. Certainly Gerald Cummings was in that category. A retired trucking company executive, he lived only a few blocks away.

But for the man whose friends call him Jerry, all of that changed late one September night. As he drove down that block of National Avenue, his attention was suddenly drawn to a young woman standing in the street frantically gesturing to passing traffic. She appeared to be in some sort of difficulty. Jerry stopped to see if he could help. The young woman jumped in the van without a word and silently pointed down the street.

What occurred next will stay with Jerry for as long as he lives. He believes he picked up a ghost. Not just any ghost, mind you, but a revenant known as Marie who haunts that particular house on National Avenue. Although Jerry

Cummings isn't entirely certain it was the ghostly Marie he encountered on that late summer night, his bizarre experience raises intriguing questions not easily answered.

The story of Marie, and the one that Cummings would eventually learn, began a quarter of a century earlier when two men—the late Paul Ranieri and his partner Jeff Hicks—found the perfect house to which they could apply their considerable restoration abilities. They'd looked for nearly a year before discovering what was reportedly the oldest brick home in Milwaukee still on its original foundation. Built between 1836 and 1840, about a decade before Wisconsin became a state, the house had at various times been a private home, an inn, a restaurant, and, its last incarnation before Ranieri and Hicks bought it, a rooming house. But during the summer of 1977 when the men found it, the house was unoccupied, neglected, and in desperate need of repair. Although it had been scheduled for demolition, the pair saw its architectural and historical value. After negotiations with the owners, Ranieri and Hicks bought it in August.

Within just a few weeks, it became apparent that along with the house came a ghost who called herself Marie, a young, attractive lady the men eventually suspected may have lived in the house decades earlier and, according to some records, had either committed suicide or inexplicably disappeared without a trace.

Marie was not shy about making it clear she loved the house, even carrying on a conversation about renovation plans. More often than not, however, Marie was an unseen presence, a hovering custodian whose arrival was signaled by a sudden, sweeping coldness in a room, as if all the windows had been thrown open on a January day.

Over the ensuing months and years, Ranieri and Hicks became, if not entirely comfortable with Marie, at least tolerant of her infrequent forays into the corporeal world.

The condition of the house was such that the men knew they could not move in for some time after their purchase. However, a separate, two-story, attached apartment at the rear of the house was in good condition and could be leased out.

Donald Erbs was the renter. He was the first person to "meet" Marie.

"I didn't see her come in," Erbs recalls of his first, startling experience of seeing an attractive young woman unexpectedly sitting in a chair across from him. "I don't know if she *appeared* . . . but all at once she was there."

He wasn't frightened. For a few brief moments, he thought there was a perfectly natural explanation for her being in the house: an outside door was not far away, and she had simply wandered into the second-floor living room of his apartment, which was separated from the rest of the house by a long hallway with separate doors to his living quarters, the main house, and the street. Perhaps she had somehow slipped quietly up the steps to his room.

He tried to ask her questions but she didn't answer, although she stared at him with what he described as a kind of dreamlike expression on her face. It was also that face, however, that seemed out of sync with the rest of the room. There was a glow about her, Erbs said, "like she was giving off a light. As if somebody had a spotlight on her . . . almost overexposed and much brighter than her surroundings."

She was barefoot beneath a sort of simple, flowing, ankle-length dress with lace at the sleeves and neck. Her long brown hair fell around her shoulders.

Then she surprised him by beginning to talk about the house.

"She told me a little about who built the house, which section had been built when, and why certain remodeling had been done," Erbs said. Just exactly how she came to know all of this he couldn't figure out and she didn't explain.

She then got up and walked out of the room. Erbs followed, but she was gone as abruptly as she had appeared. He reckons she was out of his sight for no more than a few seconds. Although she appeared to be quite real, Erbs said there is no earthly way she could have gotten away so quickly.

"A ghost, or spirit. Of that I am sure. She picked me to talk to for some reason. I don't know why." Although she appeared as a solid form, Erbs couldn't figure out how she could be a living person with the comments she made and the manner in which she acted.

Erbs gave details of his nocturnal visitor to Paul Ranieri, who confirmed that no one had been given permission to be in the house, nor did he know of anyone who matched this woman's description. He was as puzzled about the visit as Erbs.

On the following Saturday the new owners spent the day stripping yellowed wallpaper from the plaster walls and preparing the hardwood floors for refinishing. Erbs also put up a small shelving unit he'd brought from another apartment. After he was done with the job, he walked over to the main part of the house to help Hicks and Ranieri. A crash came from the room he had just left. The shelf had fallen to the floor, but a plant that Erbs had placed on the shelf was sitting intact on the floor a few feet away, as if it had been removed from the shelf before it fell.

It had been, Erbs discovered later that evening as he watched television. Without warning, the same woman appeared in a chair next to him.

Less startled than the first time, Erbs asked her if she had anything to do with the falling shelf. Yes, she allowed, but it was an accident. She had been looking around his apartment and had bumped into it. The plant she'd managed to catch as it slid off the shelf.

Erbs was satisfied with her explanation. But he wanted to know who she was, and so he asked her.

"Marie," the woman replied. She assured him she meant no harm. In fact, she was very happy that the house was being fixed up. She even told him her father was a carpenter and might be of some assistance.

Just as before, the conversation ended abruptly when the woman he now knew as Marie got up and walked out into the quiet of the night.

Paul Ranieri himself was the next one to see Marie. It was in September, after long and tiring hours of renovation. He sat in the still-unfinished front room. As he mulled over the day's work, Ranieri had the impression of being watched, of knowing in some way that he was not the only one in the room. Glancing toward the staircase in the front hallway, he drew back as the lucent form of a woman suddenly materialized, brushed past within inches of where he sat, glided through an archway, and then seemingly melted into a wall. She said nothing, nor did she look toward him.

He realized the woman was remarkably similar in appearance to the person Donald Erbs had encountered, including the dark hair and long gown.

"I wasn't really afraid," Ranieri said, adding that for a few seconds, almost echoing Erbs's first impression, he thought she was an unexpected visitor. But there was one significant difference: Erbs had described Marie as a solid figure whereas Ranieri quickly realized the person he watched was a ghost—walls and the few pieces of furniture were visible through her.

However, Erbs's next encounter with Marie, about ten days later, seemed to confirm that both men had seen the same woman.

It was about ten thirty in the evening when Erbs climbed the steps to his bedroom. When he reached the top landing, he glanced into the small living room where he had first encountered Marie. He jumped when he saw a transparent Marie standing near the door. He quickly backed away. She vanished, perhaps frightened away by his behavior.

A few weeks later, Erbs was again visited by Marie in his apartment shortly after Ranieri and Hicks had started probing around the earthen-floored basement, which was, as in many old houses, damp, small, and cramped by today's standards. It was sectioned off into several rooms with rough-hewn doors connecting them. Broken dishware, musty jars, and old furniture lay scattered about. The men wondered if it might be useful to conduct a more formal survey of the basement debris, considering the history of the house. They contacted an urban archaeologist at a local university who agreed to take a look. In the meantime, they suspended their work.

That's when Marie paid her next visit to Erbs. She was concerned that the men weren't working in the basement anymore. He gave the reason, but it didn't seem to satisfy her. She asked him to follow her and guided him down to the basement. Once there she pointed to a wall. Puzzled, Erbs walked over to take a look. He couldn't see anything interesting, but when he turned to ask her a question she had again departed.

Erbs, Ranieri, and Hicks took a more careful look at the wall the next day and discovered that a section was newer than the rest. They knocked out those bricks and started digging in a tight crawl space beyond. They found pottery shards, pieces of jewelry, and bones, later determined to be from a dog that had apparently been buried there.

Those aged dog bones may explain two other odd events during the house's early renovation. Late one night as Ranieri lay in bed reading, he noticed his pet cat cowering under a chair on the far side of the room. As he leaned over the edge of his bed to calm the cat, Ranieri came eyeball to eyeball with an aged bull terrier that looked decidedly unfriendly. Yet the only dog in the house was a Siberian Husky, and it was downstairs.

Jeff Hicks also had an encounter with a ghost dog. It was near the end of October as he worked late one evening in the basement. He heard what he thought were metal tags on a dog's collar coming up from behind him. Thinking it was their Husky, he turned around but saw nothing. The door leading upstairs was shut.

Although Hicks was the only one of the three who did not see Marie, he thought he felt her presence in another way. He had discovered a door in the basement wedged open. He tried unsuccessfully to close it but could move it only a few inches, as it stuck fast on the uneven floor. About a week later, he discovered the door completely closed. From that point on he was able to open and close the door at least halfway before it became stuck again. Earlier Marie had told Donald Erbs that her father *could help* with the restoration.

There was also the matter of the basement lights. They seemed to have a mind of their own. As often as eight to ten times a week, Ranieri or Hicks found the lights down there ablaze. The pair were doubly puzzled: not only had no one been downstairs, but three separate light switches had to be flipped on and that can only be done from the basement itself.

Jerry Cummings knew nothing of these decade-old events when on that late September night he stopped to help what he thought was a young woman in distress. And even if he had known the house's haunted history, it's doubtful that would have fully prepared him for his experience.

A lifelong Milwaukee resident who once had a tryout with the Green Bay Packers, Jerry is an unassuming retiree who lived quietly with his wife Audrey less than two miles from the house on National Avenue. He graduated from a Catholic boy's high school and went directly to work for his father's appliance delivery trucking business on South Ruthton Avenue. He worked there all his life, eventually assuming ownership of the business after his father passed away. He retired after selling the business to his son-in-law.

His life revolved around his work, his family, and that moment of glory in 1955 when he came close to playing with the vaunted Packers. It's a part of his life he disclosed early on in a conversation. But ironically it was his lack of a college education that was his downfall in professional football.

"That was a big deal. The Packers wanted college boys. A sports announcer in Milwaukee by the name of Earl Gillespie helped me get my tryout. I was very lucky. Actually, my dad was kind of against me trying out. He was afraid I was going to get hurt. At that time, football was very different that it is now. I played two positions on offense and defense, guard and tackle. That's not like it is now."

He did go on to play semi-professional football for a few years until turning his full attention to the trucking company.

Jerry's encounter with the woman on National Avenue occurred a few years before his retirement.

"The date was September 20. I was watching a bowling team my wife and I [sponsored]. They bowled a 9:00 p.m. shift, at what was called LinMor Lanes, over at the corner of Eighteenth and Greenfield. So after they got done bowling I left, probably around midnight. I went to an all-night restaurant between National and Mineral on Sixteenth Street."

He left the restaurant sometime between one and two in the morning and headed home. He climbed into his van, which was parked across the street, and drove down to National Avenue. The traffic was still considerable even at that time of night.

The young woman was standing in the street directly in front of the house Ranieri and Hicks had remodeled, frantically waving her hands, like she was in trouble. Nobody slowed down until Jerry pulled over. She appeared to be in her early twenties with dark, reddish hair falling to her shoulders. She wore a light jacket over a blouse and slacks. Oddly, she did not carry a purse or handbag of any sort.

Jerry stopped and asked her if she was all right. She nodded.

"I asked her if she needed a ride someplace. She got in the van and I asked her where she wanted to go," Jerry remembered. Strangely, the woman merely *grunted* and pointed down National Avenue in a westerly direction, the same way he was headed. Jerry couldn't understand the point she was trying to make and gave her a pencil and paper. He carefully asked her to write down her name and where she wanted to be taken.

"All she wrote was that her name was 'Mary,'" Jerry said. She seemed confused at other questions and somewhat agitated. "I felt sorry for her because I had no idea what was wrong."

He drove down National Avenue toward Twenty-Sixth Street. She frenetically waved for him to turn at that corner. A block later she again motioned for him to turn and then indicated she wanted him to stop in the middle of the block, on Mineral Street. There was no sign of life on the primarily residential street, although there are two churches at either end of the block. A large, older three-story house and garage were opposite where he pulled over. The lights were off in that house, and indeed in every other building on the block. Streetlamps from the Mineral Street and National Avenue intersections threw scant illumination on a handful of cars parked in that block.

She murmured something; he thought she said, "You nice man." Then she opened the door and climbed out. She pushed the car door but it didn't close all the way. The dome light stayed on so he waited for her to push the door shut. He peered through the passenger-side window but he couldn't see her. He feared she had fallen. He quickly got out and walked around to the passenger side.

"She was nowhere around. No place. No sign of her whatsoever. I don't know how she could have gotten away. . . . It was only a matter of ten or fifteen seconds between the time she got out and the time I got out."

Jerry didn't see any place she could have gone to in such a brief time. He looked up and down the street and listened for footsteps, but there was absolutely no sign of life on the entire block. The few houses were not close enough for her to run into, and it didn't make any sense to him that she would have been hiding.

He drove around the block still looking for her. After he gave up, he headed home to tell his wife about his peculiar experience. The color was drained out of his face. He told her the story—that he was certain he had picked up a ghost.

Jerry allowed the incident to recede from his mind until the following year, when his wife, Audrey, gave him a copy of the first edition of this book as a gift. She inscribed in it: "To My Own Ghost Hunter."

"I read [the book] and pointed out the story [of Marie] to my wife and I showed her the picture of the window of the house. She said 'For goodness' sake that says the house is on National Avenue.' I thought that had to be it," he recalled. Coincidentally, Audrey worked at an insurance company in the same block of the same street.

An old photograph of a young woman that Paul Ranieri and Jeff Hicks found in the house was included with the original story of Marie. The men thought it *might* have been Marie. It showed a young woman, probably in her late teens or twenties with bare shoulders above a low-cut gown and a bobbed hairstyle fashionable in the early twentieth century.

Jerry saw some similarity between the girl he met who called herself Mary and the one in the photograph. "The girl I picked up had longer hair, darker, to her shoulders, kind of red from what I could make out when the light went on in the van. I looked at the picture [in the book] a few times to see if it could have been her. I can't say for sure."

So what happened to Jerry Cummings on that late Friday night in September?

The simple truth is he doesn't know to this day if the woman was a *real* woman in some sort of crisis, or Marie of National Avenue asking this kind man for a ride. The destination the hitchhiker directed him to seemed pointless: no late night businesses to work at, no homes with welcoming porch lights, no parked automobile in which to drive away.

"The strange thing was that she disappeared so fast. I wasn't frightened, but I couldn't imagine what had happened to her," he said.

As one can imagine, too, Jerry took some good-natured ribbing when he told people the story. "For a while everyone thought it was a joke."

But it was never a joke to Jerry Cummings. He knows what happened. And though it remains a mystery, the possibility that he gave a lift to a ghost ranks right with his Packers' tryout as one of the more exciting milestones in his life.

Muffled Screams

There's something about an old house that invites rumors of ghosts. For instance, take that unpainted, rundown house in Milwaukee's Sixth Ward. The neighbors knew it was haunted. The place was said to be one of the oldest in the city. It stood high on the west bank of the river, southeast of the old reservoir. Its second-story windows offered a splendid view of the city—for anyone brave enough to live there—and the house itself, if not elegant, was spacious enough, with a full basement, four rooms on the first floor, two large rooms and two closets on the second, and a garret.

Yet for all the house's attractions, no one ever lived there for very long. Year after year, tenants moved in and just as promptly moved out. As a last resort after a Polish family moved out, Herman Hegner, who lived next door and had been put in charge of renting out the place, decided to conduct his own investigation. He watched the house closely on the first night it was vacant. Sure enough, shortly after midnight he saw the room in the southwest corner of the first floor fill with light. Fearing the house had caught fire, Hegner raced next door. The light blinked out just before he got up to the window where it shone through. He groped in his pocket for the key as the light sprang on again, blindingly bright, and then shut off just as suddenly.

Hegner inserted the key into the lock. The old door groaned on its hinges as he pushed it open. He moved stealthily from room to room, peering into dark corners and musty closets. Nothing—he found nothing at all. Although Hegner was perplexed, he was certain he had seen the light and equally certain that no living being was in the house to explain it.

Later, a newly arrived Czech family of five moved into the house. On their first night they settled down on the first floor. The parents were jolted awake by heavy footsteps from the floor above. A muffled scream trembled in the air, followed by the resounding crash of a heavy body falling to the floor. Though the very walls seemed to vibrate, the children did not awaken.

On the second night, the sequence of events was repeated but with increased violence. At one in the morning the terror-stricken family fled to Hegner's house to spend the rest of the night. At first light they gathered their meager possessions and left.

As word of the haunted house spread, two recently arrived Englishmen asked Hegner for permission to spend the night in the house to expose the illusion and, if possible, capture the "ghost." George Heath and Henry Jordan picked up the key on Sunday evening, August 8, 1875. Armed with nothing more than their own courage and a few warm blankets, the pair said they'd report back in the morning. Both men worked at the Milwaukee and St. Paul Railroad car shop and were considered responsible and trustworthy men.

But early the next morning when Hegner went next door to check on them, he found the front door standing open. Inside, piles of crumbled plaster lay on the floor; the bare walls were streaked with water stains from a leaky roof. Worse still, the kitchen floor was worn through in several places, exposing the square-cut log floor beams. The ladder leading to the garret was laced with cobwebs.

Hegner found a pile of blankets but no Heath or Jordan.

A newspaper reporter who tracked down Heath and obtained his story pieced together what happened that night.

Heath said that he and Jordan had checked all through the house just after sunset to make certain no one was hiding inside. Satisfied the place was empty, the men went back to work at the railroad shop until after ten o'clock. They walked back up the hill to the house and sat around smoking until they got tired and went to sleep.

"I was awakened by Jordan," Heath told the newsman. "He had heard some noise upstairs. We sat up for a moment and then heard someone walking across the floor."

Heath said they heard a scuffle, a smothered cry, and then a body hitting the floor.

"I proposed to go upstairs," Heath recalled. He was just about to relight their candle when a brilliant white light enveloped them.

"For a moment my eyes were dazzled so that I could distinguish nothing. Then Jordan pointed toward the stairway . . . through the open door. I looked but saw nothing."

Heath said the light lasted for no more than a minute before going out. He managed to light the candle and glanced at his pocket watch. It was twenty-five minutes past midnight.

"I was not frightened in the least and insisted upon going upstairs," Heath bragged. "At first Jordan hesitated but when I moved he followed. We searched rooms and closets, but found no trace of anything living or dead."

The men decided to stay awake. They blew out their candle and sat silently, waiting. Their patience was rewarded. In about fifteen minutes the stealthy footsteps could again be heard from upstairs. Then a brief pause, a muffled cry, a struggle, a fall—and silence. Within what seemed like only seconds, the brilliant light again filled the downstairs room in which the men huddled.

Heath wanted to make another search, but Jordan refused to spend another minute in the house. Heath reluctantly agreed and both men left.

The newsman asked Heath for an explanation. He could give none, but he insisted ghosts had nothing to do with it. But if not ghosts, then what was it?

Mrs. G's Boardinghouse

Nobody ran a Milwaukee boardinghouse with so much aplomb as Mrs. William Giddings. She filled her south-side home with workers from the local tannery and catered to them with calm efficiency. The two-story frame house, at the corner of Allis and Whitcomb streets in what the city called Allen's Addition, soon earned a reputation as a haven of solitude where nothing more disturbing than an occasional raised voice occurred.

But that was before one Saturday in August long ago. At nine in the morning, Mr. Giddings was at work at the tannery; his wife and their young housemaid were alone in the kitchen. Mary Spiegel, the daughter of a neighboring Polish family, was a slow-witted child of fourteen whose father brutalized her so severely that she welcomed the opportunity to be "hired out." Although Mary lived in a constant state of nervous apprehension, Mrs. Giddings treated her with compassion and dignity.

The women were making pies for dinner when suddenly spoons began leaping from their holder and flying in all directions around the room. Only momentarily startled, the older woman continued to work—until a trap door in the kitchen floor began to rise and fall. Mrs. Giddings asked Mary to stand on it. When the youngster was unable to hold down the heaving door, the woman knew some prankster had gotten into the cellar. She lifted the door and descended, but saw no one.

Climbing back into the kitchen, she found everything in commotion. Dishes flew from the china closet and smashed on the floor. An oil lamp soared from its shelf and shattered. Chairs rose to the ceiling, and one broke upon hitting the floor. The stove danced. One of the pies fell from the table, a dish of beans spilled, and eggs whirled out of the pantry that was open to the kitchen. One egg turned a corner to hit Mrs. Giddings where she sat.

Mary, greatly frightened, was sent to get the neighbors, Mrs. Mead and Mrs. Rowland, to come sit with them. As the women approached the Giddingses' house, a pail of flowers at the door leaped over a wooden fence the height of a man and into the next yard. One of the neighbor women brought it back but again the flower pot flew over the fence.

Once inside, the four women sat in a circle. Mary began peeling potatoes for dinner. As she talked, the knife flew out of her hand, along with the potato from the pan in her lap; both hit Mrs. Rowland. A moment later a dish on the table cracked in two. None of the group was near enough to the table to have reached it. One piece fell to the floor; the other remained on the table. Corn, boiling on the stove, leaped out of its pot.

The resolute Mrs. Giddings tried to keep her composure, but Mrs. Mead lost hers. Visibly upset, she announced she was going home. No sooner had she reached her yard than a heavy stick of wood was hurled over the fence at her. Mary was at the far end of the Giddingses' yard and the stick would have been too heavy for her to lift.

Pails of water also traveled over the fence and back again, and yet no more than one pail in four was spilled.

Curiosity soon brought throngs of neighbor women to the house, where they remained, riveted by fright. Finally, the bewildered Mrs. Giddings sent Mary to fetch George W. Allen and his brother, Rufus, owners of a nearby tannery, the Wisconsin Leather Company. The men were at their offices and came promptly, bringing with them two doctors, including Nathaniel A. Gray, an eminent Milwaukee obstetrician.

While George Allen tried to calm the women, a stove-lid lifter flew off the wood stove, hurtled ten feet through the air, and struck him on the leg. No one was closer to the stove than he. Then, a pie rose from the table, flew past him, and smashed against the stove. To avoid further bombardments, Allen left the room.

By this time the floor was littered with the debris of broken dishes, splintered wood, shards of glass, and spilled food. Mrs. Giddings asked Mary to sweep, and as she did so, one of the doctors kept a close, scrutinizing eye on her. From where he stood, he had a full view of the pantry and of the servant. As he watched, a small china dish sailed horizontally out of the pantry. He dodged it and it fell to the floor, dumping the playing cards it held but not breaking.

Mary then began to wash the floor, but the pail of soapy water skated to the outer edges of the room into the crowd of frightened onlookers. As Mary got off her knees to chase the pail, she was hit hard on the head by a bowl flying out of the pantry. The men searched the pantry, the kitchen, and the dining room but found no person or thing that might have propelled the objects.

The strange events continued until late afternoon. By that time, reporters from the local press had arrived to interview the men and the women still present. They questioned each eyewitness independently and were completely satisfied that there had been no collusion. Since the phenomena occurred only in Mary's presence, there was some speculation that she might have thrown some of the objects. But the careful observations made by the witnesses and the unnatural ballistics of the moving objects exonerated the girl. That the phenomena had indeed occurred without human agency was vouched for by scores of well-regarded eyewitnesses whose testimony was considered unimpeachable.

One reporter also had a talk with Mary. He found her a pitiable creature fearful of staying in the house or of doing most anything. She could not explain the events, but denied all responsibility for them. The reporter also learned that the child would sometimes get up in the night to fight imaginary enemies. Mrs. Spiegel, who was present during the interview and who spoke no English, thought that the note-taking newsman was a law enforcement officer gathering evidence to support a charge of witchcraft against her daughter. She scolded Mary repeatedly, and the girl huddled deep in her chair, trembling and in tears.

By Saturday evening, the Giddingses decided that they could not keep the girl in their boarding house and told her to go home. She begged to stay, and when her pleadings were of no avail she hid herself in the woodshed. Her father found her there, and beat her severely.

Sadly, the next anyone heard of Mary Spiegel was her attempted suicide in the river. An unnamed gentleman rescued her, soaked and shivering, and took her back to the Giddingses' house. When asked why she had tried to kill herself, she said she was so hounded by everybody that she could no longer endure her life.

Again her former employers sent her back to her parents, and the charitable Mrs. Giddings sent along a dish of food. The next day Mary returned the empty dish. No sooner had she put it on the kitchen table than the teakettle leaped off the stove, hit the floor, and was damaged beyond repair. Giddings, hearing the commotion and fearing further destruction of his property, drove Mary out of the house.

Two days later Dr. Chauncey C. Robinson, a prominent physician of the city who had taken an interest in the girl and wanted to question Mrs. Giddings about the strange phenomena, took her back to the house. The family and the boarders were eating dinner; the moment Mary and the doctor entered the room, knives and forks flew off the table.

According to news accounts, Mary was finally taken into the home of a well-known physician in the Seventh Ward.

Was Mary the source of the upheaval? Parapsychologists believe that neurotic conditions are factors conducive to poltergeist activity, and it was the consensus of the time that Mary was neurotic at least; today she would likely be diagnosed with multiple disorders. Did her neuroses and somnambulism facilitate the unconscious release of paranormal powers? Was it mass hallucination, or was it simply fraud?

Because all normal explanations for the outlandish incidents seemed preposterous, the poor little servant girl attracted international attention. The late author Herbert Thurston, a Jesuit investigator of psychic phenomena, included the story of Mary Spiegel in his book *Ghosts and Poltergeists*. He referred to it as a "remarkable American case."

House of Evil

Violent death is often the catalyst for the appearance of a ghost. Those who die at the hands of a murderer or take their own lives are frequently said to leave behind strong energy impressions that may manifest in the activity of a ghost or poltergeist.

Present-day Milwaukee residents passing the corner of Twelfth and State are unaware that they are within a few feet of the location of one of the city's most famous haunted houses. The brick building is gone now, but its sinister reputation persisted for many years. It belonged to one Major Hobart. He departed the earth too soon and his house, which was never the same again, came to be known as the "house of evil."

Hobart, a former army officer, calmly hanged himself for unexplained reasons one afternoon. He was found swinging from a chandelier in the large two-story home. After Hobart's demise, many families lived in the house, but not many remained for more than a few months. The terrified residents reported doors opening and closing without human assistance, footfalls clattering up the staircase when all were in bed, groans wafting from various rooms, and chains being dragged across the floors.

When the house was vacant—which was often—neighbors would notice lights through the dusty windows, solidifying the house's reputation for evil.

After several years, no realtor could sell the brick mansion, so infamous had its reputation become. At last it was razed, and with it was lost the last, unearthly traces of Major Hobart, late of the U.S. Army.

Face on the Bedroom Curtain

Early one Saturday morning in September, Milwaukeean Mary Tubey died. Although the circumstances of her death were not unusual, her youth made her passing especially poignant to her friends and family.

A block away, on Hill Street between Seventh and Eighth, her stepbrother, Dan Connell, had finished his lunch and was sitting in the front room, silent and alone with his grief. The door to the bedroom was open, and from where he sat he had a clear view of the curtained window in that room. Suddenly he saw Mary's face appear on the curtain. The longer he looked, the clearer the face became.

Connell called his wife, and she too saw the strange likeness. They tried to divert their uneasiness by keeping busy in the house, but their curiosity impelled them to check the curtain several times during the afternoon. The face was always there—shimmering, smiling—in exactly the same place. Had Mary returned to say good-bye, or were the Connells, in their sorrow, imagining her presence?

We don't know precisely what it was the Connells saw that led them to believe Dan's stepsister had made a stop at their home, but later that day the story got out, and neighbors by the dozens swarmed through the front and back doors of the small, brown cottage. Some glanced at the curtain and, seeing nothing, held in their laughter until they got outdoors; others were profoundly moved by what they believed they saw. A policeman who visited the house that afternoon said later that he had never seen anything plainer in his life.

When the size of the crowds became unmanageable and the Connells were chilled to the bone from the cold air blowing through the open doorways, they barricaded the entrances and refused to admit more visitors.

The next day, Sunday, the crowds swelled into the hundreds, including several reporters drawn by stories they'd heard on the streets. The doors were opened again and the curious callers filed past the window curtain. At dusk the face vanished but the visitors did not. From all parts of the city they came, and many were deeply disappointed upon learning that there was no longer anything to be seen.

The following week, a local reporter called on Mrs. Connell and also interviewed a number of neighbors who claimed to have seen the face on the curtain. Some said emphatically that they could not have been deceived, and all cross-questioning failed to shake them. That group was so solemn about the affair that the reporter decided it was foolish to tell them their imaginations may have gotten the better of their judgment.

The Restless Servant Girl

Dr. Gerhard Bading and his wife lived in a rental house on Upper Wells Street between Twenty-Fifth and Twenty-Sixth Streets, on Milwaukee's west side. It was a large clapboard house with double stairways typical of the era. One staircase connected the front of the house to the upstairs hallway; the other descended from the same hallway to the kitchen in the rear. Rear staircases often led to a sleeping room for the maid or cook and were used by that staff to reach the kitchen without going through family rooms. The hallway and both stairways were carpeted. That year, the Badings decided to take a short trip, and, not wishing to leave the house unattended, they asked their friend Dr. E. J. W. Notz to live there in their absence.

Notz moved in on the appointed day and that night went upstairs to bed and promptly fell asleep. Shortly after midnight he was awakened by a thundering crash followed by footsteps in the hallway. He sat up in bed, then he thought he heard someone going down the rear stairway. He felt certain he was not alone in the house. He got up quickly, turned on lights, and searched the attic, second floor, first floor, and basement. There was no one anywhere, nor could Notz find evidence of anything else that might have caused the disturbance. Satisfied and much relieved, he went back to bed and fell asleep, until . . .

A sudden crash, then hurried footsteps across the hall and down the stairway awoke him again. He got up, searched the house for the invisible prowler, but again found nothing.

The commotion erupted a third time before morning; the same sequence occurred during Notz's second night in the house. When the Badings returned, Notz told them of his experiences, but they showed no surprise. They said they had heard the same thing so often that they weren't greatly disturbed by them.

Later, Notz learned that people in the neighborhood believed the ghost of a servant girl who had committed suicide on the premises haunted the house. She had been sent to the house early one autumn day to open it up and get it ready for its owner, the proprietor of a resort hotel in the Waukesha Lakes area. The girl was apparently suffering from depression and, upset at not being able to complete her work, killed herself. It was her restless ghost that roamed the hallway and staircases, terrifying each family who has lived there ever since.

Ghostways

The gentle rise in Dane County's Burke Township—known to locals as Ghost Hill—was most appropriately named. For years on end, and at the stroke of midnight, a lean figure clad in white appeared astride a pale horse racing across the top of the knoll going in the direction of Blooming Grove. Neither the harshness of the weather nor the darkness of the night kept the horseman from his appointed rounds. He, or rather *it*, could be seen plainly, a white cape fluttering in the breeze like some sort of spectral streamer.

Early Burke Township residents could not recall the origin of the mysterious specter—called that since there was general agreement it was not of this earth. Ghost Hill itself was on the former Messerschmidt farm in the northeast corner of Section 19 on the old road from Madison to Token Creek.

Some witnesses thought the horseman was the angry spirit of an early pioneer who had been robbed and murdered near the hill. The man's ghost was condemned to wander through the night, seeking revenge for his brutal death.

At least one effort was made to identify the ghost—or at least verify its existence. George Armbrecht of Madison told a newspaper reporter in 1936 that he and several other brave companions camped on the hill one night to see the horseman for themselves. Midnight arrived, but unfortunately on this occasion no ghost appeared.

The hill was partially excavated when a quarry opened to supply stone for the Dane County airport. With the changes to Ghost Hill, the legend of the horseman slowly faded from memory.

Madison Sheriff Van Wie held the kerosene lamp high as he made his last rounds on that late November day of 1873. The nine prisoners were either fast asleep or resting on their beds. All seemed well. Sheriff Van Wie returned to his own quarters in another part of the jail complex and went to bed.

A wild shriek slashed through the silence. Wie leaped out of bed in his nightshirt, grabbed a lantern, and raced to the cellblock. Two young prisoners named Foster and Sheevy were thrashing about in their bunks, their eyes wide with fright.

Wie unlocked the cell door and demanded an explanation. The men said they'd just settled down for the night when they heard a noise in the doorway at the far end of the corridor. The sound increased in intensity, then it seemed to move through the iron bars of their cell. As the noise surrounded them, a blindingly strong light filled the cell. Then, they claimed, an ill-defined form screamed and brushed against their beds.

Wie thought the men had obviously concocted the tale, but he conceded the young men seemed genuinely frightened. They demanded to be moved. Wie refused. He said the men could work out their own salvation.

The next night came and the disturbances continued. But this time Wie remained snug in his bed. Foster and Sheevy did get their chance, however, to tell their tale to a reporter. They claimed the light had again filled their cell. To escape both it and the wild wailing, they dived onto their bunks and wrapped their heads in their blankets.

Wie thought Foster had had a hand in the commotion. Young Foster had been accused of setting fire to several of Madison's flourmills. Sheriff Wie was convinced that Foster spent his time behind bars planning pranks to frighten the wits out of Sheevy, apparently quite a superstitious man. Yet both men seemed genuinely frightened by the experience.

The episode—and the men—gradually faded from the news. There was no follow-up investigation, so it will never be known whether it was an attention-getting device on the prisoners' part or truly the vestige of a long-forgotten prisoner sentenced to roam forever the cold, gray halls of Madison's old jailhouse.

Albert J. Lamson was a farmer who lived near Lake Wingra in Madison. On one particular dark and starless spring night early in the twentieth century, Lamson stepped out onto his front porch and heard the unmistakable thwack of an ax—the clear, ringing, rhythmic swing of an expert woodsman at work.

As Lamson listened, he was certain the sound was coming from Bartlett Woods, later known as Noe Woods, on the southwest side of what is now the University of Wisconsin Arboretum.

Lamson couldn't figure out why anyone would want to fell a tree in the middle of the night. Yet he knew he was not mistaken. He heard the blade bite repeatedly into the trunk, pause on occasion, and then resume its steady rhythm.

The next morning, Lamson's curiosity got the best of him. He climbed a fence near the present-day Curtis Prairie and the Arboretum Administration Area. Though he searched the area, he could not find any recent ax marks on the trees, nor wood chips anywhere on the ground.

Several nights later, he again heard the sound of wood being chopped. He summoned his hired man—who also claimed to have heard the axman at work—and together the pair hiked into the woods to investigate. But again, they could find no evidence of recent timbering. Lamson questioned his friends and neighbors. Several said they also heard the noises and some, like Lamson, unsuccessfully searched the woods for its source.

Periodically during the summer and fall, the mysterious sound returned. Travelers who heard the story avoided the "ghost road" that ran by the woods. A search party with lanterns was finally organized to go into the forest at night to locate the woodchopper. But after several faint-hearted volunteers dropped out, the hunt was called off. Lamson was too superstitious to go back into the dense woods after dark.

The woodchopper—or whatever it was—finally abandoned his nightly encroachment. His identity and the purpose of his endeavors remain a mystery to this day.

There is more than one "ghost road" in Madison. Seminole Highway is now a mostly residential street of homes and wooded acreage crossing the Beltline near the University of Wisconsin Arboretum. The only ghost one is likely to see here is a young child costumed for Halloween. But when the highway was known as Bryant Road, tales were spread that unearthly apparitions appeared to teamsters and pedestrians alike.

Most described the ghost as a luminous white vapor that would appear suddenly from the brush on either side of the road, follow the unsuspecting wayfarer for a short distance, and then vanish as quickly as it had appeared.

A few others claimed the vapor was in the shape of a Native American astride a pony, and that he would walk his horse behind them for a little way, and then disappear. Sometimes late at night people fancied they heard the clatter of a pony's hooves as the ghostly rider charged up and down Seminole Highway in pursuit of an unseen quarry.

The phantom never harmed anyone. Nor was his identity learned. Some said he was a Native American who had been killed in battle and was seeking revenge. Others thought he was a man who had been buried in the cemetery near the old Bryant barn at the east end of the highway. But if that's the case, no one knew his name or why he had returned.

By the time the horse and buggy gave way to the Model T, the troublesome ghost had disappeared, leaving stories of Madison's "ghost road" alive only in the memories of the older generation.

Terror in the Night

Darkness wrapped the old clapboard farmhouse near Cedarburg on that early March night in 1975. Barb Yashinsky lay sleeping. The late winter day had been long and exhausting after her family's move into the rural home they had just purchased. At two o'clock in the morning Barb was jerked awake.

"I thought it was a cat fight," she later said of the noise, noting the time on the bedside alarm clock. "And you know what they sound like."

Barb was now listening intently. She decided the sounds were more like those of a weeping child. She wondered if her daughter, Kate, had awakened and become frightened by the strange surroundings. Barb got up, crossed the darkened hallway, and opened the door to her daughter's bedroom. The two-year-old was sound asleep.

Then Barb thought she heard a woman's voice blending with the crying. More curious than frightened, she walked downstairs and looked around the house. Everything seemed in order. She even fetched a flashlight and went outdoors to look around the yard.

Satisfied that there was nothing amiss, she returned to the house. But the muffled crying and indistinct voice persisted. At times they seemed to be coming from a closet in the bedroom she shared with her husband, Michael, who was sleeping soundly. No more than twenty minutes later, the sounds subsided and Barb drifted back to sleep. She decided not to tell her husband about the episode.

Within less than two years, Barb and Michael would finally come to grips with what their brains told them was not possible—that they had moved into a haunted house.

The house was well over a century old when Barb and Michael Yashinsky moved in. There was still much work to be done to convert it into a comfortable and cheerful home. Barb was eager to get the remodeling underway. They had bought the house from a man who restored rundown homes for resale, yet he had made only minimal cosmetic changes to this place. Barb and Michael had bought it "for a song," as they described it, after it stood empty for nearly a year. New wiring and central heating had been put in before their arrival, but there was still a great deal of painting to be done outside and in. It would be a busy spring and summer. Barb was a schoolteacher and planned to return to work in the fall, so she was most anxious to complete work on the house.

But the hard days of painting and cleaning did not bring the anticipated rewards. Unaccountably, Barb was nervous and restless during those early months.

"I was never satisfied with anything, which isn't like me. I couldn't find enough to keep me occupied. [I thought] what I was doing was boring. I found lots of reasons to yell at the baby for no reason at all, but I thought I just needed to get back to work."

The couple was able to finish most of the necessary work on the house by late summer. Barb returned to her classroom job on schedule. Michael was a chef who worked night shifts and cared for their daughter during the day. Barb's mother, Margaret, filled in for an hour or two on those days when her daughter wasn't able to get home before Michael left for work or on those evenings when Barb had a school function. Yet a return to the classroom did little to alleviate Barb's self-described "nervousness."

One night in November, Kate awoke crying with what her mother thought was only a nightmare. It was odd in that she had always been a sound sleeper. Barb went into her room to see what was the matter.

"I felt the closing in of fear and apprehension, which I was to experience many times," Barb remembered. She took her daughter into her arms. Kate asked if "the man" would come again. Barb didn't know what she was talking about and shrugged it off as the figment of a young child's lively imagination.

The next night Barb was again awakened by Kate—only this time the girl was screaming in what seemed like utter terror. She told her mother that "the man" had come again, although this time he had brought frightening circus animals.

Kate was a bright and very vocal child, according to Barb; yet she could not provide any sort of description of the man or the animals. Barb held her tightly until she quieted down and fell back asleep.

Barb was left with many questions and an equal number of fears.

The next night, Michael had decided to stay downstairs watching television when his wife went to bed. She had not been asleep long when she felt a stinging slap across her face.

"Barbara!" a deep male voice cried out.

She flung an arm out to defend herself. It fell across the other side of the bed, where Michael slept. He wasn't there.

"I was frozen to the bed," she recalled. "I do remember praying and then getting enough courage to move. But I [felt] real heavy. I couldn't get myself up. I always scoffed when you see heroines in movies that can't move. I thought this was silly—you can always do anything you want. Your own will is stronger."

Barb finally made her way downstairs, where she confronted Michael. She still thought he was responsible. But he was as astonished as his wife; he had been watching television the whole time.

Michael remembers that night as if it were yesterday. "Barbara isn't the type to dream. That's why I couldn't figure it out. I'm a very logical individual. I couldn't figure out the logic for something like that. Knowing her as I do, she never lies. It just wasn't Barb."

Meanwhile, Michael began noticing other oddities in the house. Intense cold often filled the kitchen, the upstairs hallway, and Kate's bedroom, which was situated directly over the kitchen. At first Michael and Barb reasoned that the drafty old windows were the cause. But modern, carefully sealed windows did not lessen the chill, especially in Kate's room. With hot air pouring from the register in Kate's room, Michael could still see his breath. "I'm so cold," the little girl sometimes complained to her parents in the middle of the night.

In the upstairs hallway, newly applied wallpaper kept peeling. No amount of glue or pressure could keep it sealed to the plaster.

One morning in the spring of 1976, Michael had an especially disturbing experience.

As he awoke, Michael saw a vaporous, whitish haze flowing into the room from under the bedroom door. It didn't look or smell like smoke, perhaps something closer to steam or fog, a heavy, damp thing, transparent. He could see its edges as it receded back under the door and into the hallway.

Michael nudged Barb and asked her if she smelled anything. But she only murmured and continued sleeping. When he looked back toward the bedroom door, the vapor was gone. Michael finally roused Barb, and she got up to check on Kate, who was sleeping peacefully.

A few days later, Michael awoke to find a similar blanket of vapor, but this time it surrounded the bed.

"It reminded me of a screen completely encompassing the bed," he said. "You could look through it. But this time it had no [dank smell]."

Michael's personal experiences upset Barb even more.

"The next months left me fighting a battle to remain calm in the evening. We didn't seem to notice anything during the day. I rarely went to bed without Mike. I'd sleep on the sofa until he'd come home. I'd check on Kate a great many times."

Barb and Michael had kept their peculiar experiences to themselves yet continued to search for answers. The events were usually spaced far enough apart that they came unexpectedly, which only added to the couple's distress. Neither one believed in psychic phenomena; they had no interest in the subject. But all that changed early the following fall of 1976 as Barb was starting to teach again.

Her mother, Margaret, was a straightforward woman in both her speech and manner. One day she asked her daughter directly if she thought something was "wrong" with their house. Margaret said the kitchen was often so bitterly cold that she had to put on a sweater while she cooked or did her crossword puzzles. Yet at the same time the adjoining living room and dining room were very warm.

Barb took some relief in knowing that her mother thought something odd was going on. "She's the most stable person I have ever met, a very calm, quiet, sedate lady full of common sense and very much in control of her surroundings."

Her mother suggested that the house be blessed, but Barb was hesitant. "This person or whatever it is isn't aggressive or violent," she reasoned. "Who knows why it's here?"

The house was never blessed. And that may have been a mistake if an event the following January was any indication.

Michael had been playing with Kate before her bedtime. When she got tired he scooped her into his arms and carried her up the stairs, her head snuggled against his shoulder. He hadn't bothered to turn on the lights. When he opened the door to his daughter's room, he stopped short. A squat, vaporous form shimmered in the middle of the room. Clearly it was the figure of a small man.

"The [out]lines of it were moving, vibrating. I've never seen anything like it. You could see somewhat through it but nowhere near like the [vapor] around the bed. I reached over, turned on the light, and it was gone."

The room was intensely cold.

Nevertheless Michael put Kate to bed. He did not tell his wife of the experience until much later.

The sensitivity of animals to reported supernatural events is well documented. Household pets such as dogs, cats, and even birds seem to be more sensitive to the unseen world than their human companions.

Such was the case with Benji, the Yashinskys' massive Great Pyrenees. He slept on the floor in the master bedroom. His behavior one night was another signal to Barb and Michael that all was not well. The couple was sitting on the edge of the bed talking. Benji was curled up on the floor. Suddenly the dog leaped to his feet, looked toward Barb, and growled. She was momentarily frightened, thinking he "had gone nuts or something."

However, in one great leap, he bounded past her and into the corner of the room, facing the closet where Barb had first heard the crying voice. Benji growled for a few moments, then, looking as if he had made a fool of himself, returned to the couple with his head lowered and a rather woeful look on his large face. Neither Barb nor Michael had heard or seen anything out of the ordinary, yet they could make little sense of the way their dog had acted. All they could figure out is that the room had been in near total darkness so perhaps it had been a passing shadow. The couple said that was the only time their dog ever acted oddly in the house.

On January 13, less than two years after they moved in with high expectations, the Yashinskys packed up the furniture and moved away.

"We wanted to get out of there," Michael said. "Whatever it was seemed more and more disturbed."

Barb was convinced that if they stayed in the house, their lives would continue to change for the worse.

"It might start throwing pots and pans, rumpling bedding, or become hostile in some way. It's silly to talk about it like this, but you wonder. If Kate saw a man bringing animals maybe he was [a ghost] just interested in her as a child."

Or maybe not. That was her great anxiety: their unknown and unknowable future if they continued to live in the house. Was the "presence" merely curious, or might it become even more aggravated and dangerous?

Before they moved away, the Yashinskys had tried to discover something of the history of the house. The original homestead apparently stayed in the builder's family for nearly a century except for one brief period of time. The last member of the family had been a reclusive bachelor who died in the place. He reportedly never saw any outsiders save for his widowed sister-in-law; he heated only a few rooms downstairs and closed off the second floor.

A descendant of the original family provided another intriguing bit of information: a miserly ancestor was thought to have hidden a sizable quantity of old coins somewhere in the house. At least one search by his descendants years earlier included knocking out some walls.

A neighbor family to whom the Yashinskys confided their troubling experiences said they'd never seen or heard anything odd in or around the house. Yet their daughter often babysat for the Yashinskys and habitually turned on every light in the house when she was there.

The short, squat figure Michael had seen in the bedroom might have been a member of the builder's family—the descendants Barb was able to track down were strikingly similar in that they were all small of stature.

The couple could find no leads on the identity of the sobbing woman or child Barb heard.

"It's changed my ideas about people who I previously thought were crackpots for seeing ghosts or trying to film ghosts," Barb concluded, finally coming to terms with what she determined was the supernatural basis of the "problems" in her home. "Although our experiences weren't particularly frightening, you . . . want to forget. We'll probably wrestle with this the rest of our lives."

Michael agreed.

"I've gone over and over it in my mind, many times. I'm not an extremely well-read person, but I know what I know and I know what I saw. Nothing will ever change that. This happened to me."

In the years following their adventures in the old farmhouse, the Yashinskys found their new home blissfully terror-free. Even little Kate noticed the change. "Oh, mama," she often confided in her mother, "it's so nice and warm in my room."

The Legacy
of Mary Buth Farm

The weather was warm for the last day of December. Wispy strands of fog clung to the gently rolling fields of southeastern Wisconsin as the thermometer hovered near thirty degrees. At the end of a long, paved road near Germantown, Tom Walton and his family prepared to celebrate New Year's Day in their 140-year-old farmhouse. The clock struck midnight. Family members and several guests toasted each other for success and happiness in the coming twelve months.

But, as Tom later said, the evening had not been cheerful. There had been a tinge of something sinister, something almost evil intruding upon the celebration. The whole evening had been very strange. Small things happened at first. The house suddenly cooled for no apparent reason. A candle burned much faster than its twin sitting nearby. The television set lost power—without explanation. And then, outside the wide living room window, she appeared: an old woman, dressed in a rough black dress, staring in at the assembled family and guests. Before Tom could react, she was gone.

Who was she . . . that vague, dark phantom staring in at the startled assemblage? Tom had a hunch—a guess that led back in time to 1838.

In that year, John and Mary Buth built the farm as one of Wisconsin's pioneer homesteads. The Buth cabin and land also were used as a trading post for early settlers and traders. Near the farm, Indians camped by a small stream. The decades have brought innumerable changes to the original log cabin, but a section of it forms a part of the present two-story frame house. Sturdy log ceiling beams now support a segment of the second floor. The place is still known as Mary Buth Farm.

John and Mary Buth had three children: Herman, who died at age seventy in 1917; Carl, who died at age seventy-four in 1923; and Mary, the only daughter and the farm's namesake, who died at age seventy-six in 1926. None of the children married. An overgrown cemetery near the farm holds their remains.

How does this explain the eerie events of the Waltons' New Year's Eve gathering? The Buth farm has a long history of being haunted. The ghosts of the younger Mary Buth and her mother were said to roam the farm by day and inhabit the house at night. Tom had heard neighbors tell stories about the farm. When Walton and his family moved there, they didn't place much faith in these tales until that night about four years later.

It was then that Walton changed his mind. The fleeting apparition outside the window left him perplexed. The next morning he discovered that a pepper plant near the window had wilted leaves on one side while the other half remained green and healthy. The other small incidents that night added to the mystery.

Over the next several years, until the family moved away, the Waltons were to have other baffling experiences. An overnight visitor told Tom that he had seen a young girl in the yard vanish into the early morning mist. The Buth farm is quite isolated from nearby houses, making it unlikely she was a neighbor.

One afternoon, Tom was alone in the house when violin music floated through the house. No radio was playing. The stereo was turned off. Later, Walton learned that Herman Buth had played the violin as a hobby.

On another occasion, when the kitchen was being remodeled, the Waltons' plumber said he had heard footsteps walking across the upstairs floor. The plumber had been alone in the house at the time.

What caused these phenomena? To find out, Tom asked author and expert in the supernatural Mary Leader to visit the home. After a session with a Ouija board, Leader said at least two ghosts haunted the Buth farm. She identified them as the two Mary Buths—mother and daughter. The daughter was an evil ghost lurking outside the home and searching for her missing lover. According to local lore, Mary had been left standing at the altar on her wedding day. The mother was the "inside" ghost protecting the house from her daughter. The psychic could not explain the violin music Tom had heard.

Some neighbors scoff at the idea of the two women coming back to haunt the house. The younger Mary, according to one long-time resident, "just wasn't the type who would come around and haunt [the farm]. Sure she was an old maid and probably a little eccentric, but she had a good heart." Mary reportedly cared for mentally disabled people in the vicinity during an era when they were shunned by most of society.

Few contemporary accounts remain of the elder Mary. She was ninety-three at her death in 1899, outliving her husband by forty-six years.

After their parents' deaths, Mary and her brothers were hardworking farmers who cut wood with a handsaw and offered the use of their farm as a resting place for peddlers traveling to and from Milwaukee. Is it possible that one of these itinerant salesmen proposed to Mary and then jilted her when a new territory beckoned? It has been known to happen.

The Strange Case
of Henry James Brophy

At noon on Tuesday, March 9, 1909, schoolboy Henry James Brophy, age eleven years, arrived home for lunch. He opened the side door of his home in Mount Horeb and was immediately struck in the back by a snowball that broke and splattered across the kitchen floor. The boy spun around, but there was no one in sight.

At the same time the next day, the same thing happened.

Early on Thursday evening of that week, cups suddenly flew from the dinner table and crashed to the floor. Glass lamp chimneys disintegrated. Spools of thread unwound. Bars of soap soared through the air.

And so began one of the strangest cases of alleged poltergeist activity ever recorded in Wisconsin.

Little Henry Brophy lived with his grandparents, Mr. and Mrs. Knut K. Lunde, in Mount Horeb following his mother's second marriage, to Patrick Trainor. It is not known what happened to Henry's natural father or why he was unable to live with his mother and stepfather.

The boy attended the village grade school. A shy, delicate child with few close friends, Henry possessed no extraordinary talents . . . or so everyone thought. But he was soon at the center of a series of events that led those in the community to believe he was either psychically gifted or was a superb manipulator and clever fraud. Which conclusion was correct has never been satisfactorily determined.

217

On Friday, March 12, Henry's mother came from Madison to attend a family funeral and spend the night with her parents, her son, Henry, and her sister, who still lived at home. Early that evening, Mrs. Trainor is said to have sat down to play the organ. In that instant, household utensils allegedly took to the air, banging against the walls and crashing to the floor. Knut Lunde became so agitated that he sent for a local minister, a certain Reverend Mostrom. When the minister arrived with a friend, Sam Thompson, a hymnal that had been sitting on a windowsill near the door fell to the floor at their feet.

"There, you see it!" Knut Lunde said.

Reverend Mostrom listened attentively as the Lundes explained what had been going on. Since most of the unexplained events occurred near Henry, Sam Thompson kept the child by his side.

"Look out!" Henry shouted as a butcher knife flew from the kitchen table, arced through the air, and fell at Thompson's feet. The man said later that the boy could not have touched it. Later, a hatpin retraced the knife's arc. Neither Thompson nor Mostrom understood what had happened.

Nightly thereafter, the family and a steady number of curiosity seekers reported objects flying around the house. Doors crashed to the floor after screws in the hinges were mysteriously loosened. Glass lamp chimneys shattered. A stove lid toppled to the floor. A drawer under a sewing machine came free and soared high into the air, knocking plaster from a wall and scattering bobbins, thread, and needles in every direction. Mrs. Lunde had to duck when a table knife leaped through the air at her before clattering to the floor.

News of the strange phenomena spread rapidly beyond the confines of the little town, attracting the attention of newsmen and self-described clairvoyants from across the Midwest. On a single night in March, an estimated two hundred people left muddy footprints as they tramped through the house. No one in that group reported seeing any paranormal manifestations.

If the Lundes and their visitors could not explain what was happening, some of Mount Horeb's residents believed they could—even if their reasoning was a bit unusual to say the least.

Two prominent citizens came to the Lunde house and singled out the recent installation of a telephone line and electricity as the source of the disturbances. The house had been "electrified," they insisted, and therefore cutting the electric wires would put an end to the troubles. The distraught family, however, apparently feared darkness more than chaos, and so they demanded that the visitors leave.

The family had concluded early on that Henry was somehow responsible for the turmoil—either by natural or supernatural means. The phenomena always occurred in Henry's presence and the flying objects seemed to travel toward the child. His family reasoned that if the child were removed from the house and the strange events continued, perhaps then "electricity," or something other than Henry anyway, was the cause after all.

Thus it was that Henry was sent to stay at the homes of his uncles Hans and Andrew Lunde in the settlement of Springdale. Henry spent one day at Hans's house during which only a few small items took flight. But it was a far different story later at Andrew's home. No sooner had Henry walked in the door than a pail of water began spinning, then spilled across the kitchen floor. After the mess had been mopped up, Henry spied a mirror on the wall. "You'd better take that down," he warned. Andrew laughed. A moment later, the mirror crashed to the floor.

Meanwhile, all was peaceful at the Lunde home in Mount Horeb. Rather than take this as a sign that little Henry had been the source of the mischief, Mrs. Lunde insisted that there must be a supernatural explanation. A Mount Horeb cheesemaker told her that in the Old Country a bag of salt was the time-honored "remedy" to exorcise evil spirits. Accordingly, she sent word to Springdale, and Andrew Lunde put a small bag of salt in Henry's pocket.

But that didn't seem to work. A neighbor boy who came over to play was hit in the face by the salt bag when it supposedly flew out of Henry's pocket. Later a set of marbles the boys were playing with disappeared. Henry found them hidden around the house, even a few tucked deeply between bed quilts.

Andrew tried an experiment after the neighbor boy left. He put Henry in a chair and then held a cigar box full of marbles in front of him. The marbles leaped from the box, though the uncle swore Henry could not have touched them.

That night Henry complained about noises coming from the wall next to his bed. His uncle took a look around but could find nothing to explain the sounds. The next morning, however, Andrew found a large hole in the plaster wall next to Henry's bed. By this time, Uncle Andrew was tired of the problems his nephew was causing and talked his brother Hans into taking him back to Mount Horeb.

"I took a basket of eggs along and set them on a chair in the house," Hans later said. "While we were standing there one egg flew out of the basket and struck Henry in the face. I saw it leave the basket with my own eyes. There was no one anywhere near the basket. Two more eggs jumped out . . . on the floor and one jumped off the table."

Physician and Spiritualist Dr. George Kingsley of Madison also examined Henry. The Spiritualist movement in Wisconsin was still quite renowned at that time with a major center in Whitewater. During the short time Henry was in Dr. Kingsley's office, the doctor pronounced the boy a "splendid medium" for his age, destined to become one of the world's "greatest Spiritualists." He said that although the boy did not yet have the "spirits" under control, he would gain power over them later on.

Other clairvoyants were more specific in their assessment of the child. Some claimed they saw three spirits—two women and one man—hovering near him. They did not explain who the spirits were. Henry's mother recalled that when her son was quite small, two female Spiritualists had cared for him, one of whom later died. Some people thought she had passed her supernatural powers on to Henry before her death.

The seers also said that the three spirits were "oppressed" by crowds; for that reason, the manifestations never occurred when Henry was in school or when large groups of people came to the house.

But the Lundes came to another, even more amazing, conclusion. They told Mert P. Peavy, then editor of the *Dodgeville Chronicle*, that Henry had been hypnotized by someone and left in a trance.

If many accepted the notion that Henry was possessed of strange, supernatural powers, others did not. Henry's family had consulted a number of physicians in addition to Dr. Kingsley after they noted he seemed to be running a high fever and was losing weight. His mother said he was also experiencing mood swings; at times he would not talk to anyone.

Among those who concluded Henry was a fake were Dr. N. C. Evans and former sheriff G. E. Mickelson. The two men visited the Lundes one night at the peak of the excitement. They were seated with their backs to the kitchen doorway when two pieces of sausage, a bar of soap, and several chunks of coal flew into the room from the direction of the kitchen. They knew Henry was in the kitchen. Dr. Evans whirled around and asked Henry, who stood in the doorway, if he had thrown the articles. The boy did not give a direct answer. Instead, he hid in the kitchen because, as his grandparents said, he was "shy."

On another evening, Dr. Evans was in the sitting room and Henry was again in the kitchen. Suddenly a ball of yarn sailed into the room. The doctor was convinced that Henry had thrown it from the kitchen.

Another medical man at the time, Dr. Clarke Gapen, was asked for his opinion on the case.

"It is nonsense to waste any time on such cases unless it be to explode or expose them," Dr. Gapen was quoted as saying. "They can always be explained away and have been time and again exposed."

However, churchmen in the community were far less certain. A prayer meeting was held at the Lunde house to exorcise the demons, but, according to those present, the services only resulted in an increase in the phenomena.

What are we to believe in the case of Henry James Brophy?

Parapsychologists insist that many cases such as his cannot be explained away and that young children are often the focus of poltergeist activity. Some research suggests that children unconsciously create such disturbances in order to vent repressed hostility. That may make some sense in this case. Henry had lived with his grandparents since he was two years old. The loss of daily contact with his natural mother and her remarriage may have had a negative effect upon him that was then unconsciously expressed by propelling objects through the air.

It was also noted that as a baby, Henry had been struck by a horse-drawn wagon. Although he had mostly recovered from his crippling injuries, he remained delicate and sickly throughout his childhood. Poltergeist activity has sometimes been attributed to youngsters with histories of physical weaknesses.

Henry left Mount Horeb sometime around 1914 or 1915. No one is quite certain what happened to him in later years. Some thought he had married and moved to California, others that he had left for Madison or perhaps Milwaukee.

In the years that followed the Brophy case, community opinion was strongly divided about its authenticity. One local woman who knew Henry and the Lundes, Josie Evans, thought the whole thing was a fraud. Her brother, Jake Evans, thought it had perhaps been real. They both agreed that neither really knew what had gone on. Another resident at the time, Mabel Espeseth, said many of the stories were "made up." She later lived in the old Lunde house and claimed that she had never given a thought to supernatural activity. But Jan Kogen, who also later lived in the house, recalled that strange things did happen—she said a camera the family owned kept taking pictures on its own and finally had to be replaced.

The only point on which all agree is this: Henry James Brophy created a sensation more than a century ago in that little town west of Madison. Wittingly or not, Henry built a memorial to himself that no one who knew him or of him has ever forgotten.

Always Time for Ghosts

The premiere ghost hunter in southwest Wisconsin should be expected to have had at least a few supernatural experiences. In this respect, writer and folklorist Dennis Boyer does not disappoint the expectant listener: he has ghosts skulking about his own farm near Dodgeville.

Boyer lives on the mile-and-a-half-long Bethlehem Road, he said by way of setting the scene at his home. It's a dirt road that doesn't have much else along it except the abandoned Bethlehem Lutheran Cemetery. The church that used to be there burned down a long time ago. But that doesn't mean there isn't still activity there . . . of a sort.

"One day as I passed that cemetery [I] saw a young woman who looked to be in a lace nightgown out in the middle of the cemetery, kneeling down. Now, I can't say that what went through my mind was 'ghost,' but it seemed like an odd occurrence. What was she doing out there? It was toward dusk, but there was sufficient light to see."

Boyer soon discovered that the out-of-place woman in the cemetery might in fact have been a ghost. A neighbor told him that some sixty years earlier a young woman who had been incarcerated for some reason in a nearby county-owned facility escaped and sought refuge in the now-vanished church next to the cemetery. She is thought to have been responsible for burning it down.

The other ghost frequenting Boyer's neighborhood is an irascible old man who some believe is Tommy Lee, an early pioneer who farmed and fished.

222

"People see an older man," Boyer said about the sightings in his farm's woodlot. "It's taken on a life of its own. About a dozen people have seen him in the woods wearing his old blue coat."

Alas, Boyer has yet to catch a glimpse of that apparition.

For a man who has been an avid listener to people's stories for most of his life and a serious collector of ghost stories and folktales for nearly two decades, Boyer is not terribly surprised to encounter specters so close to home.

"I'm open to a lot of different possibilities. I don't know what the explanation of these things might be. Who knows? Maybe science will provide some of the answers. But ghost stories are one of the most durable forms of folklore."

Boyer grew up in a Pennsylvania Mennonite family with a tradition of storytelling dating back several hundred years. Many of the stories he heard as a child were from his coal miner grandfather who enthralled his grandson with tales of apparitions still hanging about long after the French and Indian and Revolutionary wars in the eighteenth century. Boyer had ancestors in both those conflicts.

But a pivotal experience in his childhood came to be the defining moment in his lifelong pursuit of American folk stories. Boyer was in the first grade. He had just learned about Abraham Lincoln and George Washington when his grandmother took him to see her own great-aunt who was over one hundred years old at the time and living in a nursing home.

The older woman started reminiscing about her father taking her down in the direction of Philadelphia to see Lincoln's funeral train pass by. She talked about the African American freemen and the Union soldiers crying in the rain as the bands played.

"She had a vivid memory of that time," Boyer explained. "That really struck me because it was such a very long time ago. But she was there! That impressed me."

Boyer says his great-great-aunt noted his astonishment.

"Then she talked about how her own grandfather told her about seeing the Pennsylvania Militia escort Washington away from the Continental Congress on that same road her father had taken her to see the funeral train."

Even though he was a young child, Boyer found himself profoundly moved by the woman's stories. He set off on a course that would include successful careers in law and in lobbying, as a social activist and environmental preservationist, but all the while maintaining an abiding avocational interest in documenting the stories, legends, and folk beliefs of ordinary people, and then sharing them with the wider world through his writing.

Although Boyer has a broad interest in all sorts of folklore, ghost stories are among his favorites, especially those that occur in the open countryside, far away from the traditional haunted mansions of legend. Many of Boyer's best stories come from men and women responsible for enforcing hunting and fish regulations. He said conservation wardens "see everything." If someone has seen odd creatures in the swamps, or spotted UFOs hovering over a lake, someone has told the region's DNR (Department of Natural Resources) officers. Boyer has found the officers to be "wonderful" storytellers themselves.

Unfortunately, conservation officers also end up as the supernatural subjects in some stories. Boyer knows of one "warden ghost" and another legendary specter of a "warden's special," that is, an auxiliary conservation officer. Both ghosts are from northern Wisconsin, above what Boyer and others have termed the "tension line," a boundary sometimes placed along U.S. Highway 8, which slices across the top quarter of the state from St. Croix Falls in the west to Iron Mountain in the Upper Peninsula near Lake Michigan. North of there, the character of supernatural tales seems to change. He said the highway might also be called the "story line."

"Things are kind of pastoral south of there, in a rural sense. North of there stories get edgier; either they have macabre content or they incorporate themes that may not necessarily be supernatural but are the source of some discomfort and dissatisfaction."

Some northern ghost stories even contain what might be termed "political" content. The storytellers have complaints about government or big business, and those gripes are incorporated into the stories they tell.

Boyer remarked that people he has talked to are angry at the DNR, or at the U.S. Fish and Wildlife Service, or at the pulp and paper and mining companies. He thinks it's inevitable that when such people tell stories they incorporate their grievances into them. And up north he finds more of that sense of resentment.

Northern Wisconsin also hosts a fair number of lumberjack ghosts, given that the logging industry took quite a human toll in its early days. In other parts of the state, Boyer explained, ghost stories are generated by what he terms "industrial themes" such as railroading, which has resulted in tales of vanishing brakemen and ghostly steam trains.

Phantom hunters seem to be a bit more prevalent in Wisconsin than, say, phantom hitchhikers, one of the most frequently recurring ghost tales in other parts of the globe.

Hunter ghosts are common owing to the frequency of tragic accidents or other, more sinister events.

Boyer believes these particular hunter stories have an underlying theme. In feudal Europe all wild game belonged to the crown or aristocracy, and commoners caught hunting could be prosecuted for poaching. The punishment could have been imprisonment, torture, or even death. Therefore, immigrants to Wisconsin had little tradition of hunting game upon which to build but embraced it "with a vengeance," Boyer explained.

"Ghostly hunter stories are told with zeal. And people can be proprietary about them. They're told within families. The family goes to the same hunting shack every November and grandfather tells the story" of the ghost hunter who's still seen out in the forest.

Boyer quite naturally points to his own region, southwest Wisconsin, as being particularly rich in ghost stories.

"Among those early lead miners there was a wild west environment that didn't exist elsewhere in Wisconsin, and probably one that didn't exist much anywhere else east of the Mississippi. It was almost a Dodge City milieu. When you hear about the knifings, the shootings, the card brawls, it was pretty wild and woolly. And there were public executions that drew thousands of people in a way that doesn't even seem like Wisconsin."

For all the abundance of Wisconsin's ghosts, however, most of them are more temperate beings than those found in other regions of the United States.

Boyer said ghost stories he heard as a child on the East Coast had an edgier, more macabre quality. "[In Wisconsin], people look at [ghosts] like guardian angels. By and large their experiences are fairly benign. I've found only a few in the tradition of 'The Legend of Sleepy Hollow,' where there's some relentless pursuer. Other than that, they are watchful, sentinel types that appear to be looking after things. Even the ones that are agents of mischief don't seem that malignant."

In 1962, folklorists Robert Gard and L. G. Sorden claimed that Wisconsin had more ghosts per square mile than anywhere else in the United States. While a supernatural census has never been attempted—and is probably not even remotely possible—Boyer thinks Gard and Sorden were right.

"I don't think there's anyplace else that on a statewide basis has more ghosts, from the Illinois state line right up to Lake Superior."

Although he cautioned that most of his conclusions are tentative, Boyer believes the reason for Wisconsin's supernatural abundance may have more to do with the state's diverse ethnic mix than with a climate particularly well suited to visitors from the beyond.

"I think that as people came up from Missouri, and the Yankees were coming out here, at the same time you got all the settlers from Norway and Germany bringing with them lots of traditions."

But that's only part of it, Boyer said, especially for those ghost stories with strong rural themes. He pointed to a strong Native American presence in Wisconsin, for instance, much stronger than in Eastern states where the Native populations are remote from the present in both time and space. In the American West, the settlers and Native populations were antagonistic, the transition to white settlements more violent and unsettled.

"Here in Wisconsin, despite the Blackhawk War and the short-lived Winnebago War, there were more protracted interactions [between Native Americans and white settlers] from as far back as the time of the French voyageurs. Because I focus on the environment, many Native American legends [interconnect] easily [with non-Native ghost stories] because there are many natural themes, such as the names of places where spirits are alleged to inhabit."

Boyer noted that when European Americans retell stories that began as Native American legends, they tend to lose the spiritual character with which the Native Americans may have originally invested them, and to assume the light-heartedness more typical of European stories. The ghost at the center of the tale shifts from being a religious symbol to being merely the source of a good scare. That's particularly true of the spirits who evolved from benevolent beings in the original Native American accounts into malevolent specters in the European versions.

Whatever the source of the ghost story, Boyer believes most have served a specific purpose in their repeated telling. He said they reinforce values, or let people know what the "rules" might be. A ghost story may *dissuade* people from engaging in some activity, such as to keep children away from an old mine shaft or uncovered well, or a dilapidated barn. There are clearly other values as well, he added—pure entertainment being one—but he's found there's an "uplifting" or spiritual function too, though some storytellers "are loathe to use that word in this way."

Among Boyer's favorite yarns are those he has culled from people on the lower Wisconsin River, roughly from Sauk City down to Prairie du Chien. He said there is a story milieu there that exists in only a few other places in the state. It is also along the river that he has found a recurring character under various names—sometimes just the Old Man—but who could be Wisconsin's variation of the trickster, a prank-playing spirit found in legends of various cultures over the millennia. The Wisconsin variant ascribes misfortunes of most any kind to the one-eyed Old Man.

He sometimes steals the biggest fish a person catches, sometimes causes accidents at the boat landing, and sometimes even capsizes a boat if he's irritated enough.

According to Boyer, any sort of mishap gets attributed to the Old Man. Boyer's theory is that the character might have had its beginnings with some older Ho-Chunk trickster.

"There must have been a time when these people who lived outdoor lives, trapping and so forth, must have come in contact with Native Americans. I have a feeling the [trickster] story started in the area around that time."

The trickster tradition in the American ghost story is rather common. Boyer has found different versions among Native American peoples as well as Europeanized accounts from along the Wisconsin River. But today, the story may be used more as a "cover" for a practical joke than an authentic ghost story. "Some guys delight in getting a friend to put his boat in the water and then getting him off on some sort of errand. When he comes back, he discovers that his boat is filled with water." His friends try to persuade him that a "ghost" was responsible.

Nevertheless, the ghostly trickster is still often blamed for human failings: "In farming country it's what sours the cow's milk, it's why the ham is missing from the smokehouse, never mind that the hired man left yesterday for parts unknown."

Boyer, an attorney by profession, said that he is not particularly concerned with "truth" in his avocational pursuit of folktales.

"I would never look at a ghost story in the same way that I would look at an evidentiary matter in a worker's compensation hearing. I couldn't treat them in that fashion. I do believe that most of the people I've talked to are sincere, that something did happen to them. It's then a question of interpretation. Often what they saw were variables—an unusual light in an abandoned house, or a noise in the barn, or some recurrent physical phenomenon outdoors—a glow maybe."

That's not to say, however, that Boyer has not been gripped by a first-person account of the supernatural. After all, he has had his own experiences in that realm. But the one anecdote that sticks out above all others in his mind was told to him several years ago as he was collecting stories along the Wisconsin River.

"An elderly man in Avoca, on the southern shore of the river, told me a story of what happened to him when he was a young man . . . [during] World War I or . . . before. One morning he was trapping in the backwater when he walked across the ice and fell through. He claimed to have just about given up that he was ever going to get out when a hand reached down and pulled him out. He thought he saw an old man in front of him on the bank. He coughed and sputtered and wiped his eyes but nobody was there."

Arthur, the Impudent Ghost

Shortly after A.J. Nielsen moved into her house at Sparta, she wished she had not. She was to recall many times over the next months the odd hesitancy of the previous, elderly owner before agreeing to sell even though it had been vacant for fifteen years. A.J. had been attracted to the well-kept, two-story house for reasons that even she sometimes could not understand; though she especially admired its charming and spacious rooms, there seemed to be something else pulling her toward ownership.

The troubles began almost immediately; A.J. and her two children confided in each other that they felt "uneasy" sometimes. Within weeks, their disquiet intensified with a distant scratching that the family attributed to mice or bats in the large, walk-in attic that occupied a third floor, except that searches never revealed any evidence of rodents or flying mammals.

But that all changed one night when A.J. arrived home from work at ten in the evening. She found her son and daughter armed with baseball bats, their faces pale with fright. They said they had been watching television when they heard something jumping up and down from somewhere on the floors above. The chandelier in the dining room was actually swinging back and forth, they said.

With flashlights and baseball bats, the trio climbed the staircase to search the bedrooms and attic above.

"The chill was terrible upstairs," A.J. remembered. "We all held our breath as we opened the attic door."

Stacks of unpacked boxes were exactly where they had been placed earlier. Nothing had fallen. Nothing had been disturbed.

But later things got much, much worse.

Small items placed on a table one minute went missing the next. Locked doors swung open. Doors left ajar suddenly slammed shut.

"When I was in the bathtub there would be doors slamming and footsteps all over the house," A.J. recalled with a shudder.

Every family member was awakened during the night at one time or another by scratching noises or loud, thumping sounds. A.J.'s son often bounded downstairs to say he had felt some presence at the top of the stairs icily staring at him. His sister thought she sensed her brother standing nearby on the stairs one night as she watched television. Expecting him to pop into the room and play a joke on her, she flung open the door that led out into the hallway and staircase. A blast of cold air hit her in the face, and then a hissing. The girl ran upstairs and found her brother fast asleep in his bedroom.

Early one morning, A.J.'s daughter awakened to the pressure of a hand pushing against her side. "That was the last straw for her," A.J. said of her adult daughter. "She moved out and got her own apartment."

The Nielsen haunting also affected the family's social life. A.J. hesitated to invite friends over, given the nightly commotions and sudden, unpredictable chills that swept the house. Two acquaintances who did drop in told A.J. they had felt uncomfortable during their visit.

An electrician hired to rewire the house started on a day when A.J. was not home. From then on out, he refused to work there unless she was home. He told her he felt someone breathing on his neck, watching from over his shoulder as he worked.

A.J.'s former husband stopped by one day to visit their son. The boy had not yet returned from school, and A.J. had left the house to run an errand. When she got back, her ex-husband was standing outside, pale and shaken. "I don't know what happened," he told her, "but something made me get out. It's just like ice in there."

So onerous was her life there that A.J. began to doubt her own sanity. On a day when the turmoil seemed unceasing, she ran to the bone-chilling attic and fell sobbing to the floor.

"Why are you doing this to me?" she cried out. "I have never hurt you. I have no other place to go!"

And then a remarkable calm filled the room. She felt the pressure of a hand on her shoulder, but this was a reassuring touch that conveyed warmth and understanding. A.J. thought that at that moment a kind of truce had been reached with whatever the source of the haunting had been.

But if A.J. thought it was over, she was mistaken. Although the unexplained noises and sudden cold spots subsided, she was to face a new ordeal.

An apparition materialized in the form of a slight man in a dark suit and white shirt. His pant legs were narrowly tailored; a large, orange cat stood by his side. The faint image was always wrapped in mist.

In the days and weeks to come, A.J. caught glimpses of her resident ghost sometimes gazing out a window or sometimes slipping quietly up the staircase. She took to calling him Arthur, for no particular reason, and even held one-sided conversations with him. Occasionally, she asked him to watch over the house while she was gone!

One week there was no sign of Arthur, but the ghostly cat was still very much around.

"He'd rub against my legs when I was cooking at the stove," A.J. said. "When I'd look down I'd see this shadowy figure just disappearing" through the doorway. Sometimes she'd hear him jump to the floor from a windowsill, the curtains fluttering at the sudden movement.

A.J. knew Arthur had returned when she heard the front door slam shut. She came into the hall just in time to see his murky form going upstairs carrying a leather valise with strap bindings.

Although A.J. had begun looking for another place to live, she continued to fix up "Arthur's house." He seemed to approve of the work, and was even helpful and protective toward her.

On one occasion, she slipped off a ladder but unseen arms caught her and lifted her to safety. Another time she was running late for work and misplaced her car keys. She called upon Arthur for help. There was a slight *clunk* and the keys were on the table beside her.

A.J. found another key when cleaning the kitchen cupboards. It didn't appear to fit anything in the house, but she slipped it on her key ring anyway for safekeeping.

After her watch broke, A.J. said Arthur guided her to the attic, where she found a small, gold wristwatch with a woman's strap in the middle of the floor. In all of her trips to the attic, she had never seen it. A jeweler told her that all the watch needed was a good cleaning to run like new. A.J. wondered to whom the watch had belonged. Perhaps it had been someone important in Arthur's life and now he wanted to share it with someone else.

Though A.J. longed to ask the former owner questions about Arthur, she kept to herself. After all, she reasoned, if word got out that the house was haunted, who would buy it?

With the passing weeks, Arthur became even bolder in his appearances. He often sat on the kitchen stool when A.J. was baking or washing dishes. The conversations were still one-sided—A.J. chatted away; Arthur remained silent. He seemed to like her but still resented her friends. When they visited, the chandeliers swayed and icy breezes swept through the rooms.

A.J. became quite fond of Arthur, yet she knew she had to move away. She yearned for a normal lifestyle, one free of unwanted ghosts. At the same time she was fearful that he might in some way try to prevent her from leaving. She need not have worried.

Finally she found a suitable new house, bought it from the builder, and moved right in. A.J. claimed that to her astonishment the key she found in her kitchen cabinets fit the lock on the front door of her new house!

During the months before the old house was sold, A.J. made regular trips back to clean and keep it secure.

"I could still feel his presence," she said. "But he was much quieter than usual, almost a little sad."

Arthur made far fewer appearances during her infrequent stops at the house. Eventually the house did sell, presumably ghost and all.

On the day when the new family was moving in, A.J. paid her last visit. Two little girls were playing outside.

"Look," one of them called out. "There's a man in your upstairs window!"

A.J. looked up. Arthur stood gazing down at them. His cat was perched on the sill. "Good-bye," she whispered. He raised his hand to say farewell and was gone. The cat remained in the window a moment longer and then he, too, was no more.

Cassandra

Not all family ghosts are kept in the closet or stalk about the house frightening residents or startling visitors. Take the case of B. T. Jutes * of Crawford County for example. Hers was the live-in kind of ghost: a friendly, solicitous woman who watched over the children and helped B. T. with her genealogical research.

According to B. T., the ghost's name was Cassandra and she first appeared in a kind of psychic tableau on a bedroom wall one frosty January night. She wore a shimmering, swirling red dress and, with her bearded companion, stood before an open, horse-drawn carriage. Her jet-black hair was parted severely down the middle and pulled back tightly over her ears; dark eyes twinkled above a veil that concealed the lower half of her face. She suddenly dropped the veil and stepped into the carriage with her partner. With that, the image vanished.

"I kept thinking I was dreaming, but yet I knew I was awake," B. T. said. "My husband was snoring all the while this was going on. I was awake. And I was frightened."

She got up, checked on her children, and then walked through the entire house, examining the security of each window and door from the basement to the top floor. Still uneasy, she went back to bed but slept poorly.

The next night the identical scene returned to the wall, but this time in black and white rather than the colorful depiction of the night before. This time, however, there was a new twist—the mysterious woman lowered her veil, turned to B. T., and smiled.

Sometime later, B. T. was invited to attend a séance. When she told the story of the mysterious woman and her companion, she was warned by the others present that because of the veil the woman was a negative spirit and not to be trusted. They suggested she put a mental "red circle of truth" around herself, her loved ones, and her home.

It was after midnight when she returned home. "I was scared to death. I wanted to leave all the lights on," she recalled. The mental red circle of truth she had been advised to create didn't seem adequate.

"I knew I wasn't keeping anybody out because they were already in!"

As B. T. opened her front door, the woman from the ghostly montage was standing in the hallway. She looked exactly like she had looked on the wall, except that B. T. could see through her.

"Why are you so afraid of me?" asked the vaporous visitor. Before B. T. could reply, the specter sprung another surprise on her: she was, she said, B. T.'s great-great-great-grandmother, Cassandra, and she had lived as a child in Virginia and Maryland a century and a half earlier.

B. T. thought she certainly didn't seem like an evil spirit; in fact, Cassandra offered to guide and protect the family.

Later that day, B. T. told her husband and children about their spectral guest. Although none of them would ever see her, they sometimes felt her presence, like that of an invisible babysitter.

Little Danny, four years old at the time, was particularly unperturbed. "I know she's here to help me," he said. One morning the boy awoke in his top bunk bed with his back bruised and cut. The ladder to his bed was on the floor and there was a fresh dent in the bedroom wall that B. T. believed was made by the force of the falling ladder. Neither B. T. nor her husband had put their son back into bed after his apparent tumble. Danny had no recollection of the incident. The boy also survived a near drowning in a local swimming pool, B. T. maintains, with Cassandra's help.

B. T. was a veteran genealogist when Cassandra first made her appearance. However, she had been unable to trace several branches of her family. B. T. found that in those years before the explosion of interest in genealogy and the advent of the Internet, some birth certificates could not be found and important marriage records were seldom available. Her ancestors had not kept a family Bible in which they might have noted family names and significant dates. B. T. claims Cassandra supplied the missing links, providing facts about family members that she was later able to verify through official documents.

B. T. believes that might have been the reason for Cassandra's appearance. Ghosts have been known to leave familiar surroundings, traveling great distances to provide missing information or intervene in a crisis.

For instance, Cassandra disclosed her own maiden name and the date and place of her marriage. B. T. followed up.

"I wrote to that county in Ohio and I [now] have her wedding license. When I gave a photocopy of the certificate to my grandmother, she was flabbergasted because she didn't know this woman's maiden name."

Cassandra also supplied the names and birth dates of all her children. B. T. went directly to the census records and was able to confirm the number of children she had and their names.

Sometimes names and complete addresses of living relatives came to B. T. "out of a clear blue sky—people that I had no inkling of any connection with us. I didn't even look up the addresses. I just wrote."

More incredible still is B. T.'s claim to have twice visited Cassandra's home. On each occasion, B. T. was transported there instantaneously. "I disappear and I am there," she maintained. The two women have talked in Cassandra's sitting room. B. T. has even seen Cassandra's daughter, Mary Jane, who was killed in a horse-riding accident.

B. T. said that when she was in Cassandra's home, the experience felt entirely real, but when she is with the ghost in her own home, "everything is in a haze."

Some parapsychologists say people can leave their bodies and describe people and places they have never actually seen.

B. T. believes she could detect Cassandra's presence in the home long before she appeared on the bedroom wall. Cassandra seemed to spend a lot of time by the front door, watching the children come and go. She also followed B. T. upstairs to tell her the phone was ringing or that someone was at the door.

Cassandra was a real and loving presence for B. T. Far from being the evil spirit others warned against, Cassandra was always a positive force, bolstering B. T.'s spirits in times of need and pushing her to do more than she ever thought possible.

The Ridgeway Ghost

The year is 1842. Wisconsin is still six years away from statehood. Towering pines hover over the virgin forests, the lumber industry is still in its infancy, and settlers are only just now reaching the remote corners of the wilderness that stretches endlessly across the horizon. Valuable lead deposits have been discovered in the rolling limestone hills of southwestern Wisconsin. For a young nation, still struggling for survival, the soft, bluish-gray substance represents a valuable commodity on the world market. Perhaps more importantly, the veins of lead could help furnish the bullets and other products with which Americans would tame the rugged wilderness.

The opening of the mines attracted rowdy, tough, dangerous men whose job it was to wrench the lead from the earth's grasp. From Ireland, Wales, and Cornwall, and from Germany and the American South, miners came to the lead district surrounding the pioneer outposts of Mineral Point, Dodgeville, Blue Mounds, and other small villages. At the height of the mining boom, nearly forty thousand pounds of lead would be hauled each year to markets in Milwaukee, Dubuque, Chicago, and Galena.

Roads were cut through dense forests over which the lead wagons would roll. Alongside the rutted paths another industry grew—the saloons and roadhouses catering to the raucous appetites of the miners. These establishments had names like McKillip's (about five miles west of Ridgeway), the Messerschmidt Hotel (five miles west of Dodgeville), and Markey's (two miles west of Ridgeway).

There were more than twenty-two saloons on the main thoroughfare, called Military Ridge Road, between Blue Mounds and Dodgeville, a distance of only twenty-five miles, and roughly along what is now Highway 18/151.

Drunken fistfights, robberies, murders, or an occasional clubbing were not uncommon along that rough thoroughfare. Various criminal elements along with gamblers and prostitutes, their lives often tragically short, joined the immigrant miners. Burial services for the unluckiest ones were informal, the corpse dropped unceremoniously into a convenient grave with a few hasty words mumbled before the dirt was shoveled in. A modest wooden slab with the victim's name crudely etched into it might be stuck into the ground.

For over two decades, wagons carrying lead for the processing mills rumbled along the road. The saloons, bawdy houses, and inns thrived. But all that ended in 1857 when the Chicago and Northwestern Railroad completed a branch line into Mineral Point. Lead could now be shipped out more easily by rail, and traffic along Military Ridge Road consequently declined. The notorious roadside lairs eventually closed down.

At the height of the mining era, however, wagon masters and wayfarers sometimes had more to fear than a chance meeting with a highwayman. Beginning in about 1840, a series of bizarre, often puckish, and generally inexplicable encounters with ghosts and phantoms beset those who lived or worked along Military Ridge Road. In particular, the small community of Ridgeway, halfway between what was then called Pokerville (Blue Mounds) and Mineral Point, became the center of activities for what came to be known as the Ridgeway Ghost.

This infamous ghost, it must be said, was not one spirit but rather a mischievous phantom that could change its appearance at will. It was known to appear as a dog, a horse, a pig, or a sheep, and it even took several different human forms, including that of a headless horseman. The ghost roamed the countryside, frightening farmers, miners, and travelers alike. The thing might shadow buggy riders or lead haulers as they ventured out along the road after dark, terrify farmers returning from their fields at dusk, and generally frighten the wits out of anyone unlucky enough to cross its path.

But is there any basis in fact for these stories of a ghost haunting the countryside around Ridgeway? We will never know the answer with certainty, despite the scores of stories that have come down to us. We must go back to the early 1840s to begin exploring the tales of the Ridgeway Ghost.

One of the seedier establishments was Sampson's Saloon and Hotel. Many a traveler risked his earthly future in this pit of human depravity. The Ridgeway

Ghost may be the earthbound spirit of one doomed wayfarer who checked in and never left.

The man was a peddler who stopped by Sampson's after a long day's ride, unaware of its unsavory reputation. He was seen entering his room but then vanished. Early the next morning, his fully saddled horse tried to enter the saloon hotel. The animal failed in its attempts and was chased off, never to be seen again.

Soon after the peddler's disappearance, people began reporting a bizarre apparition on the road near the hotel. A black horse would gallop along the roadway, and on its back was the torso of a headless man mounted backward in the saddle. The horse and rider kept pace with and sometimes pass frightened travelers. If anyone tried to converse with the macabre apparition, unearthly groans would issue from the decapitated body.

One buggy driver encountered the horseman in a most unusual way. As the driver rode along, he heard an approaching horse. Turning in the wooden buggy seat, he saw a stallion upon which rode a figure in black—backward, and minus his head. Instead of passing the buckboard, the horse reared and planted its front quarters firmly in the wagon box. Frightened nearly senseless, the driver whipped his team forward but the horse and rider kept pace. The beast's front legs were still in the wagon, only inches away. When—or if—the wagoner reached safety isn't known. Perhaps he's still whipping his team forward trying to reach the comfort of home.

McKillip's was the name of another even more notorious tavern about five miles west of Ridgeway on what is now Highway 18/151. Some accounts of the origin of the Ridgeway Ghost stem from a horrifying incident at this saloon.

Two teenage brothers, aged fourteen and fifteen, ambled into the establishment one winter day and promptly became the subject of jest by the drunken customers. The ridicule soon turned to murder when one boy was grabbed and thrown into the blazing fireplace and burned alive. The other youngster managed to escape but was never heard from again. The next spring his frozen corpse was found in a field.

After the boys' murder, a small, gray-haired woman would be seen wandering aimlessly along the road near McKillip's. She would vanish when strangers approached. Those who saw her speculated that she might be the mother or grandmother of the murdered boys looking for their bodies.

Variations of a female specter abound in the Ridgeway vicinity.

A retired railroad man, Lyle Kramer, told a story passed down by his father. The elder Kramer said he often saw two old women on an isolated section of the railroad tracks flagging down a passenger train near Military Ridge Road. When the train stopped to pick up the women, they floated away into the forest.

On another occasion an unidentified man was driving his team of horses near Ridgeway when he sighted a woman directly ahead. She was going in his direction, but walking down the center of the road. He yelled at her to move but she didn't respond or turn around. The horseman moved over to pass, but as he did so the mysterious woman moved to the side to block his approach. He urged his team into a faster gallop to get around her, but the woman always somehow managed to stay ahead. He halted his team—and she halted too. When he started again, she did likewise. After several miles of this frustrating exchange the woman vanished.

Others said an old woman would appear shuffling along the road. She would then disappear into a ball of fire.

McKillip's Saloon also figures in another Ridgeway Ghost tale. A local man was riding home after a visit to the village. As he approached McKillip's he passed a large white oak tree. A sudden gust of cold wind enveloped him. His horse reared, nearly tossing its rider onto the ground. The man managed to hang on as the animal raced wildly all the way home.

The death of the pastor at Ridgeway's Catholic church gave rise to another version of the origin of the ghost.

The priest was walking down the steps of the church when he fell and struck his head on the stone steps. He died shortly thereafter. For many years, on the anniversary of his death, people claimed blood would appear on the steps of the church and hideous sounds reverberated from within.

The church mysteriously burned to the ground several years later.

Whichever version one chooses to believe there is little doubt that the Ridgeway Ghost is the subject of more tales than any other legendary specter in the state. It showed no favoritism, assuming various disguises to frighten unwary victims. The following stories recount some of the Ridgeway Ghost's more infamous appearances.

The long-vanished Messerschmidt Hotel in Ridgeway was the scene of several ghostly visits.

The hotel's founder, George Messerschmidt, was a member of the county board. A railroad was to be built from Warren, Illinois, to Mineral Point, and board members had decided to raise the necessary capital by issuing county bonds.

Soon after Messerschmidt decided to sign the bonds, a strange creaking and groaning sound filled the hotel at night. Messerschmidt couldn't sleep.

Night after night the uneasy noises grew in intensity. Sometimes a voice cried out in the night, "Don't sign the bonds. Don't sign the bonds."

Perhaps a disgruntled taxpayer had discovered a political use for the Ridgeway Ghost. Or perhaps the spirit realized the railroad would take away the traffic along its favorite haunt, Military Ridge Road.

Throughout the hotel's history, customers heard moans coming from the walls accompanied by the sound of dragging chains.

An early Irish settler named Kennedy accumulated quite a sum of money and used part of it to build a large home on land he owned near the old Porter Grove cheese factory.

One evening he visited the nearly completed house. Kennedy unlocked the front door and strolled through the many rooms. Upon entering the dining room he saw a person's misty form seated at the table. The old man fled in terror, never to return. He built a smaller house nearby and lived there the rest of his days, convinced the Ridgeway Ghost had taken up residence in his mansion.

Other stories are told about Kennedy. He had a penchant for burying his money. His favorite hiding spot was close to the railroad tracks, where he could check on its safety each day. One night after visiting the cache, he was walking home when he saw a light mysteriously dancing up and down, one moment dim, the next quite bright. A train? A flagman? Perhaps. But Kennedy didn't wait to find out. He fled across the fields.

In the end, Kennedy's death was attributed to the nightly visitations at his earthen bank. As the years passed, his hearing deteriorated. One night a train struck and killed him as he sat on the tracks. No one knows for sure what became of the money.

Years later a local character named Rocky Jim Ryan moved into the old Kennedy house. Jim claimed that at night he could hear the old man's boots tromping through the rooms. He finally moved out the morning after "something" pulled the covers off his bed.

The old Reilly house stood near the Catholic church in Ridgeway. But when it was built more than a century ago the house was located several miles west of Ridgeway near the railroad tracks. A ghostly history is connected with the house.

An old gentleman named Peavey once lived at the house's original location. After he moved away, the place burned down. Another house was built on the foundation, but the new owners left within a few days. A large black dog would appear, tired and panting, under their dining room table every night after dark. The animal would then disappear as suddenly as it had come.

The house was eventually moved to its current location in Ridgeway. The dog never reappeared. Some people think the canine apparition was connected somehow to the location of the original house.

But a couple who have lived in the Reilly place more recently have reported other unusual events. When their daughter was young, she would become frightened at a noise coming from the attic that sounded like children playing with marbles. The "marbles" rolled across the floor for several minutes on end. Nothing was ever found that could explain the sound.

There are two versions of Evan "Strangler" Lewis's mysterious death.

Lewis was a well-known local wrestler of immense size with a fearlessness that matched his physical strength. When he wasn't winning bets in the wrestling ring, he supported his family by farming and helping neighbors butcher their animals. It was after a day of such butchering that Lewis took a fateful walk.

He had been warned not to travel home after dark because of several recent appearances by the Ridgeway Ghost. He sneered at the reports, citing his strength, agility, and the butcher knives he carried as protection enough against any would-be phantom.

According to one version of the tale, Lewis was walking across a field when a white horse pulling a driverless carriage charged at him. Lewis jumped out of the way and as he did so the horse and carriage rose and disappeared into the sky. He ran all the way home.

The second tale likewise has Lewis crossing a large field. He suddenly felt something warm breathing on his hand. Lewis turned and found himself staring directly into the red eyes of an immense black dog. He tried to chase it away but the beast kept following him at a distance. A few yards farther along Lewis again felt the panting beast at his heels. This time he aimed a kick directly at the dog, but his foot flew through the empty space where the dog had been only seconds before.

Fleeing the scene, Lewis thought safety was within his grasp. The darkness was almost total as he crashed through the brush. His cabin only a hundred yards away, Lewis again felt the pressure of the black beast at his back. Lewis drew one of the butcher knives and slashed at the dog, but hit only air. He continued attempting to fight off the dog until within sight of his house—when the canine disappeared.

When Lewis reached home he was dripping with sweat, shaking, and exhausted. His family sent for the doctor. Upon examining the still-traumatized

Lewis, the physician claimed that his heart had moved nearly two inches from its proper location.

Lewis died two days later.

All sorts of strange animals have been sighted as part of the Ridgeway Ghost stories—pigs, sheep, horses, dogs, and "critters."

One night, a Mr. and Mrs. Buckingham were returning home from a day of shopping. As their buckboard approached Markey's Saloon, two miles west of Ridgeway, Mrs. Buckingham noticed what she thought was an animal on the road. Her husband squinted into the gloom and said it looked like a breed of dog he'd never seen before. Whatever it was, the couple claimed the entire area around the animal was illuminated with sparks flying from its back. The horses nearly bolted at the sight. The apparition slowly vanished. The Buckinghams never encountered the creature again.

Boo Tesch and his dog were returning home just after midnight after an evening at a friend's house. As they passed a low bank of earth, Tesch heard a sound; looking up on the ridge, he saw a giant, snarling dog crouching as if ready to spring at any moment.

Tesch's dog took one look at the creature and scampered away down the road, whimpering, tail between its legs. Tesch was left alone to face the brute. He looked for something to use as a weapon and found a stone, which he hurled at it. The rock missed and the dog began circling the vulnerable Tesch. And then, just as suddenly as it had appeared, the dog vanished.

Until his death fifty years later, Tesch could neither forget nor explain what he had seen that night.

Sailor Dave Jones often courted his future wife at her home in what is now part of Governor Dodge State Park, just north of Dodgeville.

Jones was returning home on horseback one evening when he heard sheep bleating on the trail behind him. He stopped his horse, and a herd of sheep passed on either side of the startled rider. Behind the sheep rode two silent men. They did not look at Jones or say a word. The sheep and their stoic herders faded into the distance. Later, a group of men examined the trail but could find neither sheep nor riders.

George Russell, a farmer near Ridgeway, had arranged with another man to purchase a pig. Russell agreed to meet the man in Ridgeway to pay cash for it. The two met, the pig was placed in Russell's crate on the back of his wagon, and the seller departed. Russell finished a few errands in the village and finally hitched up his team for the drive home.

At his farm, Russell backed the wagon up to the chute and opened the crate but, instead of the pig, a large dog jumped out. To this day no one knows how the exchange took place, whether it was the work of the Ridgeway Ghost, or whether a practical joker was having some fun at Russell's expense.

Interestingly, a phantom pig or drove of pigs was a quite frequent encounter in the Ridgeway area.

One particular teamster reported that he encountered several on Military Ridge Road. As he approached, they dissolved into a cloud of dust.

Wagon drivers would often stop at one (or several) of the saloons for a shot of bottled "courage," despite knowing they were within the stomping grounds of the Ridgeway Ghost.

John Riley was one such frequenter of a particular saloon near Ridgeway. His team of oxen would stand outside with a load of pig lead destined for Galena.

One night after finishing his brew he stepped outside the door to find that his oxen had been rehitched to the rear of the wagon. And walking down the road was the Ridgeway Ghost with a whip in one hand and a lantern in the other.

Riley spent the night in the tavern.

There was a "haunted grove" west of Ridgeway on Highway 18/151. During the era when the highway was known as Military Ridge Road, a phantom would often appear there to startled passersby.

One story describes a man on foot who encountered a team of huge black stallions pulling a black carriage. The apparition charged directly at him but, incredibly, flew directly overhead, leaving him lying prone in the dirt, dazed and frightened but unscathed.

Other travelers passing through the "haunted grove" reported that a strange white apparition flew out at them from the forest before disappearing into the brush. Some heard an eerie, wailing scream from the bowels of the grove. No one ever ventured in to investigate.

One old gentleman didn't believe in the Ridgeway Ghost. The fellow took a shortcut through the local cemetery one evening. A bright light suddenly shone upward from a tombstone, and ghastly screams pierced the nocturnal air.

From that day forward the elderly gent was afflicted with a nervous disorder.

A young girl was returning home from a visit to a neighboring farm when she saw a light coming from within a barn her family used as a stable. Thinking it was her father checking on the horses, she walked up to the barn—but the light suddenly vanished.

She found no one inside. And yet she claimed to have felt a presence. Perhaps the Ridgeway Ghost was looking for a new horse?

The Ridgeway Ghost also took on various human forms.

A young man named Jim Moore was visiting his sweetheart near Blue Mounds. The young lady lived in a large house with an exterior stairway leading to her apartment on the top floor. It was dusk when the suitor arrived to see her. He paused at the top of the stairs to catch his breath before knocking on the door. From there he looked down and saw an old man perched atop a rusted stove lying in the yard. Moore had never seen the elderly man before and thought there was something strange about him. Moore went inside and told his girlfriend about the man in the yard. She was concerned and, as the night progressed, tried to persuade her beau to spend the night. Moore didn't think it was proper and declined.

Moore started home on foot. He didn't see the man in the yard at first, but then suddenly the old gentleman was at his side, matching Moore's stride step for step. The vaporous figure did not speak a word and stared straight ahead. As Moore neared his own house he heard a small explosion and the old man vanished.

Moore broke into a run and made it safely home. As he leaned panting against the kitchen door, it dawned on him that the Ridgeway Ghost had escorted him home.

Jim Moore never visited the girl again.

In the era before automobiles, young couples would walk short distances to visit friends. So it was that a young man and his new bride accepted an invitation to a party at a home a few miles away near Wakefield.

The night was dark and still. The only light blazed from their swinging lanterns, pointing the way through the heavy woods. The air had not yet cooled from an unusually hot day in early autumn. No breeze stirred the air. Freshly fallen leaves formed a carpet upon which their steps made a faint rustling sound.

Without warning, something stirred in the path a few yards ahead. Thinking it was a neighbor also walking to the party, the young man called out a greeting, but there was no answer. Abruptly the night air turned cold. Their lanterns' glow reflected upon leaves fluttering in the air for no apparent reason. The sound of footsteps reached their ears, and looking down they clearly saw the imprints of a man's shoes.

Although they saw nothing, the couple claimed to have felt a presence in the forest. The Ridgeway Ghost was out for an evening stroll.

Willy Powell passed a pleasant evening with his girlfriend in Ridgeway and was returning home in his buckboard, hitched to a fine pair of silky black horses. The winter night was particularly cold, with masses of swirling snow drifting across long stretches of the road.

Hurrying the animals along, Powell turned into the drive, which led to the warmth and safety of his cabin. Without warning, his horses reared suddenly and the wagon overturned, tossing Powell into a snowbank. As he looked up he saw the object of his horses' fright: a towering shadowy figure standing in the doorway of his barn. Powell scrambled to his feet and raced for the cabin to rouse his brother.

The pair returned to the barn to find the door closed and no sign of an intruder. The horses were not found until several days later.

An old man who lived alone reported that the Ridgeway Ghost visited him one night as he was doing his chores.

The fellow had walked out to the pump to fill several buckets with water. On his way back to the house he turned and saw that the pump handle was still vigorously moving up and down. At once he realized the ghost was getting a drink. The terrified farmer ran back inside to his kitchen and bolted the door.

Country doctors were regularly called out at night to isolated farms to deliver babies or look after the sick. Doc Cutler, who tended the people of Ridgeway for years, took the ghost stories quite seriously. The ghost, it is said, was particularly attracted to anyone who worked with blood.

Doc avoided the main road if at all possible since the ghost was known to frequent the area. On those occasions when he had to travel along the highway, the Ridgeway Ghost always kept him company. The phantom would spring from the brush and perch on one of the doctor's horses or stand on the tongue of his buggy. Cutler tried whipping his horses into a faster gait, but the ghost could not be shaken off, all the while staring with hollow, vacant eyes up at the frightened physician.

After one late-night call Doc Cutler claimed he had overtaken a man walking alongside the road. He asked the stranger if he wanted a ride, and the man climbed into the doctor's buggy near the edge of town but then suddenly vanished a short distance later.

Doc Cutler was convinced he had given a lift to the Ridgeway Ghost.

A man was riding home one afternoon in the hills near Ridgeway when he thought he saw movement in a deserted cabin. He dismounted and walked into the ruins. Sitting in a chair was a gauzy, vaguely human figure the visitor immediately recognized as the Ridgeway Ghost. He struck at the phantom with his whip, and the ghost vanished.

The next day, the man noticed there were clear impressions of his fingers in the handle of the whip—so tightly had he gripped it in fear.

Johnny Owens, a Welsh miner, was out for a stroll early one evening on Military Ridge Road. Rounding a bend he saw several dark objects swinging from the limb of a tall oak tree. As he drew nearer, the moonlight revealed three human bodies hanging by their necks. Owens ran all the way home.

The next day when Owens returned to the spot with three stout friends there was no sign of any bodies, dead or living.

One day in the late 1840s, a lead miner encountered the Ridgeway Ghost on the road west of Ridgeway.

As the miner trudged along, he realized he was being followed. He turned and saw an indistinct form some distance behind—he figured it was the Ridgeway Ghost. He quickened his stride. So did the phantom. Always keeping the same distance behind the frightened miner, the ghost matched his lengthening strides step for step. The miner began to run. So did the ghost.

Finally, after several hundred yards, the exhausted miner slumped down on a log at the side of the road. The ghost sauntered up and took a seat at the other end. For one of the few times in its history the ghost spoke.

"That was some mighty fine running you were doing back there," the spirit said.

"Yes," panted the miner. "And I'm going to be doing some more here in a minute . . . soon's I catch my breath." And with that off he sped once more, the Ridgeway Ghost at his heels.

Three men were sitting in a Blue Mounds saloon, nearing the end of a stud poker game. The stakes were high and a considerable sum of money was riding on this final deal. A miner with a full house won the pot. As he reached across the table to gather up the winnings, a stranger suddenly appeared in a vacant seat, grabbed up the cards, and began to deal. The uninvited stranger wore black clothing with a wide-brimmed hat pulled down low over his eyes.

The cards began flying from the stranger's fingers and seemed to dance across the room before floating down to the table.

The innkeeper dove behind his polished bar and hid for the duration of the stranger's visit. The poker players were thoroughly frightened at the card antics and stumbled over each other in their headlong rush for the door.

The money on the table vanished, along with the phantom in black.

When traffic declined on Military Ridge Road following the completion of the railroad in 1857, the Ridgeway Ghost also became less active. In fact, it is said that the phantom was seen leaving town on the cowcatcher of a freight train passing through Ridgeway. Others claim the ghost died in a 1910 fire that consumed nearly the entire Ridgeway business district.

But there are others who say the ghost has never left.

Jeanie Lewis from near Wakefield collected stories about the ghost for many years. She was never convinced that the ghost truly departed, citing several bizarre experiences that otherwise seem to defy explanation.

Once shortly after the birth of her first child, Mrs. Lewis arose in the middle of the night to give the baby an early feeding. As she sat rocking the child in the darkened living room, Mrs. Lewis heard the kitchen door open. Turning to look, she saw newspapers that had been placed on the freshly waxed floor floating through the air. She could hear the steps of someone approaching, but no one came into the room.

Mrs. Lewis ran to the bedroom to rouse her husband. Together they heard the footsteps again and then the kitchen door slammed shut. The couple cautiously looked around the kitchen but found nothing disturbed. The newspapers were still arranged neatly on the floor, and the damp ground outside the door bore no impression of footprints.

Mrs. Lewis's next incident could be called "The Case of the Wandering Jacket." Her husband once owned a jacket given to him by a former girlfriend. About three years after their marriage, the coat disappeared from a clothes hook in the stairwell where it was always kept. Mr. Lewis insisted that his wife had destroyed it; yet she no less strenuously denied any involvement. Mrs. Lewis searched the house thoroughly but could not find it.

Several years passed. Then one afternoon as Mrs. Lewis walked down the stairs she saw the coat hanging, as always, on the peg. But the garment was nearly in shreds. It was as if someone had worn it nearly every day since its disappearance.

An old schoolhouse in Wakefield has been converted into a recreation center. This new center, along with the Folklore Village Farm, provided neighborhood youngsters with a great gathering spot. But some rather peculiar incidents took place there.

At about the time the school was undergoing its renovation, Jeanie Lewis, who lived within sight of the place, happened one evening to glance toward the sky. On the eastern horizon she noticed a bright, colorful object directly over the Wakefield cheese factory. It hovered for a while and then began to descend. Then it took off to the north and stopped over the old schoolhouse, before seeming to descend into the school's chimney.

Several times since that night, children and others visiting the schoolhouse have reported strange sounds from within that chimney. It is said the Ridgeway Ghost visits there every so often.

According to another legend, a bleak, abandoned farmhouse on the old Petra property is the permanent residence of the Ridgeway Ghost. It sits surrounded by weeds past the pioneer Ridgeway cemetery south of town and looks just like the sort of place a ghost would inhabit. Doors hang from single hinges, windows are broken—altogether an ideal haunted house.

Was there really a Ridgeway Ghost? Or did the Old World settlers bring their superstitious beliefs in ghosts and banshees to the new land? The Ridgeway tales and any truth upon which they might have been based are now lost in the mists of time. We will never know for sure, but the legends will live as long as there are listeners willing to believe.

Selected Bibliography

Books

Boyer, Dennis. *Driftless Spirits: Ghosts of Southwest Wisconsin*. Madison, WI: Prairie Oak Press, 1997.

Chapin, Earl V. *Earl Chapin's Tales of Wisconsin*. Compiled and edited by M. Wayne Wolfe. [River Falls]: University of Wisconsin–River Falls Press, [1973].

Cole, Harry Ellsworth, and Louise Phelps Kellogg. *Stagecoach and Tavern Tales of the Old Northwest*. Cleveland: Arthur H. Clarke, 1930.

Conard, Howard Louis, ed. *History of Milwaukee: From Its First Settlement to the Year 1895*. Vol. 1. Chicago: American Biographical Publishing Co., [1895 or 1896].

Gard, Robert Edward, and L. G. Sorden. *Wisconsin Lore*. New York: Duell, Sloan, and Pearce, [1962].

Gilman, Rhoda R. *Historic Chequamegon*. [La Pointe, WI]: n.p., [1971].

Holzhueter, John O. *Madeline Island and the Chequamegon Region*. Madison: State Historical Society of Wisconsin, 1974.

Lewis, Jeanie. *Ridgeway: Host to the Ghost*. Dodgeville, WI: [Lewis], 1975.

Napoli, James. *The Coasts of Wisconsin*. Madison: University of Wisconsin Sea Grant College Program, 1975.

Norman, Michael. *Haunted Homeland*. New York: Forge Books, 2006.

Norman, Michael, and Beth Scott. *Haunted Heartland*. Madison, WI: Stanton and Lee, 1985.

———. *Haunted Heritage*. New York: Forge Books, 2002.

Owen, A. R. G. *Can We Explain the Poltergeist?* New York: Garrett Publications, [1964].

Schoolcraft, Henry Rowe. *Schoolcraft's Indian Legends*. Edited by Mentor Lee Williams. Westport, CT: Greenwood Press, 1956.

Strait, William E. *Campfires at La Pointe: A Historical Journey through the Centuries in La Pointe*: n.p., [1976].

Stresau, Marion. *Tomorrows Unlimited*. Boston: Branden Press, [1973].

Thurston, Herbert. *Ghosts and Poltergeists*. Edited by J. H. Crehan. London: Burns Oates, 1953.

Periodicals

Bednarek, Jim. "The Legend of Mary Buth." *Germantown Press*, September 1, 1977.

Bennett, Joan. "Ghostly Events Change Granton Man's Life." *Eau Claire Leader-Telegram*, March 29, 1980.

Burnett County Sentinel (Grantsburg), October 4, 1889.

Cummings, Gerald. "The Mysterious Hitchhiker." *FATE Magazine*, August 1992.

Daily Milwaukee News, August 9, 1874.

Dayton, Scottie. "The Haunted Inn Ghost." *Wisconsin Trails*, September/October 2003.

Doehlert, Betsy. "Do Ghosts Walk Arboretum Glades?" *Capital Times* (Madison), October 31, 1977.

"Does Ghost of Adam Bobel Haunt the Hotel Boscobel?" *Boscobel Dial*, October 29, 1987.

Dunn County News (Menomonie), September 13, 1873; October 25, 1873; November 8, 1873, November 2, 1994.

Durand Weekly News, September 12, 1873; September 26, 1873; October 3, 1873.

Franklin, Dixie. "New Light Shed on Odd Light." *Milwaukee Journal*, August 6, 1978.

"The Ghost Hunter's Handiguide." *Wisconsin Week-End*, October 1978.

Heinen, Thomas. "Tragedy Stalks a Farmhouse." *Milwaukee Journal*, October 25, 1977.

Henningfield, Julie. "The Double Meaning in Spirits." *Excursions*, October 22, 2000.

Hirsch, Stephanie. "Ghost Stories Alive in Brodhead." *Monroe Evening Times*, August 29, 1989.

"History of the Kewaunee Inn Property." Photocopy in author's possession. N.p., n.d.

Hollatz, Tom. "'Haunted House' Alters an Author's Life." *Minocqua Lakeland Times*, April 21, 2006.

———. "Summerwind: A North Woods Haunted Mansion." *Lake Superior Magazine*, September–October 1988.

Hudson Star and Times, December 8, 1869.

Lenz, Elmer. "Have You Seen the Light?" *Milwaukee Badge*, July 1977.

Madison Daily Democrat, December 5, 1873.

Miller, Willis. Editor's Column. *Hudson Star-Observer*, September 14, 1944.

Milwaukee News, October 16, 1873.

Milwaukee Sentinel, August 11, 1875; September 26, 1878; February 14, 1897.

Mount Horeb Times, March 18, 1909; March 25, 1909; April 1, 1909; April 8, 1909; April 11, 1909; April 15, 1909.

Olson, Kathy. "'Something' Is Out There in Flowage." *St. Paul Pioneer Press* (Minnesota), July 5, 1992.

Orton, Charles W. "The Haunting." *Wisconsin Trails*, Autumn 1976.

Orum, Alma. "Octagon House Has Spirit, But No Ghost." *Milwaukee Sentinel,* January 3, 1960.

Oshkosh Weekly Times, November 25, 1873; December 3, 1873.

Pease, Harry S. "A Different Northern Light." *Insight Magazine (Milwaukee Journal* supplement), November 30, 1980.

Peterson, Gary. "Time Plays Tricks with Memory of 1909 Mt. Horeb Poltergeist." *Capital Times* (Madison), October 26, 1978.

Pett, Mrs. W. F. "A Forgotten Village." *Wisconsin Magazine of History,* September 1928.

Pooley, Will. "Haunted? Once Called Summerwind, an Old House Stirs Controversy." *Milwaukee Journal,* October 30, 1983.

Rathbun, Andy. "Where Things Go Bump in the Night: Western Part of State Has Seen Its Share of Ghosts." *St. Paul Pioneer Press* (Minnesota), October 30, 2009.

Reuschleim, Harrison. "Mischief on High Hill Where Jenny Lies Buried." *Wisconsin Week-End,* December 7, 1977.

River Falls Journal, September 23, 1873; October 31, 1873; December 12, 1873.

Rogo, D. Scott. "More about the Poltergeist: The Power behind Teenage Tantrums." *Human Behavior,* May 1978.

"Sanford Syse, U Speech Prof, Dies at Madison." *River Falls Journal,* December 6, 1973.

Smith, Susan Lampert. "Where Ghosts Gather: Book Describes Spooky History of Iowa County." *Wisconsin State Journal* (Madison), June 14, 1993.

Starks, Norm. "Hotel Has Everything, Including Own Ghost." *Beloit Daily News,* July 12, 1989.

———. "Hotel Loses Its Haunt." *Janesville Gazette,* January 25, 1991.

"Terrifying Tales of 9 Haunted Houses." *Life Magazine,* November 1980.

Tschudy, Kim. "Explanation of Light in Barn near Postville." *Monticello Messenger,* November 20, 1991.

Waukesha Freeman, July 18, 1918; July 25, 1918.

Wisconsin State Journal (Madison), August 11, 1874; March 30, 1909; April 2, 1909.

Unpublished Works

Brown, Charles E. Charles E. Brown Papers. State Historical Society of Wisconsin. HB, Boxes 7 and 9.

Christ, Bev. "Ghostlore at Ripon College: School Spirit, We've Got 'Em." April 1996, Ripon College, Ripon, Wisconsin.

Dettloff, John. "Indian Trail Resort: A History." N.d. Photocopy in author's possession.

Nielsen, A. J. "He Came With the House." May 9, 1977. Photocopy in author's possession.

Orton, Charles W. "Ridgeway Ghost Tales." N.d. Self-published.

Owens, Dick. "A Graveyard Tale." N.d. Photocopy in author's possession.

———. "The Happenings." May 8, 1991. Photocopy in author's possession.

Van Dyke, Madge Patterson. "The Story of Kilbourn and Its Vicinity." Bachelor's thesis, University of Wisconsin–Madison, 1916.

Index of Place Names